BEYOND MY WINDOW

A Collection of Memoirs, Essays and Short Fiction

Miami Sunshine Writers

ISBN: 1548799963
ISBN 13: 9781548799960

CONTENTS

PREFACE

Once upon a time, in a city by the sea— at The University of Miami Osher Lifelong Learning Institute, OLLI for short— a group of a dozen writers met. A camaraderie grew and laughter pervaded the room. Loyalty blossomed. The group continued to meet over lunch when the leader could not attend during regular class hours.

This is a volume of memoirs, essays, short fiction and performance poetry produced by these OLLI authors. The reader will discover each writer's unique voice.

The cover has been designed and executed by Ellen Leeds, one of the writers. Her cover-making talent is very much appreciated by the other writers.

We hope you enjoy reading these pieces as much as we enjoyed writing, critiquing, and finalizing them.

BEYOND MY WINDOW

By Elsa Goss Black

S ome of us are born to wander, some of us are introduced to it by well-traveled parents and some of us learn about the world beyond our windows, as we learn about so much else, through books.

In my case, it was one specific book, *Around the World in 2.000 Pictures*, a heavy but otherwise unassuming blue-and-black-bound tome as revolutionary to me as a fiery call to arms. From the first time I opened it as a very young girl, it beckoned me to places far from the suburban garden apartment where it sat on one of my father's bookshelves.

Again and again through my young years, I would thumb through its pages, losing myself each time in the reverie of foreign lands and distant shores. My deep-seated desire to see these countries, to meet the people who lived in these exotic places and to make them real, was born during those childhood daydreams. The hours flew by as I imagined the pictures coming to life for me someday.

The odd thing is that in these tech-savvy times, even the most curious child might find the book dry and dull.

Originally published as two volumes, the book we owned had two parts instead, the first devoted to the world at large and the second focused on the United States. Compiled in the early 1950s, it contained only small black and white pictures. Even the grass-skirted Hawaiian hula dancers living across the Pacific in a place that was not yet a state might be unappealing to young eyes accustomed to swaths of color and computer-enhanced graphics.

But I was enchanted. Big Ben! The Eiffel Tower! The Coliseum! And the palaces! All those palaces, which my girlish imagination imagined as mansions I could someday inhabit as the princess in a real-life fairy tale. In my innocence, it never once occurred to me that being a would-be Jewish-American princess would in any way disqualify me from becoming the consort of an Anglican, Catholic or even Hindu prince. Harsh realities of any kind were still a long way off.

Instead, these wonders of the so-called modern world called out to me as I both figuratively and literally held them in my lap, all becoming the siren songs to the little girl I was. But as the years have flown by, I've realized that it was more than the conventional Grand Tour tourist stops that captured my rapt attention back then.

I remember photos of girls wearing red sashes and candle-lit crowns to celebrate the dark, mid-December St. Lucia's Day in Sweden. How odd and how interesting, I always thought. I also recall a picture of a Swiss castle, the caption underneath referring to "The Prisoner of Chillon." It would be years before I understood that the reference was to a poem by Byron, that the castle, actually a chateau, was in the town of Montreux and that none of those French words were pronounced anything remotely resembling the way I thought they were.

Remembering that photo always reminds me, too, of a picture of the city Sault Ste. Marie in Ottawa near the U.S.-Canadian border. To my child's eyes and ears, it could only be pronounced *Salt Stay Marie*, and to this day I much prefer my version to the correct one, mostly because that small memory never fails to make me smile.

Likewise, from Japanese kimonos to German lederhosen, from traditionally woven Andean fabrics to Polynesian sarongs, I loved seeing what both children and grown-ups far away from me wore on a daily basis. I found them all much more fascinating than the prosaic skirt, sweater and saddle shoes I put on for school every day.

It's almost comical how those images have stayed with me and spurred my wanderlust. When I finally made it to Greece not that many years ago, I was, of course, rendered nearly mute by the history and beauty of the Parthenon and other ancient ruins. But one of my greatest hits memories was when I spied the skirt-clad guards in front of the Parliament. They were posed exactly as I'd seen them in photographs during my 1950 childhood, men standing tall and proud, looking faintly ridiculous but ramrod straight in their short, starched, pleated white kilts and red clogs with black pompoms. I couldn't wait to capture the moment with my own camera.

And so it has been everywhere I've traveled as an adult. I have never failed to be awed by the sight of one of those long-ago pictures coming to life in front of my excited eyes. Each time, it has been as if a distant dream has come true at long last.

Sadly, I don't know where that beloved book went. Somewhere in one of my mother's moves after my father died, or perhaps in one of mine, it was lost, most likely thrown out as a dusty, well-worn relic of another era.

Along the way, I discovered that in this age of Google and Amazon, I could buy one from an online seller of antique books.

But I prefer to keep the book safe in my memory, a totem of my youth, a sacred object and symbol of who I once was and all that I'd hoped to become.

Besides, I have since realized such a memory is not mine alone. For a long time, I thought I was the only one who was so deeply affected by this book of photos. I should have figured, of course, that I was not the only child whose imagination was ignited by what was obviously a widely published book of its time. Nonetheless, I was stunned a few years back to open up the Sunday *New York Times* and read a piece by a woman who named this same book as the one that made the biggest difference in her life.

My first thought was envy that I hadn't written it first. But the feeling of *woulda, coulda, shoulda* passed, replaced by a warm sense of camaraderie with this stranger. We might not know each other, but we were sisters under the skin, and I hoped that there were others who had also begun a life of travel because of *Around the World in 2,000 Pictures*.

I still think of those, similarly influenced long ago, who might still swear by the words, perhaps apocryphal, attributed to Saint Augustine: "The world is a book, and those who do not travel read only one page."

I think of Susan Sontag's wonderful and pithy remark: "I haven't been everywhere, but it's on my list."

And keeping my passport ever-current, I remain grateful for the book that lit the way.

MOVE OVER VAN GOGH!

By Kitty Winkler

I decided that I was destined for great fame as a leading avant garde artist. Something in the air convinced me. I was waking up each morning in the land of Cezanne with Mont Sainte Victoire visible from my bedroom window. Visions of Monet, Gauguin and Van Gogh, who also painted here in Aix-en-Provence danced through my head.

When I saw Studio Art on the class schedule for the second semester, I jumped at the chance. Not one to be ill-prepared, I spent 100 French francs, a huge sum for me on a student's budget, on a magnificent wooden briefcase full of art supplies. It was second-hand, from one of my classmates at the university who had taken the art course in the previous semester. However, it was like new; only four or five of the paint tubes had been opened. In my euphoria about my destiny as an artist, it never occurred to me to question why she had given up and was willing to sell her beautiful art kit.

How I loved the names—burnt umber, ochre, cadmium red—all of these conjured up images of me standing before a dazzling canvas of color with a smiling professor standing behind me admiring my work. The names were wonderful, but the smells were even better. I defy any smell to top the rich, oily, turpentine-tinged smell of oil paints. Opening one of the small tubes was like letting a genie out of a bottle. It would transport me to a future exhibit of my renowned works or to a room in the Musee D'Orsay, where one of my canvases would be hung for public viewing.

The atmosphere for greatness was just right. Classes were to take place in a 4th floor attic studio in one of the grand 16th century buildings that made up the university. On the first day of class I couldn't wait. I was in the studio at least fifteen minutes ahead of my classmates and the professor. It gave me a chance to take in paintings leaning against the walls of the room, easels everywhere, and a skylight pouring sunlight into the room.

As the time neared for class to begin, Monsieur Junot, our professor, appeared. He didn't disappoint. A maroon beret sat slanted on his almost-bald head, and he wore a beige smock with smears of paint across the front and sleeves. The studio began to fill with some of my "artier" classmates. It never occurred to me at the time that I didn't exactly fit in, radiating the aura of a conservative middle-American preppie in my plaid skirt and monogrammed sweater among all of those Bohemians.

Monsieur instructed us on preparations and gave us the assignment. To learn to be an artist, he said, you must study the techniques of the great masters. So our first project would be to copy a masterpiece.

I was feeling overwhelmed but willing to try. Monsieur gave each student a different picture of a painting to copy. Mine was a Van Gogh. It was called *La Berceuse*, the portrait of a rather lumpy lady in a green dress with red hair pulled back in a severe bun.

Start by penciling in what you will be painting on your canvas, Monsieur suggested, and most of the group spent the rest of the class period sketching what they would ultimately paint. Monsieur Junot made the rounds of the class making suggestions, giving short lessons, and occasionally correcting lines that didn't correspond to the great masters' original paintings.

I left class that day encouraged. My drawing hadn't been all bad.

In the second class session, it was time to put paint on the canvas. I noticed that my kit was pretty ostentatious compared to the four or five tubes of paint and couple of brushes most of the other students had brought to class. My professional palette board also stood out compared to the pieces of plain Masonite the others were using for palettes. However, my real focus was on the dazzling white canvas in front of me and the color palette of sweet-smelling oil paints which Monsieur Junot was instructing us on how to prepare.

Soon we were underway. Where to start? I needed advice and beckoned Monsieur Junot over. Start with the background, he advised, but be careful not to cover your pencil outline. I got that done, a fairly easy chore since the painting's background was mostly white. Then I was again at a loss. I caught Monsieur Junot's eye. Choose an area and start, he said. There was a note of impatience in his voice.

Okay, I would start with the woman's face. I began to mix what I thought would be a flesh-colored tone only to apply it to the canvas and find it was a sickly pink. I worked to subdue the pink and find a better match for the original painting, but that brought me to an important discovery. The woman's face wasn't just one color; it was made up of many colors that provided shading and dimension. I beckoned Monsieur Junot again.

I don't understand this, I said, pointing out the color nuances I had discovered.

Mademoiselle, he said, this is what painting is about. Nothing in nature is a single color; just look in the mirror at your own face.

Humbled, I studied what Van Gogh had done and tried to duplicate it. I must have put 15 layers of paint on the woman's face and nothing I did resembled the original. In the meantime, I began to panic as I looked at Monet's *Bridge at Giverny* developing nicely at the easel to the right of me. I saw that the painting in front of me of Van Gogh's *Café Terrace in Arles at Night* was taking shape. Mine looked like nothing but a grayish beige blob floating on a sea of white canvas.

When Monsieur passed by again, I wanted to hide myself, my canvas, or both. But he saw it all, and his expression showed that neither the canvas nor I gave him pleasure. Mademoiselle, give me your brush, he said, and he proceeded with two quick strokes to give the face the dimension and color that had eluded me. Carry on, he said.

I went for the lady's eyes next. With my daintiest brush, I planted a big black blob on the canvas. I tried to wipe it off. I only succeeded in wiping off the brush strokes that Monsieur had artfully placed on my canvas moments before. I wiped harder, and the face got larger and grayer, completely wiping out the pencil lines that were supposed to be my guide. I was near tears. It didn't help that everywhere I looked in the room were recognizable paintings from the great masters.

Finally, class was over. Monsieur Junot asked me to wait as the others were leaving. Mademoiselle Winkler, perhaps this isn't the class for you, he said.

Exactly what I was thinking, I said, choking back tears. I rushed for the door and went straight to the Dean's office to drop the course. The beautiful paint kit, with only a tiny bit more use than when I had bought it, finally sold for half of what I had paid.

I guess you don't have to move over just yet, Vincent.

WOMB WITHOUT A VIEW

By Zooey Kaplowitz

I n 1944 the United States was at war with Germany, Italy, and Spain. Brave and patriotic men and women had temporarily abandoned their civilian lives to fight to preserve those American freedoms that we all love. They volunteered for the Army, the Navy, the Marines, the Coast Guard, and the Merchant Marines. Others were drafted but still served proudly and bravely. They risked their lives. Some came home. Some didn't come home. They all contributed to a history that was being made daily. On September 8, 1944, Italy surrendered unconditionally and on the 10th Germany shelled Rome. Battles on three continents were being won and lost on a daily basis. On October 5, German troops were cleared from Corsica and Japanese planes were being destroyed by U. S. sea and air attached on Wake Island.

Men, women, and children were also making great sacrifices on the home front. It was an especially difficult time for me. I was finishing up a compulsory nine month sentence in a womb without a view in the borscht belt hamlet of Kerhonkson, New York. Kerhonkson wasn't a one-horse town. There were plenty of horses—and cows and chickens. There just wasn't very much to do. The town consisted of Schneck's Department Store, owned by my Aunt Lillian; a kosher butcher; a kosher deli; the shoykit, a man who ritually kills chickens. The shoykit performed all Jewish rituals, including bar mitzvahs and circumcisions. There was a drug store and a grocery store where the goyim could shop.

Seven miles away in Ellenville, there was a movie theater, The Ellenville Paramount, which showed movies such as *Tarzan of the Apes*; *See Here, Private Hargrove*; *Miracle of Morgan's Creek*; and *Hail the Conquering Hero*. But I couldn't see them because I was stuck in the womb. I couldn't read Dick Tracy or Little Abner. Life in the womb sucked. I had to get out of there. I kicked and I screamed, but no one heard me.

World War II was not a great time to be born. There were all sorts of shortages. There were gas and tire shortages. People were limited to where and when they could go. Cars were only used when necessary. Teenagers had to walk to their prom or the soda fountain. There were shortages of laborers. Farm labor had to be brought in from Jamaica. Women were being trained to work in factories. They were being called names such as Rosie the Riveter.

Doctors of all specialties were overseas patching up those who were wounded in battle. House wives were being trained to take over most of the duties of physicians. My Aunt Gussie who had worked behind the counter at a Woolworth store was now doing open-heart surgery at the Montefiore Hospital in the Bronx. These women were being called Rosie the Physicians. In Kerhonkson where I was stuck in the womb, after months of kicking and screaming, I was due for birth. There was no obstetrician available, so my mother was stuck with Mutzi. Mutzi had worked for my Aunt Lee as a domestic. But now, after ten weeks of training, she was a midwife.

My mother probably would have been better off with Rosie the Riveter.

The day came. I was about to make my entrance into the world, and all my kicking and screaming caused me to be turned around. I was going to be a breech birth. That meant I had to be turned around in that womb to get out of the hellhole. This is where the future of my life was determined. Mutzi the midwife had slept through the class on breech birth and had no idea what to do. She did not know that I had to be turned around. So she did what every former domestic would do. She looked my mother in the eye and said, "I don't do breech births. You're on your own."

This was Hell. I was going to be stuck for the rest of my life in this womb. The womb sucked. There was nothing to do. The only food I got came intravenously through my stomach. I was dying for hot corned beef on rye. I had to get out. So I turned myself around and crawled out. Free at last! Free at last! Thank God Almighty, I'm free at last. Little did I know at that time I would be spending my adolescence trying to get back in.

Eight days after my birth, my foreskin was removed by the shoykit. He remembered he wasn't killing a chicken, so my penis was more-or-less intact. One hundred and fifty people were in attendance. Corned beef on rye was served. They were not there because they were friends. There was just nothing else to do in October in Kerhonkson, and they didn't have to pay for the food.

In November 1957 I was a Bar Mitzvah. I was trained for it by the ritual chicken killer who performed my circumcision. I chanted my haftarah and led the service. I was also trained to ritually kill chickens and removed a foreskin with one hundred and fifty people watching.

MY DARLING CLEMENTINE

By Isabelle Whitfield

W hen I was six, the life-sized, most extraordinary doll arrived as a present for my April 1ˢᵗ birthday. As it happened,
on the day I was born, Easter Sunday fell at the beginning of April
and my mother often mused that I was her Easter present. Of
course, many others teased me unmercifully about being a little
April Fool. Frankly, I loved it!

Thus it was inevitable that my mother would concoct grand
and glorious joint Easter-birthday celebrations with the requisite
Easter motifs to mark the joyous occasion---Easter baskets for everyone, Easter egg hunts for colorful pastel eggs hidden throughout the rolling green yard behind trees, bushes, and sprightly
spring daffodils, papier-mache Easter bunnies located all around,
yummy vanilla birthday cake decorated with pink and green icing
and frosty ice cream treats for my young guests. And there were
lots of balloons, always lots of festive party balloons.

Amid all the fun and excitement, suddenly I spotted the biggest doll I had ever seen sitting among the Easter bunnies, and she was mine, the best Easter birthday present a little girl could ever have.

I do not remember who named Clementine, but I strongly suspect it was my mother, who most probably lifted it from the old popular folksong, the refrain of which is:

Oh my darling, oh my darling
Oh my darling Clementine
You are lost and gone forever
Oh my darling Clementine.

But *my* Clementine was not lost or gone forever, although she was missing for quite a while.

Today Clementine sits comfortably in a vintage white highchair in a corner of the breakfast room of my beloved grandparents' home. She is a happy reminder of my carefree childhood summers spent in a small southern town in the heart of Alabama's Black Belt.

At the time she came into my young life, Clementine was the most enormous doll that any of my friends or I had ever seen. Today she might be considered a version of a ragdoll, but she was so much more. She was not floppy like a typical Raggedy Ann doll but she was stuffed with something that made her sturdy and solid. She was not the type to be dragged around, and when in a standing position she was almost as tall as I was when I was six. I could barely pick her up!

Clementine had bright blue eyes framed with whimsical long curling eyelashes stitched with chocolate brown yarn on her fabric face, which was embellished with a little nose, heart-shaped smiling red lips, and powder pink rosy cheeks. The long thick pigtails surrounding her friendly face were braided with matching dark brown yarn. Her brunette pigtails were almost as long as my blonde braids. We were quite a pair.

She was clearly the main attraction for my playmates around town, who, like me, realized what a unique doll she was, and they often begged their parents to come over to play with Clementine and me. This led to many happy hours of special enchantment only little girls can know.

I have a fleeting memory of the last time I saw Clementine as a little girl. She was sitting in a deep rose velvet Victorian chair by the fireplace in the living room. She quietly observed as my white-haired grandfather got down on his hands and knees on the beige sculptured Oriental rug to review the ABCs with me, to my great delight, by carefully forming big letters with brightly colored marbles.

But time marched on. Eventually I outgrew dolls, lost track of my precious Clementine, and those happy, hazy summer days faded away.

Sadly, I do not remember wondering in the ensuing years whatever happened to Clementine. I suppose I thought she must have disappeared with the other long-lost memorabilia of my childhood---the famous big blue tricycle all the boys liked to ride, my large comic book collection, my favorite stuffed puppy dog from Japan named Fuji, the red Radio-Flyer wagon I pulled my little brother around in on hot summer days.

Then one day, over half a century later, after our mother, in her nineties, had peacefully slipped away, it seemed time to explore the large dark attic of the home my brother and I had inherited. As children, we were rarely allowed to go up the steps to what was a very mysterious place. Who knew what curiosities and lost treasures might be hidden up there? It was a large cavernous room under the high rafters, covered with black soot and without much light, a place where cast-off furniture, clothes, old framed photographs and records, 1920s travel trunks, broken china, dented pots and pans, and all sorts of miscellany ended up when my grandmother decided such items were no longer useful but not yet determined to be useless and thus thrown away.

So one sunny afternoon when rays of sunlight streamed through the high dormer windows, allowing better visibility, I made my way up the attic stairs. I wandered around for a while trying not to touch things because of the black soot blanketing everything that was not covered up.

Then, when I opened one of the old trunks that had been stashed away for years, *lo and behold,* I could hardly believe my eyes to find the lost treasure of my childhood---*it was Clementine!* Somehow she had found her way to the old trunk and had been sleeping there, undisturbed for decades, where someone had placed her so long ago for safe-keeping, hopefully to be found again someday. How it gladdened my heart to see Clementine after so many years!

At first glance, Clementine looked just the same as I remembered her; she had fared quite well during the intervening years except some brown yarn bangs were missing over her forehead and her rosy pink cheeks were slightly faded. Someone had dressed her in a sweet cotton summer frock with faded blue eyelet trim, rather dusty now, that I suddenly realized had been mine once upon a time, a dress that my grandmother had made for a three-year-old me. Her chocolate brown pigtails were tied with light blue satin ribbon bows. She wore on her feet a pair of white lace-up baby shoes that might have been mine, too. Overall, Clementine was amazingly well-preserved.

It was truly a joyous and sentimental reunion with my one-of-a-kind childhood friend. I picked her up and suddenly wished she could talk so we could reminisce about those happy days we spent together that seemed, at the time, to be days that would go on forever. I wished I could remember more, wished to re-live those magical summer days with Clementine, to greet each

new day again with that sense of wonder and innocence so charac-
teristic of the young.

But, discovering Clementine unlocked a flood of long-forgotten
memories, of a cacophony of colors, scents, sights, and sounds, of
flashbacks to a time and a place and people that exist now only in
my memory.

Suddenly the childhood memories came rushing back---of that
eagerly anticipated early summer day when we could finally go
barefooted and first feel the cool green grass between our toes,
of playing bicycle chase all over town, of collecting and trading
baseball cards of our summer heroes such as Jackie Robinson,
Roy Campanella, and Duke Snider (not noticing the first two were
black), of playing baseball with the boys, of roller skating all day
long, causing my skate wheels to wear out and getting a new pair
every Christmas, of climbing trees and engaging in peashooter
wars hidden up in leafy branches and hitting unsuspecting victims
below, of finding that surprise at the bottom of the Cracker Jack
box, of hearing the jangle of the small silver bell rung by our dear
cook and housekeeper, Hannah, summoning us for dinner (the
noon meal back then), of oftentimes whiling away the afternoon
reading on the cool screen porch and sipping a coke float, of suck-
ing the sweet taste of honeysuckle blossoms, of arriving home by
dusk, tired and dirty, after telling ghost stories up at the cemetery
while perched obliviously on the tombstones of long-forgotten
Confederate soldiers, of rushing home before dark in time to
catch twinkling lightning bugs in a jar with holes punched in the
top so our little captives could breathe, of finally climbing into my
four-poster bed and falling asleep, all the bedroom windows open,
and cooled by a black, oscillating GE fan on a hot summer night.
It was a glorious childhood!

Although Thomas Wolfe once famously noted that "you can't
go home again," I may be one of the lucky few who can. Whenever
I drive up to the dark green house accented with white trim,

wrap-around concrete porch and heavy banisters, with the white swing I was rocked in as a baby and white rocking chairs on the front porch, I feel the ever-present spirits of my beloved grandparents, of my wonderful mother, and of dearest Hannah roaming the rooms still, all there to greet me, to welcome me home.

And, of course, there is Clementine, sitting patiently, waiting for me in the breakfast room, an authentic and precious guardian of an idyllic childhood, of that magical and cherished time when I had the very best doll of all.

FINGERPRINTING

By Beatriz La Rosa

I follow the man to an inner room, where the only people there are he and I. He says, "Take off your shoes and your stockings." I am not sure this is right, but I do as I am told. After all, he is helping me become a permanent resident of the United States of America. I follow his instructions—this Immigration and Naturalization officer who seems to be in his forties—and sit on the chair he has pulled over for me. He is standing in front of me.

I bend over to take off my shoes, and out of the corner of my eyes, I take a glance at this area I am in. I notice the vacant, empty desks, forgotten papers cluttering their surface. Empty boxes. A disarray of things. This room looks more like a storage area than an office for conducting official business.

I have been living in the United States—Miami to be exact— for the past month. My sister Adriana and I had arrived in January of 1961. We left La Habana on a direct Pan-American Airlines flight to Miami. The two of us came alone and are staying with my sister's future in-laws. My parents left Cuba and are living in Guatemala, waiting for papers to enter the United States.

I am sixteen, my sister eighteen. This morning we are following a process required by the INS to become permanent residents of the United States. If we do, becoming a U.S. citizen is the next step. In order to start the wheels turning, we need to complete paperwork—which includes fingerprinting—at the INS building on Biscayne Boulevard and 79th Street. This procedure of completing paperwork allows our status to be changed from Political Refugees/Parolees to permanent residents.

This is an important occasion. I, therefore, want to dress properly, remembering the advice from my family that people judge you by how you present yourself. As I ponder what to wear, I hear generations of female voices telling me "You must dress like a lady." I pick my attire carefully. The clothes I select are, I hope, representative of who I am: a middle-class, Catholic, Cuban young woman.

For this first encounter with the officials of the INS, I choose an apple green wool suit that was made to measure for me in La Habana by a well-known tailor, and a cream colored silk blouse. I probably wear the fake pearl necklace—I always wanted the real thing like my other wealthy girlfriends wore, who received a string of real pearls from their parents when they turned fifteen—and tiny pearl earrings. Stockings are a must, and I wear them, even in the Miami heat, with round-toed brown leather pumps. I complete the look by pinning my hair in a French twist. I also wear the glowing red lipstick I bought before I left Cuba. It is DuBarry's Raining Rubies and according to the advertisement, it is a *A torrent of Red drenched with implications.*

Sometimes I wonder if this red lipstick was the cause of all my troubles.

I can hear the silence of this backroom where I am alone with this officer. The absence of sound in this room, and the isolation I feel, is in sharp contrast to the babel noise of the outer area, where the crowd of Cubans who were in line on the sidewalk in the early morning are now being processed. The outer room is a large area with desks everywhere and where each station is manned— all of the officers are male—by an agent of the Immigration and Naturalization Services. This is where the initial intake takes place, and after finishing the paperwork, applicants are then fingerprinted.

My agent has just finished taking my fingerprints. The tips of my fingers are still somewhat stained by the ink, and I am careful, as I follow this man, not to blemish my silk blouse. I am aware that the situation is odd. That I am the only woman who has been taken out of the main area into this secluded room. But I am so terrified of looking stupid, of making a mistake, of ridicule, that I remain silent and follow this man without questioning him. After all, I don't know how things work in this country.

I have enough trouble buying cigarettes from a machine and not a person —a dumb look in my face when the cigarettes don't appear as they are supposed to. And I buy frozen pizza in a cardboard box, follow the instructions, place it in the oven at 375 degrees, and almost burn the apartment down. Where did it say that the pizza had to be taken out of the box?

I am avoiding a rerun of the pizza affair so badly that I ask nothing, object to nothing. I am troubled, however, by what I have to do next.

I am being *foot printed*, and in order for this to happen, I have to take off my stockings. Maneuvering this—under the watchful eyes of this man—without pulling my skirt back too high up my thighs is going to be difficult. I am wearing stockings—not the modern pantyhose—which are attached to garters, which are then attached to my underwear. In my case, my underwear is the asphyxiating girdle—a Cuban chastity belt—my mother made us wear to prevent any suggestive jiggling of the buttocks. Still sitting, I get my hands under the skirt and snap open the metal clips that attach the stockings to the garters. I am not sure I am sweating, but it feels like I am. I am trying to maintain a façade of calm and composure, but I am sure my face is red.

I finally get the stockings off. I look at my bare feet which have never seen a pedicure. And I think to myself, humiliated, that if I had to bare something in front of this man, why not something more attractive than my ugly feet? These feet which have been given uneven toes, and which I used to hide under the sand whenever a boy approached me on the beach? I am embarrassed. Diminished. I feel naked, as though I have had to shed a lot more than shoes and stockings. Shyly, shrinking, and feeling inexplicably shamed, I follow the man to the back of the room where he, supposedly, is going to take a print of my toes.

My sister' s future mother-in-law, an alert, experienced woman—and a U.S. citizen by virtue of having had an American father, who was educated in the States, and who has sisters still living in Boston—has been looking for me. She enters the room and when she sees where I am standing, she signals for me to come with her, a look of utter disbelief on her face. She does not have to say anything. I put my shoes on and go to the bathroom to put my stockings on.

Why me? Was it the red lipstick?

I left the INS offices with ink on my feet. A diminutive light was extinguished in me, and a feeling of shame and inadequacy persisted throughout the years.

TRUE LOVE

By Thomas L. David

From my limited experience, primarily watching movies, it seems that special love affairs follow a pattern: each phase triggers a different emotion. The first is anticipation, perhaps combined with a little harmless stalking. You've seen her and wow! Where can you see her again? Is she available? Would we be compatible? Next comes of the exhilaration of the first meeting when it seems as if it could be a fit. Then you become an item and settle in for the relaxed pleasure of extended time together. Soon come the special moments, the unforgettable highlights of life together. Every relationship has some downside, but you salvage and repair, rejoicing in the mend. Too often, unfortunately, comes an ending. So it was with me when a true love fashioned memories that remain eternally etched into my being.

She was a bit beamy, which provides stability, and her heft in the right places promised endurance and longevity. You understand, of course, that I am referring to a sailing yacht I acquired in the mid-1970s. Some men give their yachts the name of their mistress. I couldn't afford a mistress; I called her *Finesse*, a name that fit her well. She had an upswept bow with flowing lines aft to a slightly pinched derriere. A white waterline stripe accentuated her flow. A thin cove stripe just below the deck line, slightly impressed into the dark blue hull, was painted gold to accent her elegance. *Finesse* was a C&C 30 sloop (that means one mast), the number designating her 30-foot length. Her keel was laid (that means she was built) at Niagara on the lake, a little town in Ontario, Canada, about 30 miles from my home in Buffalo, New York.

Anticipation. Cuthbertson & Cassian (C&C Yachts) located in Niagara on Lake, Ontario, Canada, was renowned on the Great Lakes for fast, high-quality, racer-cruiser sailboats. *Finesse* would not be my first yacht. So as a knowledgeable sailor and a fussy shopper, it took many months of research reading magazine articles, comparing brochures, talking to owners and attending boat shows before I concluded that the C&C 30 would be the ideal vessel to proudly fill my slip at the Buffalo Yacht Club. In the dead of a Buffalo winter, I placed an order with a dealer in nearby Rochester, New York, and was given an April production date. I was hooked when told I could actually view her being built. She deserved the best attire; therefore much of the winter was spent with catalogues picking out an anchor, marine radio, the right compass, a knot meter (a nautical speedometer) and other paraphernalia for a proper yacht. Also, sails had to be ordered. What budget? Sometimes the shopping is more fun than the owning. With *Finesse* the outfitting was bitter-sweet, meticulous so each item would be perfect. But the waiting was excruciating.

Exhilaration. A call from the boat dealer in late March announced *Finesse*'s early manufacture. Bummer. I wanted to view part of the process. The good news: I finally got to see the finished product. Of course, all appointments were immediately cancelled, and I was on the road to Niagara on the Lake. And there she was with the beautiful dark blue hull, swept back keel and a gorgeous interior trimmed with teak, and red and blue berth cushions. Now it was just the wait for the dam ice on the Lake to melt so the sailing season could begin.

She's all mine. In mid-May *Finesse* was floating at the Rochester boat dealer's marina waiting for its new owner. Her first voyage was a sail west on Lake Ontario to St. Catherines, Ontario, the entrance to the Welland Canal. The canal dates back to the 1820's. It has seven locks which lift boats the 325 feet to the height of Lake Erie. It exits at Port Colborne, Ontario, on Lake Erie just a few miles west of *Finesse*'s new home. My crew and I arrived at the marina bright and early on a Saturday morning; we began *Finesse*'s first voyage. It was cold, 60° F at best, and a bit choppy. We suffered a bit learning a new boat but finally got the right sail combination for the conditions. She sailed like a dream. The skipper—that's me!—was in ecstasy.

The Welland Canal is meant for the big guys, the lake freighters. Pleasure yachts are allowed in between as commerce permits. The first order of business on entering the canal is to call in to the dispatcher on a marine radio. Your presence is noted and you are told to stand by for instructions. We were then motoring in the entrance basin of the canal. All of a sudden *Finesse* started to shake violently. We speculated that something was caught on the propeller. *Finesse* limped to the shore as we tried to figure what was wrong. Before we even tied up, the dispatcher on the radio barked, "You can't stay there. You will get hit by a freighter." It was the first peril for my beautiful new baby. Now understand, it was only weeks before that the ice had melted off the Great Lakes. The water temperature was certainly below 50° F. The propeller was the first item to check. On *Finesse* it was under the hull just forward of the stern. Somebody had to go in the water. Love sent caution to the winds. In just seconds a sweater, jeans, shirt and shoes were off and, in only my skivvies, I was in the water and under her. A plastic bag—it probably held ice in a former life— had wrapped around the prop. It came off easily. I was back in the boat so quickly I don't remember being cold. In fact, it happened so fast I may not even have gotten wet. Could *Finesse* ever doubt my love?

The Welland Canal is twenty-seven miles long and you have to wait your turn to enter each lock and then wait for each lock to fill— it was a long trip. The locks work by the force of gravity, simple but still amazing. Each lock is still a bit of an adventure; they tuck you in a corner beside a 700-foot freighter and toss you lines to help you keep your distance as the elevation changes. It all worked out. My love was soon home, ready for a summer on Lake Erie.

Pure pleasure. In a typical summer *Finesse* provided sailboat races, day cruises with friends and clients, and on many weekends, accommodations for me, my then-wife and my three sons. *Finesse* slept six. The Buffalo Yacht Club had a summer station just across the eastern end of Lake Erie on the Canadian shore where *Finesse* spent her summer. In the protection of Point Abino the water was calm, even in storm conditions. On a Friday night after work, the trip from home to *Finesse* took hardly an hour. There we joined several other families, also camping out on their boats. *Finesse* had an oven, a stove, an ice chest and even a small dinette. It was a perfect base for a weekend outing. Not bad for what people think of as snowy Buffalo. The boys had swimming, fishing, sailing small boats and whatever else young boys do when freed from the scrutiny of their parents. They departed in the morning and returned only for meals and a place to sleep. *Finesse* ably served as a private lakeside inn for my family; so how could I not love her?

Lake Erie's sailing season runs from mid-May to mid-September. In the lonely winter yachts sit ashore on a cradle with only a heavy cover protecting them from winter's cruelty. Long suffering sailors, some just back in the house after shoveling the snow off their driveways, count the days until spring, ogling at the photos in yachting magazines, bikini-clad maidens tanning on the latest yachts somewhere in the tropical sun. When the weather finally breaks spring also blossoms in a skipper's heart and it is time to prepare for the launch of his vessel. One year *Finesse* spent the winter at a boatyard at Niagara on the Lake so that a ship's wheel could be installed in place of her tiller, an upgrade I couldn't afford at the time of her purchase. The finest yacht craftsman in the entire area worked at that boatyard. Scotty had a brogue that matched his name and took such pride in his work that he simply refused to cut corners on any job. Perfect or nothing! That was fine with me—only the best for *Finesse*. No budget. So in April of that year some weekends were spent at Scotty's at Niagara on the Lake, indulging in the joy of readying *Finesse* for her spring launch. Off came the cover. Spring cleaning ensued. The hull was waxed, and new gadgets were installed. The trip to meet her each time was a real delight. The Niagara River below Niagara Falls is a contrast in *progress*. The American side of the river abounds with commercial and industrial buildings, and middle income, or below, residential development. The Canadian side is the opposite. History gave it a pass from the economic growth enjoyed by Western New Yorkers. On the Canadian shore you find golf courses and parks maintained by a school of horticulture. As you go farther north, beautiful houses sit back from the river. The public on the road has the priority view of the Niagara. A little further and the orchards and vineyards come into view. Yes, they make wine there and proudly serve it in their gourmet restaurants. In summer fruit stands abound. Their late summer crop of peaches could be the best in the world. Of course I always took the Canadian route. Even traveling to see *Finesse* was a delight.

My work had me traveling to Florida, usually coastal cities. Each time I would buy a local marine chart to study the water depths and the location of the marinas. Though many parts of Florida have access to the Atlantic or the Gulf, none compare to Miami and Biscayne Bay. The Bay is protected from Atlantic waves and storms by reefs and islands. It has several marinas and yacht clubs that support a multitude of sailboat racing. I moved my family to Miami; *Finesse*, safely in her cradle, soon followed on a truck.

Special moments. Sailboat racing thrives on Biscayne Bay, and we jumped right into the fray. When we adapted to local conditions, *Finesse* exceled; the race trophies, usually budget silver, flowed in. The term "budget silver" fit because after only a few polishings the silver started to wear away. No problem—it's the bragging rights that count.

My competition soon envied me, having three sons. My boys were addicted to sailboat racing and each in turn mastered a sailing crew's most demanding position, the foredeck. Having three sons that love sailing was a blessing every skipper would covet. Having three smart sons, each of whom believed he knew more than his father about racing a sailboat, was—interesting. We still reminisce about the wins and losses, the arguments, and some big races that could have been won if the skipper had just listened to his crew.

Our first ocean race introduced us to the some of the wonders of South Florida waters. The race began on the Atlantic at Fowey Light, off the coast of the Biscayne National Park. Fowey is one of several towers that mark the reefs in the ocean on the way from Miami to Key West. The race destination was Ocean Reef Club, about twenty miles to the South. The shortest distance to the winner's line hugs the shore. Natural channels, deep enough to sail, are marked with buoys guiding the way. On Lake Erie you don't see the bottom but in this race the crystal clear ocean water revealed a colorful seascape of sand bars and coral. What a sight! Then there were sea turtles, some as big as three feet in diameter. The show stopper was a nautical ballet. Hundreds of silvery fish jumped out of the water, in unison, glistening in the sun, apparently on the run from something below. *Finesse* treated us to quite a show.

The hurt. Stuff happens and some did with *Finesse*. The start of a sail boat race can be hectic. The committee boat sounds a warning horn five minutes before the start. The boats sail back and forth behind the start line, marked by buoys, jostling for position in the hope of a perfectly timed cross of the line, at speed, just as the start horn sounds. One time *Finesse*'s skipper made a dumb mistake that led to a collision. Part of her rigging (that is what holds up the mast) was damaged, putting her out of commission. After several weeks in a boatyard, she emerged sporting a repainted hull and new rigging. Soon she was back to normal, sailing with her usual speed and grace. I think she forgave me.

Parting. There came a time when financial and personal exigencies dictated that *Finesse* had to be sold. The reputation for C&C yachts was strong, even in South Florida. A willing buyer was not hard to find. It would be a few years before another sailing yacht occupied my slip at Miami's Coral Reef Yacht Club. The new yacht was designed more for racing. We called her *Haztabefast*. She was an able yacht that won more than her share of races. But she didn't measure up to the grace and elegance of *Finesse*, the love that remains permanently etched in a special place in my heart.

MOM'S BLUE TAFFETA DRESS

By Ellen Leeds

For some reason when I want to write about my mother, I usually don't. I'm not sure why that is. She was a good mother, someone I loved very deeply; yet when I write about my parents, it is usually my largest-in- life dad that I grapple with. My mom was always there for me. Frequently when my dad submerged himself in alcohol, she was the person who went through all the heartbreak with me because he was gone. Not physically, but emotionally.

Bea was the name she used. Although a woman of big stature, she was quite the fashion plate. From teased, high bee-hived hairdos to cut-short pixie-style streaked with blond—she forever tried following the trends. She learned to sew in order that her size couldn't stop her from wearing anything in size 22 that size twos could put on. She sported large oval glasses, a cigarette seemingly always in her hand. Large floppy hats in summer with long colorful muumuus and bright dresses no matter the season. She was forever engaged with people, friends and family. She could circle a room faster than anyone I have ever seen, stopping to talk to any-one and everyone in her path.

She didn't work which meant she was always available for school drop-offs and pickups. She didn't drive, but with my father's help, and taxis or friends' cars, we got everywhere we needed to be. There were many bus trips with her to the city—to Brooklyn and Manhattan to visit my mom's parents. We would sit side-by-side in the bus, and she always had snacks, drinks and candy for the ride as well as a large brown bag close by for my way-too-often car sick-nesses. I would snuggle against her shoulder and fall asleep, or look out the windows whirling past, or just listen to her read a sto-rybook to me. Broadway shows and seeing the Rockettes at Radio City Music Hall were some of our favorite outings.

We would go to Girl Scout meetings and events, she as our leader. Cartons with boxes of cookies would be stacked in our living room, and she was there distributing them to the girls dropping by, and then she would tabulate the returns. Whenever one of my birthdays occurred, she was instrumental in getting things put together with a theme. A favorite memory is the Japanese-themed birthday in our backyard with everyone sitting on the ground in kimonos, fans as favors, and large paper umbrellas shading the party goers. She was a master of making adventures for me right where we lived.

My dad's mom lived with us for many years, and it was just mi-raculous how the two of them were like sisters rather than mother-and daughter- in-laws. My mom had an affinity for welcoming people and having folks get along.

The picnics, the parties, the love that she exuded. When I would come home from school and feel alone or depressed, she would sit me down for milk and cookies and try to make it all bet-ter. She knew if she heard me crying in my room when to give me space and when to barge in and engulf me with a hug.

Being an only child I was lucky to have a mom who focused her love on me and guided me around dark spaces that I thought

I wouldn't pull out of. My high school years had many such moments. I never thought I could stand another day attending classes, but I did graduate with her pushing and prodding. I never felt condemned for below average work, or at times failures, but I was lifted up as being part of the human race.

My mom made a home for me that was inclusive of my friends and that lesson I believe I carried to my son and he will carry to his family someday. Whomever I brought home, she never judged. All races, religions, sexual orientation— if they were good people she sat them down at our table and many often felt like family.

I remember her asking me if I was in love with the man I chose to marry. When I said yes, she got on board and began asking about the future wedding.

She never got to walk me down the aisle with my dad, as is the Jewish custom. One month before the wedding I was called to come by their apartment because my mom wasn't feeling well. When I got there she first wanted me to open her bedroom closet to show me her beautiful royal blue dress that she recently purchased to wear at the upcoming ceremony.

"Mom, I have time to see it. How are you feeling?"

"Fine. Just a little dizzy. Please take a look. I want you to see it."

I opened her closet. I took it out of its plastic wrapping, delighted by its beauty. A bright blue taffeta dress. It was a three-quarter length with nice long sleeves, and it had jewels spattered along the top.

"Magnificent, Mom. You might be the hit of the day!"

Then I changed the subject.

"I saw dad in the kitchen. He said you weren't feeling too well, and he wanted me to come over to help. Why don't you sit up and I will get you some water?"

"I can't sit up. I can't move."

She was looking very pale, and her skin had become ashen. Her normally bubbly smile had left, and I began to worry a little. I persuaded my mom and dad to call an ambulance to get her to the closest emergency room.

My dad was pacing the apartment by now. He was worried and began to drink. I was too oblivious to be scared.

The wedding happened a month after that, and within that month my mom was buried. She had an aneurism that day I took her to the emergency room, and due to her extremely large size, the operation was more difficult than anticipated. The doctor came out and said he didn't think she would pull through the night.

She did pull through but hooked up to a myriad of tubes. She did manage to squeeze my hand. I felt encouraged to go home, change and get a little rest. After my future husband drove me home, a few hours later the hospital called saying she had died.

I don't know how it could have been, but our wedding was wonderful. My rabbi said my mom wouldn't want it canceled, and he was right. She would have loved the balloons on every table, the flowers, the people, the cake, and I could imagine her running around from table to table talking to all the wonderful family and friends who attended. My dad was there and somehow her death catapulted him into a deep depression and then to his sobriety; which he held onto until his death. I always thought her hand somehow was still directing the show.

Oh, and that beautiful blue dress! What happened to it? I could hear her voice: "Ellen, do not bury me in that. Someone on earth would enjoy it! Find someone to wear it. I would love that."

And so with love I found the perfect person to give my mom's blue taffeta dress—a teacher's aide at my school where I taught. She reported back to me that she loved wearing it to church. Even many years later, I asked her about that dress. She still owned it and loved wearing it for special occasions.

AND IT ALL BEGINS

By Sharon Wylie

"I don't seem to be able to locate this town on the map," I mentioned to the personnel assistant sitting across from me at a gray aluminum desk which mimicked her metallic gaze. I knew the job description "personnel" noted on the sign on her door had nothing to do with her having an actual "personality." Without comment, she slid her glasses farther up onto her nose with her index finger and dismissively pushed the papers across the desk in my direction with a keen sense of authority. She managed to do all this with the minimal effort of a single hand gesture using maybe four muscles. The original Lego. I signed the contract with my new adult signature (no more heart shapes as *I* dotters) and ignored the slight—no time for recrimination. After all, I was finally employed and on the road to my first teaching job—wherever that was. I didn't want to upset her by asking too many questions. She wasn't exactly chatty and wielded such power over me at that moment. In a spurt of irritation she could deem me incompetent for such responsibility, shred the documents, and call the whole thing off!

Later after packing up moving boxes in my Minneapolis apartment, which weren't many since I had been there only a few months, I further scrutinized the map of southern Montana. Under the eye of my magnifying glass, I discovered a small, lonely, almost translucent dot indicating a town named Ekalaka, not Ekauwa, as my employment information had mistakenly read. Someone's typo. No wonder I hadn't been able to find it on the map! I also noticed the thread of road that ran into the town stopped at the dot. Bleak—maybe. Deterred—no. School was to begin in a few days. I had miles in front of me.

Waves of loneliness saturated the air as the wind pushed me across the flat, empty terrain. The journey began in the crop land where, being the onset of autumn, an occasional farmer finishing up his harvesting was the only other sentient being for miles. Combines, like massive grasshoppers throwing the chafe into the air, cut long swathes into the golden fields of wheat. The wind arched the chafe a few feet into the air before letting it drop.

That topography came to a sudden stop and made way for the rocks of the desolate Badlands. Striations of iridescent formations gleamed in the late afternoon sun settling in behind the barren crags. The layered pastel colors told archeological stories and held ancient secrets of eras millenniums ago. I wound around—east, west, up, down until escaping the labyrinth and reaching the Montana border. There the straight ribbon of road emerged and was not to be intruded upon with the likes of a speed limit. It stretched until infinity. My destination was the ranchland, the verdant fields and the silent rock were behind me now and had been replaced by soulless cattle.

I observed as I turned south to follow the sign to Ekalaka that the road switched from concrete to gravel—not a good omen. It was as straight as if it had been drawn with a cosmic ruler. The only divergence was the vertical plane into which my shocks sunk as they descended the deep pot holes and threw me into the air a few inches. Dust was stirred up and tumble weeds, the only pedestrians, crossed the road. Everything to the horizon was the color of dun.

Nestled in the soft hill, the town shot up like a mirage in a desert. Thudding down the dirt road, the main thoroughfare, 1 shuttered at the paucity of businesses: a cafe, a drugstore, and a grocery store. Two bars skirted each end of town like licentious sentinels. The south bar marked the end of the road, so to leave town, it was necessary to backtrack out. This was my home for the next nine months. Oh, woebegone! I didn't know the parking style, whether to parallel park or pull straight in since my car was the only vehicle on the street. I emerged, took a quick stretch after my journey, and pushed open the screen door into the cafe. I slid into a booth and ordered a Coke. Shortly the silence was interrupted by a voice from across the black-and-white-checked, diner-reminiscent, linoleumed room, "You the new teacher?" A pack of teenagers in various stages of adolescence swiveled their heads in my direction waiting for my answer as they sized me up. I was outed already. Just like that. I wouldn't be getting away with much in this town.

ARTICHOKES AND ASPARAGUS

By Magdalena De Gasperi

I t is April. This year it has not been too warm; the first half was normal: rainy, mercurial. In Frankfurt I saw a magnolia tree in glorious bloom and behind it one of the first cherry trees to open, its somewhat darker pink barely distinguishable from the magnolia's, almost like Siamese twins. I looked forward to wearing open shoes again and had a pedicure.

Mid-April I went to Rome for five days with our Italian ladies group. The organization is usually organic, too full, somewhat chaotic. I often think only women can survive this—our husbands would quit after the first hour. We were seven women this time: two Italians, two Romanian-Germans, an Austrian, a German, and myself as an Italo-American. Our sleeping quarters were in a rooming house run by nuns, near Porta Pia in the northeast corner of the city. My room had two bathrooms separated by sliding plastic doors: one toilet had no wooden seat, the other had a wooden seat, but the paint was chipping in large chunks and pinched your flesh when you sat on it. I figured it was better than daily flagellation. Breakfast was included but so awful that after the first morning we went to a nearby bar for our morning cappuccino and toast or brioche.

The activities, however, are usually wonderful. The first afternoon we enjoyed a private guided tour of the Palazzo Koch, the 19ᵗʰ century villa built for the Banca d'Italia. The discreet manor is full of artistic treasures that wealthy patrons gave the bank to pay off their debts. Our guide was the bank's own art historian, who explained that the Palazzo Koch (in Italian pronounced "Cockeh") is only open to the public once a year and otherwise only accessible for guests of the Banca d'Italia. The spectacular staircase, the many rare and sumptuous types of marble used for door frames, flooring, the enormous chandeliers. Two hours went by quickly, and since the tour was in Italian, it was also an excellent lesson in Italian comprehension.

The following morning we met our guide for the next three days: a Jesuit priest retired from a German academic career and now living in Rome, Professore Marx. Professore spoke fluent Italian but our Italian ladies did not like his accent, so they asked him if he would prefer doing the explanations in German. He did, and so we went through the Vatican museum and heard his erudite, often entertaining explanations in academic German tinged with a faint accent from the Rhine country. The rooms got more and more crowded as we approached the crowd magnets: Stanze di Raffaello (Raffaelo's rooms) and the Sistine Chapel. As crowded as the room is and as annoying the loud voices of the guards booming, "Silence! Keep moving," the ceiling of the Sistine Chapel has a fascination that transcends time and space. Those two fingers about to touch in the creation scene continue to be magical even after several viewings.

After the Vatican tour we learned to appreciate Professore Marx even more. Using his Nordic walking poles to maneuver his stocky, no longer young physique through the crowds, he led us confidently to a restaurant some three or four blocks away. Our ladies kept getting lost so it took us some time to arrive. He had a large table reserved for us and immediately ordered two large bottles of water and a liter of the house white. It was 1:30 p.m. He seemed to know what he was doing: lunch, Italian style.

At the restaurant entrance there was a display of at least thirty large, fleshy artichokes. Professore recommended *carciofi alla romana*, and try them I did. My plate arrived with a huge artichoke that had been deep-fried, so it tasted salty and crunchy like French fries, but the inside was soft, healthy, and green. "Can I eat the whole thing?" I asked, ready to dig in. "Oh, yes," said Professore, "all the inedible parts have been removed." How tasty it was – and filling too. After that there was hardly a meal where one of us did not order artichokes in some way or form: marinated, fried, together with pasta or risotto. If there is an artichoke capital of the world, it must be Rome.

After three more days in the eternal city, we sadly returned home to much colder weather in Germany. My husband had to have abdominal surgery three days after our return, and I spent many hours and days in the hospital. The weather turned nasty, with sleet showers and night temperatures around freezing. When I picked him up from the hospital a week later, on our way home we saw the peak of our neighborhood "mountain" covered with a dusting of snow.

Yet it is still April, and the magnolias, tulips and cherry trees are used to these weather caprioles. And as a friend in Miami had reminded me, April is the beginning of the asparagus season in Germany. My husband, who dislikes asparagus, calls it the "asparagus terror," since nearly every restaurant you enter has a sheet inserted into the menu, the seasonal *Spargelmenü*, usually offering white asparagus with new potatoes and butter or Hollandaise sauce, and optionally any additional accompaniment such as boiled or cured ham, filet of salmon or veal, but also asparagus soup, salads, or even omelets.

Germany seems to be the only country that prefers white asparagus, which is harvested before the tips penetrate the soil and begin to photosynthesize. This underground harvesting is quite laborious and white asparagus accordingly more expensive than the green variety popular in France, southern Europe, and the U.S. But Germans swear by the delicate, somewhat smoky taste of white asparagus, and consume some 70,000 tons of it during the asparagus season, which usually ends on the day of St. John the Baptist, June 24.

Actually, it is no longer April. Today is May 1 (this is 2016), and for the first time the icy wind seems to have retreated. In our village marketplace, people could sit at the outdoor café in the sun and enjoy an espresso or an ice cream – almost a bit of Italian feeling. And while I miss that *carciofi alla romana*, I look forward to another seven weeks of eating asparagus as often as I can.

NEW YORK, A LOVE STORY

By Elsa Goss Black

N ew York has always been the Big Apple of my eye.
I was still a fairly young girl when I fell in love with this city.
Taking the Wednesday *Ladies' Day Special*, first with my mother
and then with friends, I could hardly contain my excitement as
the train entered into the dark tunnel that meant we would soon
be in Manhattan. Exactly why a train which picked up passengers
from Philadelphia's 30th Street Station could arrive some 90 minutes later at a place called Penn Station never made much sense
to me.

It still doesn't.

But knowing that I would spend a day in New York was the only
thing that mattered. I loved the hustle and bustle, the skyscrapers,
the elegant department stores and the razzle-dazzle of Broadway.
I loved the sundaes at Rumpelmayer's, the clip-clop of the horse-
drawn carriages toting tourists into Central Park and the ice skat-
ers showing off at the Rockefeller Center rink in winter. I even

loved the hot soot blowing up into my face from sidewalk grates during the long, humid summers. It all meant that I was in the city of my dreams.

Back then, I didn't realize that New York was really a place of vastly different neighborhoods and vastly differing fortunes. It never occurred to me—not for very long, anyway— that people lived in places far less luxurious than the uptown apartment towers twinkling at dusk as people headed home from what I was sure were glamorous jobs and leisurely shopping expeditions. I never considered that any of them might be dissatisfied, desperately lonely or deeply in debt. They were so lucky to be living in New York— and that, to me, meant they were lucky enough.

A part of me, I have to confess, still feels that way. Just as a picture of the famous fictional imp Eloise still stands guard in a side hallway of the Plaza Hotel, the little girl I was, enchanted by everything this city has to offer, still lies not far beneath the surface of the woman she became. We have never had a full-time relationship, New York and I, living as I have in other places, not on this island. But we have had a lasting love affair that time and experience cannot destroy.

There have been years when the streets were dirty and full of uncollected trash, when the subways loomed dank and ominous even in daylight, when walking back to your crosstown hotel from a Broadway show seemed a journey through Dante's Seventh Circle of Hell. There have even been times when New York has not seemed to care about the rest of the world any more than the rest of the world cared about it.

As the *Daily News* once screamed in a 1975 front page headline, *Ford to City: Drop Dead,* when the President refused to bail out the near-bankrupt town. And during the Iowa caucuses not so long ago, Ted Cruz made short—but successful—shrift out of the notion that "New York values" are somehow too liberal, too elitist, too Jewish and altogether un-American.

Yet I don't see it, have never, in fact, seen it and don't accept it. To me, this babbling, noisy, can-do melting pot is the most American of cities, the place that most clearly showcases our national and diverse character. I concede, of course, that many hearts have been broken here and many other spirits shattered. And when I arrive nowadays, the absence of the Twin Towers soaring above the glorious skyline outside the airplane windows is a bitter realization that happy endings are not guaranteed. Not here. Not anywhere. Not anymore.

But oh, my, the sheer enduring audacity of this city still thrills my soul. The streets are cleaner and safer now, the people nicer and the renovated, pedestrian-friendly Times Square stands like a blinding, gaudy daybreak even in the middle of the night. And about the Twin Towers: the horrific ashes which rained down on 9/11 have given rise to the One World Trade Center, with its breathtaking panorama at the Observatory on the 100th and 101th floors. On the same hallowed grounds are the 9/11 Memorial and Museum, bone-chilling and yet restorative, testaments to the courage of the lives lost there and the resilience of those who remain.

And so it is throughout this city.

Yes, it's a place of startling contrasts, of mind-boggling haves and tragic have-nots, and spending even a few days here can seem like a real life game of Monopoly as the dollars flow out of your wallet with alarming speed. But it's also a place where you can buy half-price tickets for a Broadway show on a daily basis and where you can catch a rehearsal of the New York Philharmonic at Lincoln Center— Lincoln Center!—for the price of an Andrew Jackson.

Even on a crisp winter day, you can walk for miles through the glories of Central Park, enjoying buskers playing all manner of music, from tenor sax to violin to bagpipes, passing greenery that's off-limits as the signs proclaim the lawns to be "resting" until spring.

Dogs, massive, miniature and everything in-between, wear sweaters against the chill, daring anyone to think them anything less than adorable. Led by or more often, leading, owners, dog walkers or their own nannies, they saunter alongside joggers, bicyclists, society matrons and tourists, men, women and beasts all out for an afternoon stroll. Meanwhile, you can eat a hot dog, buy a magnet or listen to a choir singing in the echo chamber of a tunnel leading to the Jacqueline Kennedy Onassis reservoir. There, forlorn canoes are stored for the season and the uncrowded boathouse restaurant sits on its urban shore.

It's all there for the taking. You can sit in one of the 4,100 Central Park benches marked by small plaques commemorating a birthday, an anniversary, memories long gone and those yet to be made. In the city so often devoted to Mammon, these metallic etchings are sentimental and quiet offerings to the best of what makes us truly human, the things that make a life well lived.

In fact, so much of what brings me pleasure here are the small treasures and sly humor found on almost every corner. A tree outside one immaculate Village townhouse is still decorated with Christmas lights in February, while a small pumpkin and a stuffed Count Dracula decorate a window of the house across the street. Not to be outdone, the residents of a townhouse further down the block have strung a flock of bright red toy cardinals from the branches of their tree. Three seasons on one tiny street? Well done, I say, and smile.

Commemorating quite another season altogether is the pocket park on Christopher Street, with its duplicate of the George Segal sculpture, "Gay Liberation Movement." Overlooking it is ground zero of that movement, the still open and ready for prime time Stonewall Inn. Christopher Street itself intersects with the small, winding, deliciously named Gay Street and nearby is the hip canine fashion boutique named— what else?—"Doggy Style."

Take that, Mike Pence!

Similarly, in a nod to threats against the civil rights of us all, coffee shops across the city sported signs last weekend advertising

"Proudly Donating 15% of sales to the ACLU." And who cares about the arts? Nearly everybody living in or visiting this city, it sometimes seems.

You need only to look at the lines outside of Carnegie Hall waiting to attend a classical concert on a Tuesday night. Or to see the crowds sitting on the steps of the Metropolitan Museum on a Monday afternoon. For a timelier visit as far as current events go, walk into the Museum of Modern Art, which responded to the Muslim ban by hanging works of art by artists from seven of the affected countries in one prominent gallery. Slickly subversive, with a touch of grace, much like my view of the city itself.

Speaking of grace, unlike audiences elsewhere, who keep their cell phones stubbornly lit throughout concerts, shows and films alike, New York audiences wait patiently in the dark to be entertained. And when they like what they see, they are the best audiences in the world, staying in their seats until the last second. There's no hustling up the aisles to beat the traffic for these crowds, not when there's still magic to be made.

And magic it often is, this near-religious connection between performers and paying customers. Consider Glenn Close's return to *Sunset Boulevard*, 20 years after she first starred in it on Broadway. Still in previews, it's a red-hot sell-out, not a seat to be had in the elegant and aptly named Palace Theater. Rapturously received the night I saw it, the show was stopped cold by loud applause several times before the curtain went down. The entire cast was then rewarded with a standing ovation and several curtain calls, while the lady herself was brought back for three more solo rounds of thunderous cheers. Movie star famous or not, she literally skipped into the wings on the joy of the final one.

I knew—I know, each and every time I visit—exactly how she felt. With the Bronx still up and the Battery down, New York, New York remains a helluva town.

SPAGHETTI — OH!

By Kitty Winkler

Louise conducted several writing workshops each week for groups of eight to twelve writers at her Magic Table, the dining table where we wrote and occasionally produced magic.

We loved Louise. Always encouraging, her critiques were handed out sparingly. She and her husband Floyd were in their sixties. Both were small, gentle people with kind hearts. Louise had two successful young adult books to her credit and a number of short stories that had been published in magazines targeted for young adults. She was soft-spoken and nurturing to all of us, and we responded by continuing to sign up for her workshops year after year.

Louise and Floyd had a unique house. It had once been the stable for a large Scarsdale, New York, estate and had been converted to a house in the 1920s when the big estates were being subdivided to make room for more mega-mansions. The mansions were set back 100 to 150 feet from the road, but Louise and Floyd's house was set back much farther with its only frontage on the main road being a very long driveway. At the end of the driveway, it was like entering another world. There was a side lot that fell away steeply from the house and a small garden and patio on the same level as the house that overlooked the wild and wonderful side yard. The property was large and totally private, being far from the road and far from the mansions that were nearer the road. The wooden house had Victorian gingerbread trim. Inside, it was filled with cozy and slightly messy rooms with books everywhere. It was a great setting for a writing class; the house itself stimulated imagination, and writing ideas flowed.

One year, Louise got the idea of holding a pot luck Christmas party for the students in all her classes, about thirty to forty of us. We were all to bring dishes, and Louise and Floyd would supply the drinks. I volunteered to bring spaghetti Bolognese, others signed up for other entrees, salads, appetizers, or desserts.

Since it was December, it was pitch dark when the party started; and being in a quiet, residential area, there were few street lights. The driveway to Louise's and Floyd's house quickly filled up with parked cars, and new arrivals had to park on the road to walk up the long driveway to the house.

I was one of the late arrivals who had to park on the road. I arrived by myself with my hot spaghetti in a large, lidded Pyrex dish. I had brought oven mitts with me because the dish was right out of the oven and hadn't cooled much in the ten-minute drive to Louise's house.

I grabbed the handles of the dish with the mitts and started the trek down the long driveway. Ten or fifteen yards down the driveway the street lights were out of sight, and it became a matter of carefully groping from car to car to stay on a path through the darkness. I kept hoping another guest would arrive to relieve me of my casserole, even if only for a few minutes, but it didn't happen. The dish became heavier and heavier, and I began to rest it on the hood of every third or fourth car as I made my slow way down the drive. At last I arrived at the well-lit house. What a relief.

I spent a few minutes juggling the casserole around, trying to figure out how to open the front door or ring the bell without dropping my burden. Finally, I saw that the door was open a crack, and I nudged it with one foot to get it open. At last I found myself in the foyer, and my dish was safe.

To get to the kitchen, I had to pass through the den and dining room. I turned to go into the den and saw Floyd coming toward me with arms outstretched to take my casserole. I took a step toward him, tripped on the den threshold, and the dish sailed through the air. It landed on the carpet after big globs of spaghetti had flown out to cover anything and everything within throwing radius of my entrance.

The rocking chair and the afghan coverlet draped over its back were covered with spaghetti. The side table with its stack of magazines caught another big blob of it. The television had spaghetti dripping down its screen. In front of me on the floor was the broken casserole dish and a mound of wet spaghetti sauce soaking into the carpet. It had all played out in hideous slow motion. I couldn't have more thoroughly coated their den with spaghetti if I had grabbed big handfuls and carefully aimed each handful at a piece of furniture. Still engraved on my mind is the picture of Floyd with his kind face broadly smiling to greet me gradually transforming into a mask of horror as the spaghetti began to fly.

What can one say after a gaffe this large? Certainly nothing profound. I think I said something like, Oh Floyd, oh Floyd, oh I am so sorry. Oh, I can't imagine how I did that. And repeated it all over and over again.

I got down on my knees with the idea of gathering as much spaghetti as I could into the broken dish, but Floyd rushed to pull me up. No, no, go on into the living room and enjoy the party. Let me deal with this; I know exactly what to do. It's not a problem.

Not a problem! If that wasn't a problem, what would have been? An atomic bomb going off in the house? A flood sweeping through? A tree through the roof?

However, I was very grateful to Floyd for minimizing the obvious damage I had done, and because he would have it no other way, I went into the living room to join the party. Thinking about it later, he probably sent me away because he was fearful of what other damage I might do.

As so often happens with cringe-worthy events like this, over time – lots and lots of time – it became a funny story to tell. The first few months, however, were terrible. I couldn't walk into Louise and Floyd's house for writing workshop without mortification as the whole awful incident rushed back at me. I am sure that Louise and Floyd spent those same few months getting spaghetti out of everything they owned. I imagined the dialogue. Oh look dear, I found some petrified spaghetti in the waste basket. Well, that's nothing, I moved the lamp to dust, and there was a perfect ring of spaghetti sauce on the table. Will we ever be free of it?

The last time I was back in Scarsdale, I learned that Louise and Floyd had sold their house for a princely sum to the estate next door. The house was torn down because the new owners wanted to put in a tennis court. I found myself wondering if the demolition team found spaghetti remnants in the floorboards and foundation as the house came apart.

GUARDIAN ANGEL

By Thomas L. David

I t was late on a Saturday morning in Scottsdale, the end of a three day business meeting. The normal MO would be to hustle my bored body to the airport for a flight back to Miami.

Not this time!

A new adventure beckoned. Several friends had marveled about the beauty of Sedona, a town about 100 miles to the northwest. A motorcycle trip through the desert to Sedona: what a perfect way to spend Sunday.

I had filled many a weekend with my biker buddies exploring the lesser known innards of South Florida. My addiction to the sport even included reading the classifieds in *Cycle World* magazine. They revealed a motorcycle rental company in nearby Phoenix. It was my chance to ride in a different world: the Arizona desert after years in Florida swampland.

The motorcycle company turned out to be a compulsive little man with several rather old BMW touring bikes in the garage of his suburban Phoenix home. BMW made airplanes and motor-cycles long before the cars beemerphiles now covet. I patiently endured the barrage of trivial questions and exasperating instructions from Mr. Anality, queasy about leasing me one of his treasures with only my rental car parked in front of his home to assure I'd ever return. The routine included a direction to always conceal the parked machine with the custom "cover" he provided. The cover was so time-worn that cheese cloth would have been a durability upgrade. Finally I was on the road guiding an old BMW touring bike back to my hotel.

Tomorrow loomed like Christmas morning to a six-year-old.

To appreciate what happened next, though, you have to understand some of the mechanics of this old BMW motorcycle. It had an opposed two-cylinder engine with one-cylinder head sticking out of each side of the engine compartment. The rider sits with his shins behind the cylinder heads and his feet on pegs just below. A couple inches ahead of the left side foot peg is a gearshift lever. You change gears by flipping the lever up or down with the left toe of your boot. This is the common gear-shift mechanism on most motor cycles. Shifting becomes second nature in no time at all. Different, though, on this bike was the fuel system. Just above the gearshift lever was a fuel bowl, a sturdy glass bowl about two inches in diameter hanging off the engine. The gasoline passes through the fuel bowl on its way to the carburetor which routes the gasoline into the cylinder where it ignites creating the force that turns the motor and moves the bike. It made your day to hear that, right?

This is going to make your week.

Any dirt in the gasoline falls to the bottom of the bowl and is visible through the glass. A simple clip under the bowl holds it in place and easily flips open to clean out any residue. Good German engineering, right?

Motorcyclists, like most hobbyists, are suckers for gimmicks and gadgets. Count me in. I often succumbed, including buying steel-toed motorcycle boots; better to protect my toesies should an errant stone threaten my foot while zooming down the highway. Really good, too, when going through metal detectors in airports. A few minutes into the ride back to the hotel the bliss evaporated. The motor began running so rough I couldn't continue. A call to my nerdy friend and he said he thought he knew the problem. "Sit tight."

A few minutes later my friend showed up in his car holding a glass fuel bowl in his hand. He found it along the side of the road. I unknowingly kicked off the clip with my steel-toed boot while shifting and the fuel bowl fell off. The gasoline flow to the left cylinder was interrupted causing the roughness. A demo on how to reattach the fuel bowl and another lecture from Mr. Nerd on how to shift and I was on my way.

The next morning I was off to Sedona on a deserted two lane road, gawking at the beauty of the desert: the sky seemed higher, the plants looked eerie and the occasional gnarled tree that refused to succumb to the lack of water. About a half hour into the ride I had to stop and park the bike to inspect the saguaro cacti. Amazing plants! Some were taller than Lady Gaga on Wilt Chamberlain's shoulders. They have delicate white flowers that open at night and close before afternoon and they offer hollows that accommodate small birds, all in a setting that survives without rain. Then, back on the bike.

Sedona here I come.

As I shifted into high gear, guess what the klutz with the steel toed boots did? You've got it. I kicked the clip and the prodigal fuel bowl decided to do its own exploring. The motor ran so rough I couldn't continue. I pulled over and parked the bike in a desert, which no longer seemed captivating or adventurous. Nothing I couldn't handle, though. Just find the fuel bowl, replace it and continue to Sedona. As I walked back down the road in search of the little bugger, a pick-up truck stopped and out popped a rather fit young man. My eyes immediately shot (no pun intended) to the holster and pistol at his hip, not something I was used to seeing in the city. Why is it again that I thought I didn't need to carry a gun for self-defense? The young man approached, with a smile, and said, "Is this yours?" In his hand was the errant fuel bowl. While following me he saw a spray from below my bike, apparently when the gasoline in the fuel bowl escaped. He retrieved the fuel bowl from the side of the road. He, too, was a motorcyclist and we motorcycle guys look out for each other. As Honda said, "You meet the nicest people on a Honda." Or on other motorcycles.

The pistol, you ask?

He was on his way to a shooting range.

The rest of the trip to Sedona and back was less eventful. But, wow! As you approach Sedona the mountains turn red. It is like entering a fairy-tale land. Almost with the charm of a New England town it has little shops, quaint eateries, but adds tales of miners. I stopped for lunch and a little shopping, faithfully covering my ride with the cheesecloth—I mean custom cover. Then I enjoyed the ride back to Phoenix. Somehow I lost the cover and my nerdy little friend insisted that I pay for a new one. On objection he played the guilt-trip card. "I'll take whatever you think is fair," he whined. I partially succumbed and paid half the cost of new cover. But, I left him and Arizona that night with a smile frozen on my face.

DIANA OF CUBA

By Beatriz La Rosa

I watch Diana die from the sanctuary that closed doors offer, through the wood bars of the window painted in a bright blue color. Foaming at the mouth, her jaws withdrawn into a grimace of death, blood staining her black and white coat, she rests under my baby brother's crib, a place where she has slept many times before.

She has been shot on this glorious fall day in 1948. She is mortally wounded, and as she dies, she hears my mother's lament—her death song—of God God what have I done?

At five years old I am one of five children—four girls and a boy. The youngest is the boy sleeping in the crib. He is the incarnation of my mother's prayers to San Antonio, her patron saint, who after giving her four girls, took pity and gave her a male child. Diana is the family dog, a sweet English pointer bitch who is not only the family pet but also a hunter of birds and other game.

I live on a sugar cane plantation, Santa Petrona, in the province of Matanzas, Cuba. This land has been in my family for generations, and my father inherited this land from his father. The farm is close to the Cienaga de Zapata, the wetlands where Playa Giron is located, and the site of the Bay of Pigs invasion.

I am told that on certain days the peace of the marshes of the Cienaga is broken by a mirage, that of a cloud which is both lucent and sepulchral. The cloud ferries the souls of the one-hundred and seventeen young men who will die in Bahia de Cochinos in 1961. I cannot tell you where the cloud is taking them.

My father hunts in the Cienaga often, and Diana is the one retrieving the birds as they fall to the ground, their flight interrupted by the pellets from my father's shotgun. When Diana and my father come back from a day of hunting—my father's hunting belt heavy with quail—I see Diana smiling, proud of the game hanging from her master's belt. I eat quail for days.

Santa Petrona had a sugar mill at the time of my grandfather. The mill is gone, but some of the structures remain. The barracon—the barracks that were used to house the sugarcane cutters who had no families—still remain. Early in the mornings, I visit my friend Perico, who lives in one of the rooms. He takes care of my father's gallos finos, or fighting cocks.

The barracon is a long wooden building with an empty space at the center—tools and machinery are kept here—and rows of rooms on either side. This building, and several bohios, are part of the batey, which is a hamlet that developed around the mills. My house, which sits at the center, presides over its less fortunate subjects, which are huts with thatched palm roofs and dirt floors. My home is a handsome stone house with whitewashed walls, a tile roof, and floor-to-ceiling latticed wooden windows and doors which are painted a bright blue. The floors are paved in colorful Cuban tiles, which feel cool on my feet as I step on them barefooted in the mornings. A covered porch serves as dining room and is next to the kitchen.

The farm is isolated. We have no electricity and there is no glare from nearby towns to interrupt the blackness of the moonless nights. I delight in the tiny points of light dancing in the darkness, those fireflies that I sometimes catch, placing them in a prison of glass, for my enjoyment. Some nights I can see the glow and smell the smoke from nearby sugarcane fields which have been set ablaze—sometimes by troublemakers—but always before the harvest.

Diana sits at my father's feet for the evening meal. Dinnertime is when tales of ghosts, specters, the dead, Santeria rituals, the latest band of outlaws, and blood-drinking sorcerers, are told. I am shaken by these tales, and haunted by the memory of those burlap bags filled with blackened pennies or bloody beheaded chickens which are left on the steps of the porch from time to time. I look to my father, two seats away from me at the head of the table. His black revolver is resting on the table, to his left.

As the family settles for dinner, the illumination from the gas lamps imparts a soft glow. This light creates a shelter around me, much like the halo I have seen encircling the bald head of San Antonio de Jesus, my mother's patron saint, in the religious prints she keeps on her bedside table.

The gas lighting is from a recently installed system, an Estados Unidos innovation my father bought from Union Carbide. This consists of a tank which is filled with a blue, chalky, smelly power, which I learn is called calcium carbide. This gives me a bright light—in spite of the fact that I am scared of this menacing tank, believing it is a close relative of if not the devil himself—my amulet against the beings who populate the impenetrable darkness surrounding the house. I can hear a punto Guajiro coming from the battery operated radio in the living room. Sometimes it is a baseball game that is being transmitted from the capital, La Habana. The music, the voice of the announcer as it yells, "Jon Ronnnnnn!" and the aroma of the chunks of pork being fried in the kitchen—using the lard rendered by the unwilling sacrifice of their kin—is a gift from my saints and from the hallowed red earth. I am safe.

The morning Diana is shot, I wake up to the clatter of the rusted windmill blades and to the incessant chatter of the hens, who are picking the ground in search of food. A murmur of voices reaches the bedroom, the sound riding the aromatic waves of the coffee being boiled and strained through a colander, Cuban style, in the kitchen. Fresh milk is frothing in an old pot, its bottom blackened by use. It sits on a coal stove, the fire started anew this morning with that one lonely ember that once again endures its overnight vigil—its only duty to sustain the fire that sustains me—linking my days in a continuum of life.

I wear a cotton dress, a hand-me-down from my older sisters, frayed by many washes, and which feels soft on my skin. I grab the brown booties and a pair of yellowed socks, their whiteness marred by the dirt that is ingrained in the fabric. I tie my hair with a silk ribbon in anticipation of the visit by the primaria school teacher, a young man who arrives on horseback, wearing a guayabera, a jipijapa hat, and a thin black moustache. I am dazzled by this man. He rides the horse, his body erect on the saddle, legs straddling the mare's sides, his body melding with the horse's body in the rhythmic cantering of the animal.

As I step out of the bedroom, Ramira—the fourteen-year old girl who helps my mother with the chores—is standing on the porch, my mother next to her. Ramira is scrubbed clean, her dress starched and ironed, her skin the color of ebony. She has high, prominent cheekbones, a broad nose, thick lips. Her black eyes are set closely on her face, her budding breasts glimpse through the soft fabric of her dress. Her hair is neatly braided in two pigtails. She glistens in the morning sun.

She is the youngest in a family of seven—five men and two women. They live in one of the bohios close to our home. Her brothers are macheteros, young strong men who cut the sugarcane by hand, using the strength of their arms, wielding machetes that cut the sugarcane close to the ground. Often I look for them in the nearby fields in pursuit of the sweet sugarcane which they cut for me in chunks and which I guzzle, the juice running down my chin and staining my dress as I bite into its fibrous meat.

Ramira's oldest sister killed herself, drowning in a water well in the same fields where the sweet crops grow. No preguntes my mother admonishes as she walks around the house, addressing no one in particular. Eventually, through whispered conversations punctuated by sighs, signs of the cross, and Ave Maria, que pena, Dios nos libre, which I hear in fragmented sentences from the adults, I devour the crumbs which I have been hungering for. Bitter food is what I ingest, the tale of a young woman fallen from grace. A narrative full of sorrow, lost honor, shame, a child, and of men, veritable hijos de puta, who take advantage of women.

I take my seat at the table, where a steaming pitcher of milk and some bread and butter have been set. From here, I can see the laurel tree, verdant and bright against the morning sky. Its branches sprout from the trunk sideways and up, arms in prayer, worshiping the Yoruba gods, paying homage to the spirits who dwell in its core. Its roots claw the earth. Laurel Nobilis has planted its limbs deeply into the red clay of Santa Petrona, claiming this land as its kingdom.

This giant, a sometimes visitor in my childhood dreams, offers refuge and respite in the hollow that forms at the center of its trunk, as it bifurcates, creating a favored place for hens to lay eggs and for children to hide and to dream.

My father, a veterinarian, leaves to vaccinate cattle in a neighboring ranch. He does not own a car, so he rides on horseback to the neighboring farms.

The roads connecting Santa Petrona to the Carretera Central are not asphalted, and during the rainy season, the mud is so deep that automobile tires get swallowed in its thickness. If the family needs to reach the outside, we travel in ox-drawn carts—the same carts used to carry the sugarcane to the mill at Tinguaro—sitting on taburetes that are placed on the wood planks for our comfort.

Diana follows my father for a while, gives up her chase and roams around the batey. I visit my friend, Perico.

As I walk towards his room in the barracoon, the stink of the outhouse overpowers everything, and I cover my face, revolted by the awful smell and by the memory of the one time I decided to explore it. I also walk by the hen house and by the valla, the small arena where my father's fighting cocks are trained.

Perico is the color of café con leche. His skin is leathery, with deep grooves coursing his face like rivers on land. His hair is white and curly. He is thin, wiry and with strong, callused hands. He lives alone.

I am silent as I enter his room—the last one in the barracks—through the one door which is open by the time I arrive. The room is bare, with dirt floors and one small window providing ventilation and some light. One taburete—the chairs made with cowhide and rustic wood—stands next to an old table. The cot he sleeps in is against the back wall, as is a small coal stove. He uses the outhouse, a bucket of water that he draws from the nearby well, to wash with. He holds my hand as we start the morning round.

Perico loves me.

My father's cocks are special, and Perico takes care of them. They are fed a prescribed diet, which he prepares for them. Perico trims their spurs and fastens the detachable, longer spurs used in the fight. He trims their comb and wattles, and conditions them for the ring by engaging them in mock fights that take place daily in the valla. Their feathers are clean and shiny, their training just as demanding as those of highly priced pugilists.

This bloody sport is a favorite with my father, who travels with Perico throughout the Matanzas and La Habana provinces, engaging in matches that take place periodically. Perico is a respected man, a trainer of gallos finos.

My mother is visiting Chencha, a woman more or less her age—early thirties—and who just gave birth to her fourth child. Chencha lives in one of the huts in the batey, and is married to Pedro, a white Spaniard born in the Canary Islands. Pedro emigrated to Cuba as a young man, in search of a better future in America. His quest brings him to Cuba, where he becomes a guajiro, a landless white peasant.

Though not today, I have accompanied my mother on these visits before. Chencha, my mother's age, looks old and worn. She has lost some of her teeth, has matted, dirty hair which is already turning gray. Her clothes are old and torn and unlike Ramira's dress, hers is dirty and tattered, as if she is too tired to wash it or mend it. Her fair skin is weather beaten, her hands are rough, and her blue eyes have a dull, distant look. Her feet look dirty, the soil of the floor embedded on their soles.

A soft ray of sun filters through the cracks of the palm roof, alighting on Chencha's face. She is sitting on a rocking chair, the newborn on her lap. The variegated light dissolves on her countenance, revealing a sliver of beauty that still remains on the broken surface that is her.

Does she remember the young girl she once was, in love with Pedro, full of hope for that illusive future that young people dream of?

I notice the filthy surroundings, the bits of food on the dirt floor, the smell of urine coming from the chamber pot kept in the back room, and another, less definite and bitter odor, which is perhaps the essence of despair. There is one bed in the middle of the room, and it is by squatting and holding herself on the iron frame that Chencha delivers her brood. The children, all of them quite young, walk about the room with threadbare shirts and no bottoms, culito al aire, stomachs distended by parasites, their sad eyes looking at me from booger-covered, dirty little faces. I want to flee, hide, and will myself small, hoping to disappear. My mother's look nails me to the taburete. Malcriada!

Pedro is lazy. He has a small plot of land behind the bohío, and he could plant a crop. But no, all he does is singar and make Chencha pregnant. Ramira's father has a vegetable garden, and his family is well fed and clean. Pedro is un haragán. I hear my mother complain. She brings Chencha old dresses and food.

In the aqueous alliances that form between siblings, my three older sisters are banding together this morning. They are probably gathering the eggs laid by the hens in several places throughout the batey, an enterprise which is a favorite of all the children.

Ramon, the overseer and my father's right hand in the running of the farm, spots Diana in one of the paths that crisscross the batey. She is running wildly, foam at her mouth. He tries to approach her but she growls at him. Alarmed, he goes back to the house, goes to the armoire where my father's guns are kept. He takes one of my father's shotguns and runs back to where he last spotted Diana. On the way, he alerts Perico, who is with me, and finds my sisters and sends them home, tells them to go inside, and to close the doors. He also goes by Chencha's house and alerts my mother.

Ramon is scared and not sure what is wrong with Diana. Fearing that she has been infected with rabies, he pulls the trigger. Diana, mortally wounded, the blood staining her black and white coat, runs back to the house, to her refuge under my baby brother's crib.

My mother had left my brother with Ramira, and thought that he was sleeping inside, in his crib in the bedroom. She bolts the doors and gathers her children around her, Ramira included. But when she asks about Pablo, she realizes, too late, that he has been left outside in the crib, and that Diana, the trail of blood staining the colorful Cuban tiles, is going directly to where the crib is. She dies there, comforted, I hope, by the presence of the baby who is sleeping peacefully above her.

My mother cannot forgive herself. She forgot her only son, left him in harm's way. But the baby is unharmed and she thanks all her saints, God, and San Antonio her patron Saint, in particular. She atones her sin of forgetfulness by relinquishing, forever, her favorite dessert: guava paste.

As a child, I feared extinction from the spells of the malevolent beings I was sure inhabited the darkness outside my bedroom window, not yet knowing that death, and sometimes sorrow, come from those you love the most.

At the end of days, when the shadows fall over the land of my birth, and the setting sun summons the hallucinatory hour of apparitions and ghosts, I see a soft glow under the laurel tree. A congregation of luminous, transparent beings is gathered under its canopy in a procession of souls. I recognize Ramira, glistening in the morning sun. Perico, looking at me with loving eyes, hand extended, a lustrous rooster nestled on the crook of his arm. Chencha, who is now the young and lovely girl she once was and Pedro, her husband, a young man full of hope, boarding the ship that would take him to the New World. Diana is wagging her tail, happily coming home after a full day of hunting at the Cienaga. The school teacher is smiling at me, erect on the saddle. My father is dressed for the hunt, chaps coming to his knees, his young body in the cream-colored riding pants and white shirt he always wears, black revolver in his belt. My mother is young, and her dark hair surrounds her lovely face like a halo. She is holding a small statue of San Antonio, her patron saint, in her hand. Theirs is an ephemeral presence against the solid stance of the tree, who reigns over the batey, limbs deeply planted in the sacred red clay of Santa Petrona.

THE WRINKLES OF TIME

By Elsa Goss Black

G etting older is a time of letting go. You begin to say goodbye, once and for all, to the child and young adult you were, to the dreams you once had, to the person you thought you'd turn out to be at this stage of life. Not that this is altogether a bad thing, mind you, or even a totally depressing one.

It's simply a time of reflection and all that it entails.

If you've learned anything along the way, you've begun to live more and more for the moment and to enjoy what you have, rather than mourn what you don't. You've learned who and what you like and perhaps more importantly, who and what you don't. You put your fears in proper context and suddenly realize that, within the bounds of time and money, you can do a surprising amount of what you please.

What really, at this point, are they going to do to you: send you to the principal's office or put it on your permanent record? They could, I suppose, ship you to "the home." But that's why God invented trusts, codicils and the smart lawyers who write them. Woe be unto those money-hungry heirs who try to shuffle off our mortal coils before our time.

And woe, too, upon those politicians who think the hippie liberals of the 60's have all mellowed into duffers and mah-jongg players. Maybe some of us have, but the pols would also do well to remember that dermatologist-approved golf visors can be switched to pink pussy hats at the drop of a sun hat. We see older men and women in the mirror, but retain the ferocity in our souls, and we understand the truth behind the slogan, "Nevertheless, she persisted." For many of us, it's the story of our lives.

And yet. And yet.

Along with feeling our oats—or is it eating our oatmeal?—and sporting AARP membership cards, we also have an amber-tinged nostalgia for the things and people who share our boomer history. We are no longer the kids we were, but a part of that fresh-faced gift of youth endures, if only to show us how far we've come.

It isn't regret that we feel or a fervent wish to be back in the "good old days." We have all come to realize that for some people, in some households, life was far from good. There were unhappy marriages, wives who were abused, spouses who cheated. I knew people like the Mullins family, with a quiet, lovely blonde-haired mother, two well-behaved, tow-headed kids—and a father who unzipped his pants and showed me a hairy nest of something I wasn't old enough to understand as he sat on a bench near our neighborhood playground.

Then, too, there were, among the growing upper middle class affluence, pockets of near-poverty, and in the sea of white-owned and rented homes, a blacks-only section of our suburbs, albeit one named after the abolitionist Lucretia Mott. We've certainly learned in the intervening years that none of our hometowns was perfect.

But we're mature enough now to realize that it's—mostly—all right to look back in amusement rather than anger. That was then, this is now, and remembering it is okay. In fact, it's kind of fun.

Facebook was invented, and first used, by college kids decades younger than we are. But while Gen Xers accumulate thousands of friends like so many notches on an online bedpost, retirees often use Facebook for pleasant blasts from our pasts through reconnections with old high school and college buddies. It's the modern-day equivalent of spending hours rehashing the day with friends after school on a brand-new princess phone.

I haven't seen, or even thought of, some of my friends, older in years but new on my Facebook page, in something like half a century. Some of them, I'm sad to report, I only vaguely remember. But I find myself smiling at pictures showing what they look like today and where they've retired, and happily agreeing with more than a few of their political opinions. Like so many of them, I've joined our nostalgic high school Facebook page and dutifully look through posts asking, "Do you remember when?"

And I usually do.

Taflin and Schwartz, the old-time drugstore at the corner of 19th and Cheltenham, owned by two brothers-in-law whose wives hated each other? Check. Lee's Original Hoagie House, right next door, mouthwateringly full of onions, oils and cheeses mixed with meats not found in any kosher kitchen? Ditto. Willow Grove Park, the old-fashioned amusement park that started featuring rock groups like Gerry and the Pacemakers when times changed? You betcha.

There were summers spent "down the shore," a peculiarly Philadelphia term for the South Jersey beaches from Cape May to Long Beach Island. Driving there wasn't as easy as it is now, but the feeling of rolling down the windows as you approached Atlantic City and beginning to smell the distinctive salt air is exactly the same. I have been at beaches nearly all over the world and none of them herald the approaching ocean in the same way that the shore does. It's a tug at the scent of memory as enticing as the taste of Proust's madeleines.

Much closer to home and during the school year, the local hangout was the new-at-the-time Cheltenham Mall, with its Horn and Hardart's and Gimbel's anchors and the joy of entering a locally-owned bookstore where you could browse for hours. It was on the street next to the mall where Jack Kennedy rode on the backseat of an open convertible before the 1960 election, hatless and movie-star handsome, waving to shouting crowds and beguiling us with an impossibly wide, white and wholly welcoming smile.

I remember the Howard Johnson's, a short, truant's walk under the bridge next to our high school, and the hot dogs improbably served in toasted lobster rolls. I also remember the outrageously named Beaver College, the female teachers' school across the street. Most of us didn't get the joke back then and it was such a sign of a more innocent era that the college didn't change its name to Arcadia University until 2001, when it began offering graduate courses and admitting men.

In hindsight, you have to ask, "Were we *ever* that young?" Yes, indeed, we were, and now we're not.

But so what? There is still a pride of place, a wisdom born from knowing how our childhood touchstones made us who we are today, wrinkles, warts, age spots, aches and all. It wasn't totally good and it wasn't totally bad, at least for most of us. Nonetheless, it was nearly all we knew back then and it provided the jumping-off point for who and what we subsequently became.

We're all over 65 now, those of us who were part of the Class of '69. That's another sex joke that many of us didn't get until well after graduation. But as today's popular TV show would put it, "This Is Us." And I have to say, "Yay!"

RUSSIANS NEVER SMILE

By Sharon Wylie

The wet laundry was lifted from the washing machine, and two ruble coins were left lying at the bottom having fallen out of a pocket. Three rubles total—what could I have bought with that, a matryuska doll? No, 3500 rubles. Those little Faberge eggs? Nope, 5200 rubles. A black, lacquered box? Not that: 8000 rubles. So nothing really. The useless little coins lay there, separated from their homeland probably forever, serving only as a strong reminder of my recent trip to the land of the tsars.

The tour groups pushing through the streets of whatever town we were visiting were like huge mosh pits, pulsing forward, shoving family and friends in front of a statue or an ancient church to snap a picture to substantiate they were actually there. They followed a leader identified only by a flag on a pole, an umbrella, and, occasionally, a large plastic flower on a stick—genus and specie unrecognizable. The groups were set apart mostly by language, but also by behavior. Sometimes it was picture taking tendencies.

The Americans used more cell phones than cameras and occasionally you'd have your view blocked by an iPad thrust in your face—anything to get the job done with as little effort as possible, even if the composition, the exposure, or the subject of the picture was grossly wrong. Such is the problem with the digital age. Shoot and delete. Pixels are free. The Asians were scrappier—maybe because their cameras were bigger and that gave them more chutzpah. Anything is a fine subject for them. Standing in front of a bus at a rest stop. Shooting into midair if the guide points a finger in any direction.

A fight broke out during our tour of the Hermitage Museum in the Dutch painters gallery in front of a portrait by Raphael. A hoard was pushing forward toward the *Madonna and Child* painting to get a closer look at probably his fine brushstrokes when noises broke out. They were like a flock of crows fighting for the same piece of bread. Scuffling ensued. Feathers flew. I backed off for safety to witness the fray. I'd return later and admire Raphael's visual achievements with less mania. When the crowd finally peeled away, with no chastisement from their guide who stood a safe distance across the room, there was actually a man in a wheelchair in the center of the fracas. Maybe the people had been just tripping over his wheels.

Our guide, a tough babushka, hammered accusations at the ineffectual leader in Russian. "These unlicensed guides bring all these people in and then don't control them, which makes it worse for us." She'd apparently had had this gig since Soviet times. "Did he understand your Russian?" I was totally into the moment's drama. "I don't know, but I'm sure he got my point." She had previously explained to us the importance of being a babushka. It was necessary to put our American politeness aside and not allow people to push into our space. "You Americans are accustomed to large spaces and comfortable distances, pulling away if people crowd you, but you have to forego your manners and push back.

You don't say 'I'm sorry' and let people push by. You have to be assertive and push back with a strong, 'Excuse Me!' You have to be like a babushka." She was a babushka in every sense of the word, weathered and sinewy, but still attractive. Blond with a scarf thrown around her neck in a coquettish way, but never smiled. Russian women like to take control. In front of the Church on Spilled Blood, she warned us of the hackers. "Don't look at their wares. If they give you something to hold, don't be nice and don't take it. Just walk by them and avoid making eye contact. They see weakness and they will harangue you until you get back on your bus." She'd worked these grounds before, a voice of experience. I tried to follow her advice. I bought only two post cards and a fringed babushka scarf I will never wear.

That was the St. Petersburg guide; however, the Moscow guide was not a babushka. She met us on the cold Russian morning wrapped in a winter coat and scarves. She resembled a bundle of rags. She was what one would expect from a woman raised on potatoes and goulash—plain, overweight, bad hair--closely cropped and dyed red. Her voice had no inflection or expression. She ensconced herself on the front seat of the bus and from that vantage point launched a monotoned description of every building in the city. She was especially fond of pointing out the stadiums. I suspected no one had ever come to Moscow to look at the stadiums, and when she took the mic the second day and began listing dry dates and events, I longed for a mute button. "Maybe I could bring her back to the boat and have her read to me so I might be able to finally fall asleep," my seat-mate observed.

━┼━

St. Petersburg is like a shiyr new penny, a city bright and gleaming with colorful buildings trimmed in white whereas Moscow is like the pennies minted in World War II when there was a shortage of copper: dark, gray, and gloomy. In fact, they could make a color called Moscow gray. So while St. Petersburg is pastel, Moscow is dun. St. Petersburg is water and islands; Moscow is concrete. St. Petersburg is culture and the arts; Moscow is government. St. Petersburg feels like the wealth of the tsars and summer palaces; Moscow feels like Soviet and communism. There is more of a staunch police presence in Moscow visible especially near the Kremlin. They are not the friendly Bobbies that stand harmlessly on the corners in England. The uniforms hardly move but note your every transgression. If you trespass, they blow a shrill whistle drawing attention to your mistake. For example, the road in front of Putin's offices is off limits, but one is allowed passage on the opposite side of the street. However, if you slip off the curb and even one foot lands on the street cobble, the whistle shrieks. We had a couple of instances of this low grade humiliation: my friend was about to step over the top of a low hanging chain fence that was meant as a demarcation line. It was a shortcut into yet another line. Only one foot was raised into the air when *Wheeeee!* She froze in action. Another in our company tried to sit down to rest on the granite wall around Lenin's tomb, another whistle-able offense. Rules reign supreme. In the streets everyone stays in the pedestrian lines crossing the street and cars screech to a halt. Absolutely no is one jay walking, which would undoubtedly be grounds for a visit to a Siberian gulag.

Russia prefers to have the biggest of everything, no matter its working condition. In Red Square they tout the world's largest bell even though it's never been rung because it's broken. A piece of it has cracked off revealing its innards. The world's largest cannon is located on the same square among all the cannons taken when Napoleon was defeated. It doesn't function and has never been fired. The massive two ton cannonball rests beside it. Even though the world's largest country, they would like to add to its real estate by taking back Ukraine and the Crimea. Don't forget Tolstoy's *War and Peace*, a very long novel.

Leaving Russia is nearly as difficult as getting into the country. To enter one needs a visa involving fifteen pages of instruction to complete. You're asked pages of questions including the impossible such as every foreign country you've visited and when, or where did your grandfather attend high school. Each hotel where you are planning to stay has to be contacted prior to departure, and they must send you an "invitation" to submit as part of the visa application. It's enough to deter the faint of heart. Me, I had already slapped a heavy down payment on a river cruise, so I was in. The visa company offered a "white glove" program where they fill it all out for you. I went that direction. I gladly paid for that service.

On the return home we arrived at the airport early, early in the morning and expected clear signage to direct us straightaway to British Airways. The cab stopped in front of a non-descript Moscow gray building. A wave of anxiety swept through my body and I asked the driver with a note of desperation, "Where are we?" "Departuro," he spit out. I guess he'd had Latino passengers equally dismayed who asked the same question often enough that he bothered himself to learn that single word which could work in most languages. Usually I chat with cab drivers in foreign countries who like to practice their English, but not here.

Once inside we were no less confused. No signs anywhere. The line in front of an information booth seemed worth a try. We asked the dour attendant, not overly eager to acknowledge us, where we could find British Airways. He didn't speak, much less smile— just held his hand out for our documents. Wordlessly he spread them out on his desk, took out a very thick magnifying glass, and began pouring over them. He did not seem pleased. I felt like I was in the principal's office for some unknown offense. I had a sinking feeling the papers were wrong or inadequate somehow. I lowered my eyes in supplication, not believing anything ever meets Russian Soviet expectations. He flipped the papers around while we shifted from foot to foot, and this was just the information booth. No telling what would be waiting for us in customs or God forbid immigration! He wordlessly returned our papers and pointed behind us. There, twenty feet away, was the glorious sign for British Airways. It wasn't the American flag, but it was good enough for a celebration. And the Union Jack is, after all, red, white, and blue. Once aboard after fastening my seat belt, I sighed with mixed emotions. I would miss the cabbage rolls and the borscht and the Cossack dancers and the babushkas, but I couldn't wait to see all those American smiles.

MY MOTHER, MISS LOUISE

By Isabelle Whitfield

My dear mother, who lived to ninety-two, always said, "Do not talk about your ailments; nobody wants to hear about them." And even after two hip replacements — at eighty and eighty-five — she never did unless it was some comic foible she committed but never would admit it could possibly be due to age. She had an inordinate ability to laugh at herself and often said that a good sense of humor was a useful "survival tool," especially at her "stage of the game."

Maybe it was because she was a child of the Deep South, where any discussion of a lady's age or one's ailments was not only unseemly but also ill-mannered. And maybe it was because she thought there were so many more interesting things to talk about. For example, when Carl Sagan's book, *Cosmos,* was published, she became fascinated with far away galaxies and the mysteries of the universe. Or maybe it was because she felt age and ailments were strictly private matters and did not want to dwell---as so many older people tend to do---on how old she had actually become with those often accompanying aches and pains, although she did seem, luckily, to have very few. *Crotchetiness* and *cantankerous* were not in her vocabulary, but she did have a better vocabulary than almost anyone I have ever known. (When her children encountered a word they did not know, she insisted we look it up.) A lover of poetry, she often spent an afternoon reading Lord Byron, Keats and Shelley, her beloved romantic poets.

A happy-go-lucky flapper of the Roaring Twenties, my mother, Louise, had stunning blue eyes, a thick, wavy, dark blonde bob, and she could do a mean Charleston. She attended a prominent women's liberal arts college near Atlanta where she majored in history, and although she loved English literature and poetry more, she was not about to wade through Chaucer in Middle English.

She spent more time hopping around to college dances at Washington & Lee, Sewanee (the University of the South), Georgia Tech, and West Point. My grandmother made her gorgeous evening dresses. She even had a young Nelson Rockefeller on her dance card at Dartmouth. (She allowed he was a good dancer but thought him a bit pompous.) With her love of ballet and natural gracefulness, she often toe-danced in her college theatrical productions. She was thrilled to be invited to join Blackfriars, an exclusive group in the drama department for which one had to audition.

Maybe that sunny disposition was just in her DNA, or maybe it was honed by the crazy, carefree days of being young and in college during the exciting Jazz Age. But as the fun-filled decade of the Roaring Twenties crashed into the sad, dark days of struggle and sacrifice of the Great Depression, Louise's unwavering optimistic attitude must have sustained her. My mother had the misfortune of graduating from college in that fateful year — 1929. And hers was often called the Lost Generation.

But she was not lost, at least she did not appear to think so. She had wangled a position with a small dance company in New York and, with high hopes, headed to the big city. But with crash of the stock market that October and the onset of the Great Depression, her dance dreams dried up, so she caught the train home to Alabama.

She planned to live, temporarily, with her beloved mother and father in her small southern town. Although jobs were few, Louise found a position teaching high school history. She was quite resourceful. To earn extra money, she turned the Victorian living room with its high coffered ceiling into a makeshift dance studio where she taught little girls whose parents could afford a few dollars for dance lessons, the finer points of ballet. Often in the late afternoons, the uplifting strains of "The Waltz of the Flowers" playing on an old Victrola could be heard wafting throughout the house as her little ballerinas practiced their positions.

As the country began to emerge from the Depression and rumblings of war could be heard in Europe, Louise found a job at the Army-Air Force base in Montgomery where she met a handsome young captain who became my father. After the war ended, he was stationed in Occupied Japan. My mother soon joined him with her two-year old toddler. She put me on her hip, caught a bus from Alabama, a train to San Francisco, and a military ship across the Pacific to meet my father in Japan. This launched a memorable two-year Japanese adventure for our family. To her great delight, I learned to perform the Japanese Tea Ceremony when I was four, and sang Japanese nursery rhymes taught by my Japanese nanny. (This was quite a hit when I returned to Alabama as not many four-year olds in those days had been to Japan and back.) And, of course, by this time, my mother was already happily teaching me the five ballet positions and the proper way to point my toe.

Mother climbed Mt. Fuji with me in tow, shopped with plenty of yen for great post-war bargains on the Ginza in Tokyo, and sent wonderful Japanese wood block prints, china, cloisonné vases, tea cabinets---all sorts of Oriental treasures---home to Alabama. She became captivated with all things Japanese, especially the Shinto religion which emphasized the worship of nature. We visited the magnificent gardens of Kyoto and the Great Buddha at Kamakura. My earliest memories are of the illustrated books of Japanese fairy tales she read to me. When she taught school again after my brother and I left for college, she always worked in a Japanese unit of study, including haiku poetry, and enthusiastically shared her treasures with her students. She often wrote letters to our favorite Japanese maid, telling her how much she "loved and missed your beautiful country and its beautiful people."

After we returned to America, a son soon arrived. And although our mother could become quite distant while listening to other adults complain about various ailments, she was enormously empathetic and comforting when one of her precious children stumped a toe, suffered a bee sting, or fell and skinned a bloody knee. It was as though the world might be coming to an end until all tears were soothed and the pain subdued.

When my father died suddenly of a massive heart attack, our devoted mother carried on. She made sure we always had our homework, always wrote thank-you notes, always stood when an adult entered the room. And although she would listen politely when someone recited various ailments, she never burdened anyone with hers.

After our father's death, she decided that instead of going back to Alabama, we would stay in Florida "because the schools were better." She saw both of us through high school, college, and law school---always interested to hear of our successes, our exploits, and always there to ease disappointments. She encouraged us to be philosophical, to take the long view whenever possible, and her wise counsel through the years sustained my brother and me. It seemed to us that somehow Mother always knew best.

One of my happiest memories of Mother was on a trip to France where my brother had shipped his hot-air balloon and was to participate in a big balloon rally to celebrate the bicentennial of the first hot-air balloon flight in France in 1783. As it was to be in Alsace-Lorraine, from whence her great-grandfather had come, we invited Mother to go as she had great interest in her French ancestry. After the magnificent final ascension of colorful balloons over quaint French chateaus, I will never forget her excitement when we reached the medieval village of Lorentzen and discovered, *lo and behold,* a relative of her great-grandfather sitting on his front porch! He even took us to the town cemetery to point out more French ancestors. And, of course, Mother was in heaven already with those flavorful French pastries and luscious French chocolates.

At her 90th birthday party in December, which we could not call a birthday party but instead a Christmas party---with no presents allowed and no mention of age---she flitted around in a Ralph Lauren holiday red blazer and had a grand time. She was animated and delightful with those blue eyes sparkling, sipping champagne, and laughing her unmistakable musical little laugh.

When my mother went to the hospital in Selma for the last time, she actually said to her long-time doctor that she did "not feel very well." He replied, "Miss Louise, I have been seeing you for fifty years, and this is the first time I have ever heard you say you were sick."

On a bright and sunny Sunday morning---the 4th of July 1999---while my brother held one hand and I held the other, she peacefully slipped away. And though in recent years she had given up much of her cherished independence, my brother announced philosophically, "Now Mother has her independence again." And so she did.

Miss Louise was laid to rest with two of her favorite things, a bouquet of sweet purple hyacinths and a Hershey chocolate bar.

IN THE CLOSET

By Joan Fisher

I step inside the small room and close the door behind me. My stomach lurches and my throat is dry. It's hard to swallow. I stand alone in the artificial glow of the overhead fluorescent light. I grit my teeth and clench my jaw. I cannot avoid the situation any longer. I have been putting off this odious task for too long. Today is the day that I will confront my closet.

While I am still able to return my freshly laundered clothes to their hangers and I can usually put together an acceptable out-fit on a daily basis, I have made a habit of ignoring the fact that my once-spacious master bedroom closet is now overflowing. It is tightly packed with shoes, clothes, purses, and scarves. It is burst-ing with nightgowns and bathrobes, beach cover-ups and bathing suits. It is full of athletic wear, outerwear, and underwear. I have too much. My clothes are crammed into the closet like a clown car at the circus. It has reached critical mass and it's time for a reckon-ing. My children will thank me someday.

I have been living in this house since 1983. Some of my clothes moved here with me from college and the early days of marriage and motherhood. When I look through old family photos, I recognize shoulder pads and sequins that still inhabit my closet in 2017! I have the silky negligee I wore on our honeymoon. (Is that a maternity top I had hopes of re-purposing?) I have an entire section filled with clothes that are too tight, but with heart-breaking optimism I hope they will fit again. Someday I may lose enough weight to zip those bell bottoms all the way up. I even have my daughter-in-law's wedding gown, squeezed in beside my mother-in-law's mink coat. You never know what you might need for a special occasion.

I own some shoes that are too small, some too wide, and some too uncomfortable to actually walk in. I have valet parking shoes and comfy, cozy shoes. I own so many sneakers that I can wear one pair for gardening, one pair for walking in the rain and I can even step in dog poop without fear. (I'll just toss those in the garbage). I recently discovered some shoes that I forgot I had bought. Damn you, DSW!

Purses and pocketbooks take up an entire shelf. Travel totes and evening bags wait for trips and galas. My shoulder bags and Birken wanna-be's stand at the ready. I spy a faux leather clutch, purchased from a store in Dadeland from the days when the mall was an open-air shopping center. My gaze falls fondly on the labels: Coach...Michael Kors...Fendi.....How can you toss a designer bag, no matter how frayed or scruffy?

I begin with the pantyhose drawer. I gingerly open it to view a tangle of pantyhose in nude, ecru, black, navy, gray: a rainbow of depressing neutrals stares back and I quickly close the drawer. Who wears pantyhose anymore? I move up to sleepwear. A collection of cotton granny gowns tumbles out. But what if it gets really cold? I'll need every one of those long-sleeved high neck nightgowns if global warming turns out to be a hoax. Okay, maybe I can cull a few pieces of intimate wear. Do I really need a full complement of old half-slips and stretched out Spanxx? Paralyzed by indecision, I move on to the drawer of gym clothes. Every T-shirt evokes memories of a different organization's fund raiser: the 5K at Metrozoo, the Corporate Run of 2005, a gaggle of faded Turkey Trot T's from Novembers past, the Lacrosse Club and Debate Team T-shirts from the 1990's! Nostalgia overwhelms me as I return each and every one back into the drawer. I turn to the hanging section, holding a collection of long dresses and pants suits. Luxe fabrics and silky textures beckon to me. Crisp twills and linens remind me of a corporate life from long ago. I spy a big-shouldered polyester jump suit. Vintage!

I must keep going but I feel a little faint. Is my vertigo coming back? The dresses, blouses and slacks close in on me, the fabrics and colors swirling like palm trees in a hurricane. (Aha! There are the jeans I wore after Hurricane Andrew.) I just can't do this! It's too stressful. I panic and pull open the door. I stagger back in to the bedroom where cool air wafts over me and I think about Scarlett O'Hara in *Gone With the Wind*. At least I don't have an ensemble made out of green velvet drapes. I take some cleansing breaths and begin to relax. The heck with Marie Kondo, the Japanese organizing fanatic. I'm not feeling any life-changing magic here. I can't think about this right now. If I do, I'll go crazy. I'll think about this tomorrow. Today there is a sale at Chico's and I have a coupon!

PROM NIGHT

By Ellen Leeds

She was waiting to come down the staircase of her split-level house. It was going to be a night of uncertainty and fear. Her good friend Steve was picking her up and taking her to her senior prom. This was not how she envisioned the evening would go, but she was determined to make the best of it. Her boyfriend, who had expressed his deep love for her and who had demanded her eternal love, would be taking her best friend. She wanted to profess this love but couldn't. She loved him, but eternal love at age 16 was far too demanding. She kept putting her decision off during their nightly long conversations until she just let it all spew out: "I love you, Jim, I do, but forever? I will be leaving for college at the end of summer as will you. Who knows what will happen? Please understand I can't say eternal love, and mean it. Not now." With those words the receiver went dead. She tried repeatedly to call back, but he never spoke again to his *eternal love.*

She was afraid she that she would see him again. She was fearful that her jealousy would have her make a scene where she might cry or run out of the cafeteria, leaving her glass pumps at the entrance door. Her dear friend Steve had heard all the melodrama over the weeks, and being the good friend that he always was, gallantly stepped in to make her prom special. He arrived a little early and hung out in the living room, talking to her dad. Normally, any other boy coming to her house she would have swept away quickly, but Steve and her Dad knew each other for many years, so the conversation flowed easily.

Steve arrived in his debonair white tuxedo jacket and black pants as well as the requisite black cummerbund and bowtie. He wore rented black patent leather shoes, and his light blond hair was held in place by gobs of pomade. He made sure to match her dress which, due to her rebellious nature, was a floor-length one in black with white flowers rather than the normal pastel lovelies. In his lapel his mother had placed a white carnation, and he carried a white orchid to pin on her dress. Although not in love with her, he did love her. He wanted this to be her night, and his loyalty stood fast.

She remained upstairs with her mom, primping with the makeup, her tall bouffant hair teased high. Layers of hair spray filled the air. Her mom assisted pulling the gown high over her head and gently slid it down. Next, the black pumps, and finally the bright red lip stick.

Her father kept jabbering about school, and plans for college. She knew when evening came, and he had been drinking for several hours, her father's mouth ran nonstop. Steve, being polite, was familiar with these bouts of her father's diarrhea mouth and just sat there politely listening. As she was about to dramatically walk down the stairs, all aglow as possible under the circumstances, she overheard her dad, "We love you, Steve. It doesn't matter that you're gay. You are part of this family."

She froze on the stairs. What had her father just said? Her friend Steve, gay? Not in New Jersey, and not her dear friend. How could her father embarrass her at this moment? It was the liquor talking, not the truth.

She backed up the hall, and hoped she wasn't noticed. She hoped no one actually took her dad's words seriously. It was the alcohol. She coughed and heavily stomped down the steps. Her dad and Steve stood up quickly. Her mom followed with the Brownie camera and snapped away. Her daughter alone on the steps, then with Steve, then with her, and finally with her dad.

Steve was smiling and promising to drive carefully, and said he would not bring her home too late. She oohed and aahed at the corsage, hoping all was normal. She grabbed her white shawl and followed Steve out the door. Her father's words stayed in her head for years. That evening stayed in her head forever.

After fifty years the invitation came for her high school reunion. *Is Steve Jameson going to attend?* she fired back in an email to the reunion committee? *No, so sorry but he died many years ago* came the reply. She had got in touch with him about ten years after she had graduated from college, and their meeting was sweet and wonderful. He was living in Manhattan with his partner, and he told her that her father's words were liberating. No one ever acknowledged who he truly was. Her father was the first one, and he was grateful.

She decided to attend her high school reunion. It was time finally to be at peace with her past.

THERE ARE PLACES I'LL REMEMBER

by the Beatles and Me (from the song "In My Life")
By Paul Gustman

I 'll remember the height and wind rippled surface of the dunes, how they were so much harder to climb than first imagined from ground level on Cape Cod. But we were honeymooners, armed with a super 8 camera, catching our breath while photographing each other climbing then sliding back as the sand refused to support our efforts. So macho in my football stance when it was my turn to charge upward—at 21, so incredibly young.

All my life, though some have changed
Climbing Ayers Rock, permissible 25 years ago, a serpentine train of climbers from around the world gathered in the desiccated red clay that makes the Australian Outback into an earthbound moonscape. Out of the vast level plains protruded a single mountain

whose flattened top long ago surrendered to the winds of erosion, leaving a broad red monolith as out of place as an elephant among ants. But we climbed with the others, sometimes needing the fixed ropes to pull ourselves up the steep face. My two twenty-something children went ahead as I stayed with their mother who, to my terror, climbed off the path and out onto the smooth rock face to let others pass because she felt her pace was too slow. Signs warned not to do this since climbers had plunged off. Eventually she decided that half way up was enough. At the top, my children and I signed the register, a photo memorializing the accomplishment. These days, it is publicized that Ayers Rock is considered a sacred place by Aboriginal peoples and climbing is discouraged.

Some have gone and some remain

With pre-teens in tow we descended on horseback into Bryce Canyon at sunset. Surrounded by intricately carved spires untouched by the hand of man, it was a descent into a cathedral, the red of the setting sun reflected off the endless stalagmites lining the pathway. But it is the silence I remember most. We would stop and just listen to the reverberating stillness, occasionally interrupted by the far off sound of tumbling rocks, the sound of geology evolving, a concert for us alone.

All these places have their moments

We awakened at 4 a.m. for a 4:30 pickup. The bus contained other bedraggled tourists in various states of semi-somnolence. It drove fifty miles into Australia's outback, away from what we considered civilization, fifty miles from the nearest electric light. The bus slowed in a clearing and each of us had to bend low to exit the rear door. As each person emerged, an audible sigh of surprise and wonder came forth as each saw the sky, the familiar sky, in a way never before appreciated—boasting a chandelier of twinkling stars, constellations clear as day, a light show far from the contamination of an incandescent bulb. We helped unroll the hot air balloons stretched expectantly on their sides. Then the whoosh of hot gases igniting and rushing so fast they were heard a second before the heat was felt by those gathered in the gondola. The balloons filled and lifted us into the night, toward the stars dimmed by the flash of engine flame. No power lines to entangle us, we drifted on the prevailing winds, matching our speed to the unfelt breeze. Just as we attained altitude the sun began to rise, turning the sky into a dynamic impressionist's palate with grays giving way to pink and orange and finally deep reds.

We waited until the sun had fully risen, then landed with a slight bump and had a special ceremony. We were given a chicken leg to quiet the surprising hunger that we had not anticipated but thankfully the tour directors had. We went through an ancient ceremony or so we were told, toasting with champagne, receiving mementos of our flight and were told we would be ceremoniously doused with water from the deepest outback wells. They rushed at us with buckets and threw the contents all over us. Confetti!

In My Life, I Love You More

The best trip of all was the walk down the aisle of Menorah Temple to await the arrival of a dream in white lace, her face aglow with happiness. The journey started as a 21-year-old with more optimism than appreciation of what marriage entailed, fortunate enough to have that glowing face accompany him on a fifty year adventure to **All the Places I'll Remember**, and some she remembers better.

EVERY DAY IS FATHER'S DAY

By Elsa Goss Black

"Never bury me on a Sunday," my father once intoned with a gleam in his eye. "I'd hate like hell to ruin someone's golf day."

When he died so very long ago in November 1972, too young for him, too young for my mother and much too young for me, his only child, his joking admonition was remembered with a smile. His funeral was held on a Monday instead. He'd have been wryly pleased by the gesture, I think, for he was a very special man with a very special outlook.

On Father's Day, 1974, when I was still a Bright Young Thing working on the editorial page of the *Philadelphia Inquirer*, I wrote a column beginning with those lines in my dad's memory for Father's Day. I told my readers that I wanted to remember him in print on a day "...when most fathers are being gifted with garish ties and citrus-scented aftershave."

Going on, I observed that "I always thought he deserved more than the usual tribute and inexpensive humorous card. I always thought he deserved more than he ever actually got. I think my father deserves this column."

Now, as I type those words again, I know Father's Day this year is still quite a way off. But I have long since realized that for me, all these many years later, although I am of retirement age and older than my daddy was when he died, every day remains Father's Day for me in one way or another.

I was reminded of that recently when one of the women in what I like to call my Old Farts' Writing Course at the University of Miami wrote a delightful piece about her childhood doll, the still-preserved and much-loved Clementine. Her memories brought me right back to a sweet one of my own, the after-dinner walks my father and I took together when the weather warmed up and the clocks were set to Daylight Savings Time.

I always valiantly tried to match my chubby, childish stride to those made by his long, thin legs as we swung our tightly-held hands together and sang, yes, "My Darling Clementine." My efforts must have been more successful than not, because I have never met another man—of any height—who could match my adult stride or walk as fast as I do.

When they remark on it, and they invariably do, I always think back to those beloved strolls, to the man who loved me first and understood me best, and I smile. I know my dad would feel, as I do, that there is no earthly reason why I should have to slow down when the clear solution is for everyone else to speed up.

That, in fact, is pretty much how he envisioned my life unfolding. He nurtured me, devotedly loved nearly everything I did and had every confidence I could achieve anything I set my mind to. He never considered any of my ideas outlandish or any of my requests out of line.

For instance, I have no clear recollection why "My Darling Clementine" became "our song" or why he never seemed too tired to sing that duet with me. Certainly, his own taste ran more to classical music and the lavish orchestral standards of the 50s than to this kitschy, twangy tune. But I suspect that it had something to do with my own taste for any and all of the TV westerns of that era.

I remember having a small record player on which I incessantly played a bright yellow record featuring children's songs sung by Roy Rogers and Dale Evans. The fact that my favorite tune on it was "Jesus Loves the Little Children" never made him bat an eyelash. Nonetheless, I firmly believe that for outdoor consumption in our very middle class Jewish neighborhood, he gently steered me to my second favorite tune, which was, of course, "My Darling Clementine."

It would have been just his style to find a way to grant my wish without disturbing others or breaking my budding spirit.

My father was, in so many ways, a most ordinary man, a local Blue Cross executive when health care insurance wasn't the billion-dollar industry it has become. Not well paid at all, he was neither rich nor famous. But he was also something much more, something rare and noble, both while he was alive and perhaps even more so when I measure his character against today's increasingly ignoble and uncivil times.

When material success was all to some men and women, and believe me, it was, even back in those days, my dad took pride in being able to help people navigate their medical insurance problems. I wonder what he would make of today's impenetrable morass and the cold-blooded assault on Obamacare. Some of it, the humane idea of universal coverage, anyway, he clearly foresaw.

I distinctly remember, for instance, his telling me in the months before his death that there would be a coming revolution in health care, a system he described as being very much what would become an early version of HMOs. But I know he'd be horrified by the vultures today who can't seem to make enough money out of other people's medical miseries and by the politicians who zealously guard their own cushy coverage while wielding legislative axes against everyone else's.

"Death panels"? Not on his watch, not if he could help it. A man of unblemished integrity, my father would never have tried to profit from someone else's misfortune, would never have cheated or lied to get ahead. He'd have angrily voted against any politicians who tried.

His word was his bond and his promises were sacred. Friendship, for him, was not a sometime thing based on expediency. I watched and learned as I saw how his love for the men and women closest to him engendered the same intense feelings in return. When he was hospitalized the last time, for a long and unbearably sorrowful month, cards, gifts and flowers poured in from everywhere, from close friends and family to colleagues across the country whose paths he'd crossed and whose hearts he had touched.

At a time when the only way to say "get well" was to use the phone or the post office, it was an incredible tribute to him that I finally had to stop counting the cards in his room when I got to 200 and the piles of mail became unmanageable.

For many years after he died, whenever I saw his old friends and co-workers, they looked at me with tears in their eyes. Even the most macho of them broke down a bit, saying, "Oh, how I loved that man!"

Time has passed and most of these men and women are gone now, too. But I knew then, and still do, exactly what they meant. "My Darling Clementine" remains a happy memory, although unlike the hapless heroine in the song, my dad has never been lost nor gone forever, not in any sense that matters, anyway. He lives forever, safe and always loved, in my heart.

THE FORTUNE COOKIE

By Zooey Kaplowitz

It was 1974 and I didn't meet a girl. Girls have always liked me. That wasn't my problem. My problem was that the girls I liked didn't like me. This was solidified on October 26th, my birthday, when I took myself to Grauman's Chinese Theater to see Warren Beatty in *Shampoo*. This was a movie about a guy who got every girl he looked at. I was alone and depressed when I left the theater and began my walk home. On the way there, I stopped at the Chinese restaurant next to the unemployment office to drown my sorrows. It was called The Chinese Restaurant Next to the Unemployment Office.

In the restaurant were a lot of actors that I knew from classes, auditions, plays and the unemployment line. I joined the actors at the character juvenile table. They were amusing, alcoholics, and overeaters. I ate and drank more than I needed to, paid my share of the bill and joined the ceremonial reading of our fortune cookies with bullshit positive haiku. I got the one that I knew was going to put a curse on my life. In bold letters like it was chiseled on a stone by God, proclaiming this: *You will meet many beautiful women and none of them will have any interest in you.*

I began my walk home drunk and stuffed from too much plum wine and cheap Chinese food. How could God do this to me? Hollywood had the largest population of beautiful women in the world, and he had placed me here just to fuck with my mind. I couldn't even have fantasies now because God just let me know that it ain't gonna happen.

On my way home, at the corner of Hollywood and Highland, I waited for the light to change. There were two other men waiting there with me for the light to change. They were tall, Cary Grant look-alikes wearing three-piece Brooks Brothers suits and red power ties. These guys looked like refugees from Madison Avenue. When the light changed and I stepped off the curb, they turned to each other and sighed, "Too young! Too chubby!"

This was truly awful. God was now telling me that it wouldn't even be of any value to me to be bisexual. It wouldn't broaden my opportunity to get laid. It would just place a plethora of pretty men in my path that also would have no interest in me. And this is in Hollywood that had the largest good looking gay population in the free world. There was a need for me to make a decision. I had to choose the path that I had always followed, so I stopped at Pink's and had two hot dogs, one with sauerkraut and pickle chips and the other with chili and cheese. I washed them down with a root beer soda.

I had just lost twenty-two pounds and I was looking good. Fuck those Madison Avenue queens. I was very young looking. I was twenty-six and I could still play sixteen. I looked good and I wasn't too chubby. At least I wasn't too chubby at the beginning of the evening. Who knows what I looked like after consuming all that food?

When I got home, I was still needy to have something sweet to eat. I needed two or three Hostess mini-peach pies, the ones that were made with real fruit.

I ran out of my house and headed toward the convenience store, my junk food source. As I was approaching the corner, I noticed a short hunpbacked black man dressed like Che Guevara standing there, staring at me. I knew that he was God, and He was there to watch me in my final descent into oblivion. One thought ran through my head: *My life may have sucked but it would make a great bad movie that I wouldn't be allowed to star in.*

When I got to the corner, he approached me and said, "I know where you're going and I know what you want."

"You are God!" I blurted. He knew I was going to the store to get the Hostess mini-peach pies, the ones made with real fruit.

He then walked toward me and placed his hand on my chest and ran it down my body until it landed on my dick. It was then that I realized that he wasn't God, responsible for the genesis of all my sorrows. He was a just a sad gay man who got a fortune cookie that said he would meet a lot of beautiful men and none of them would be interested in him. He thought I was going to the leather bar next to the convenience store. He was wrong. I grabbed his hand and shook it. I told him that it was nice meeting him and that I was flattered by his interest and headed toward the convenience store.

I walked into my house with the six Hostess peach pies in a brown paper bag and caught the tail end of *Gone with the Wind*. It was just as Scarlett was saying, "Tomorrow will be another day."

THE PUMPKIN PATCH

By Kitty Winkler

Children, we're going to do a harvest play, and you'll all get to design your own costumes and have parts to play, Mrs. McClellan announced. The whole kindergarten class shivered with anticipation and dread. I had only the vaguest idea what a play was, but I thought it must be something great if I got to wear a costume. And the bonus was that I got to design my own costume, whatever that meant.

Mrs. McClellan outlined the rather thin plot. Mrs. Wilson, the music teacher, would play the piano, focusing on tunes associated with growing and harvesting a garden. We, the members of the William R. Belknap Elementary School kindergarten, would play the parts of the garden vegetables in their various stages of growth. Our parents and the members of the other classes in the school would form the audience for this awe-inspiring sight.

The following day, we began preparations for the play. The vegetables, a.k.a. members of our class, were to be arranged in rows of at least five, meaning that at least five children had to select the same vegetable to portray. Mrs. McClellan gave us the choices: we could be tomatoes, potatoes, onions, turnips or pumpkins. Her selection process was to ask for volunteers first, then draft the remainder of children necessary to balance the vegetable rows.

We all fell silent, weighing the pros and cons of each vegetable. My thought process went something like this: Who on earth would want to be a smelly old onion? Not me. I have no idea what a turnip is, but it doesn't sound very nice, and besides, I wouldn't know how to make a turnip costume. That leaves a tomato, potato or a pumpkin; now which of these do I like best?

It was at this juncture that my kindergarten classmates began to volunteer. I felt a moment of panic. What if Mrs. McClellan made me an onion just to finish up the vegetable row? She was on pumpkins when my hand shot up to volunteer. I was elated to be selected for the pumpkin row, especially when my best friend Dona was drafted to be an onion because she failed to volunteer.

Once our parts were decided it was time to begin costume design. Our materials were brown grocery bags and show card paints in bright colors. Mrs. McClellan thoughtfully guided our artistic efforts by displaying large pictures showing us what the five vegetables were supposed to look like. That didn't thwart our imaginations; we had our share of blue turnips and purple tomatoes. My fellow pumpkins and I were smart enough to know that we should be orange, but that seemed a little static, so we banded together to agree that we should have green stems and Jack O'Lantern faces. The other vegetables were jealous until Mrs. McClellan announced that all vegetables had to have faces for the practical purpose of seeing through eye holes and breathing through a nose hole. She made it clear that Jack O'Lantern faces were out; faces had to be discreet and barely visible.

When our costumes were completed, we began rehearsals with Mrs. Wilson at the piano. The sequence of the play was pretty straightforward. All the vegetables started out crouched on the floor in a fetal position. As Mrs. Wilson played sunshine tunes, we would begin to grow, first to a kneeling position and then to standing. While this was going on, Mrs. McClellan would read a narrative about planting, cultivating and harvesting, focusing on each of the five vegetables in its order of ripening. This, of course, meant that pumpkins were last to grow. That made me happier than ever with my choice. I envisioned my role as some sort of grand finale to the play.

The big day came at last for a class of nervous kindergartners frightened to be on the auditorium stage in front of our parents and the school's older children. In fact, the day was almost ruined by Johnny Bowers, one of the potatoes, wetting his pants five minutes before the performance and having to be taken home.

The rest of us found our spots on the stage in our garden rows of newly planted seeds. The music and narrative began, and the rustling of paper bags indicated when the onions began their growth spurt. The other vegetables followed on cue, coming to maturity one row at a time.

At long last, it was time for the pumpkins. However, something went wrong. When I had first crouched in the fetal position, I could see perfectly though my eye holes; but, as the play progressed, I found my bag had slipped and I was a sightless pumpkin. In my panic to find the eye holes, I missed my growth cue. I heard a few giggles from the audience while I continued to search for the eye openings, mindful of not rustling my paper bag too much.

Finally, parents were coughing and children were laughing, and it finally got through to me that my time to grow had come and gone. Making up for lost time, I sprung to my full height, skipping the kneeling phase of the growth cycle. Then, dizzy from my inability to see and from having moved so abruptly, I reeled into the pumpkin on my right, causing a chain reaction of staggers and lunges down the row.

The play hadn't been scripted as a comedy, but that is what it became. Strangely, many in the audience thought the chaos I created was the intended ending of the play. I actually received congratulations as we sipped Kool-Aid and ate cookies after the performance. Gradually, my embarrassment turned to pride as I realized that I had achieved the grand finale I wished for when I first became a pumpkin.

A BLUEGRASS STATE OF MIND

By Elsa Goss Black

Still hanging my head over the near-Fascist turn this country took in November 2016, I think about the people I've known over the years who could possibly have voted this autocrat into office.

And then I recall my days in the Lexington, Kentucky of the early 70s when I was a new bride and a stranger in a strange land if there ever was one. Kentucky might have been a border state during the Civil War, but much of it was proudly and resolutely southern in every sense of the word.

It was lovely in Lexington, yes, especially beyond the city limits. Rolling hills dotted the countryside behind miles of fence-lined roads separating one horse farm from another. Long-limbed yearlings always seemed to be gamboling gaily across the fields, blissfully unaware of the million dollar purses dancing in the heads of their owners or the colorful silks under which they'd someday be racing.

These owners lived, at least part of the year, in Georgian, Federal style or Tara-like mansions approached by winding and tree-shaded driveways out of another time and place. Inside, they entertained in sumptuous dining rooms, at long tables set with bright white tablecloths, softly lit candles, inherited Limoges china and well-polished family silver.

Aging family retainers and cooks, always black, always soft-spoken, always at the ready, made sure the tenderloins, hams, the beaten biscuits, cheese grits and Maker's Mark bottles were deftly served on a clockwork basis. Often, it was the insistent tinkling of an antique bell close by the hostess's right hand that beckoned them from a far-off kitchen.

It was always an elegant and gracious scene, but one, I soon sensed, with a dark underbelly bubbling under the surface.

Other than as long-time servants, soothing stable hands or talented teenagers able to dribble basketballs up and down the court and make swishing three-pointers at the University of Kentucky's Rupp Arena, blacks were not merely near-silent, but also near-absent. Except to retain a way of life wildly out of step with a changing world, they did not exist for their genteel employers. Except as a necessity when all-white teams could no longer beat their integrated rivals, they were non-persons to demanding sports fans. And so, it became clear, were Catholics, Asians, gays, Easterners, uppity women, poor people, Jews, or, in fact, anyone who was vaguely "other."

In the same way that the much-ballyhooed bluegrass actually exists solely in the vivid imaginations of box-holders tearing up every Derby Day over "My Old Kentucky Home," real life was much grittier, and uglier, than any gracious myth.

That was brought home to me one evening during a well-oiled cocktail party at Hurricane Hall Stud. Or maybe it was at Spendthrift Farm, Three Chimneys, Big Sink, or Buckram Oak. I could go on, but the name doesn't matter now. What does matter—and what I remember most—is the moment one bow-tied man approached me, a large crystal glass of Bourbon and branch water gripped firmly in one hand. He greeted me with a jovial smile, then leaned down to speak rather intimately into my ear.

"Tell me, dear," he began before getting to his question. "Just who are your people?"

I looked at him blankly. "Who are my people? What on earth do you mean?" I honestly had no idea what information he was seeking, never having heard such a question in my life.

He stood a little taller then and took a determined half-step away from me. In a now-louder voice, he harrumphed, "Well, my dear, I mean, where do your people come from?"

Looking at my still-confused face, he went on, explaining as if to a particularly inapt pupil, "For instance, *my* people, the Clays, have lived around here in Bourbon County for generations. It's fitting, because we're descended from the 'Boor-bons.' You know, like the Royal House of 'Boor-bon' in France. Some of us even lived in the town of Versailles, as in the palace. But others, of course, were English, having come over from Windsor, as in the castle."

There was another pause, as he drew himself up even further with a self-satisfied smile. "So, tell me, then, where do your people come from?" At that, the conversation around us seemed to quiet down, as both host and guests awaited what the new Jew girl in town had to say for herself.

I don't know where it came from, but suddenly only one answer seemed to fit the moment.

"Kiev," I blurted out. "As in the chicken."

The resulting silence was deafening.

With that moment still so fresh in my mind all these years later, I connect the dots. After its citizens silently made their choices in the privacy of their voting booths on November 8, 2016, Kentucky was one of the first states called for Donald Trump. Mitt Romney had won the state in 2012 by 22.7 percentage points. Trump's margin was 62.2 percent.

MIAMI BITES

By Magdalena De Gasperi

There are two kinds of babies: those who like to eat and those who don't. I belonged to the second group. So instead of being a chubby, roly-poly little cherub, I was always the kind that harrumphed her nose (in those days still little) at whatever baby food was being offered. My mother told me that once my father was trying to feed me—I imagine it was when she was in the hospital having my sister, so I may have been some fifteen months old—and became so frustrated with my rejection of food that he threw a tantrum and started screaming, at which point I was probably scared to death and also started screaming.

After some years in Burlington, Vermont; Boston, Massachusetts; and Asunción, Paraguay, my family settled in Miami. The year I turned eleven, my father bought a house near the University of Miami main campus, and this was the house I grew up in. I have many fond memories playing weird games with my three sisters—doll contests, boarding school in Geneva, or Gidget the

Midget—but food did not play a major role in my early years. My sisters ate things like hard-boiled eggs, tomatoes, or potatoes, all of which I found revolting.

I attended St. Theresa School in the Gables and was not on the meal plan. Like many children I took a bag lunch, but mine more often than not consisted of one bread-and-butter sandwich. No box of raisins, no apple. Once in a while my mother would give me a tuna fish sandwich, but no mayo. To drink I would buy a cup of grape juice in the school cafeteria. To get home from school, we took a public bus to the Coral Gables bus terminal (sadly no longer in existence—the fire station is now the Coral Gables museum) and then had to change buses. Some of my fondest Miami food memories are from the bus terminal snack shop. There for ten cents I could buy a Hershey bar, or a small bag of Lay's potato chips. I once even made a sandwich at home: Lay's potato chips between two slices of white Farm Stores bread.

It may have been the onset of the counterculture that changed my palate. I remember going to Arby's on U.S. 1 with my first boyfriend and having some (maybe not all) of a roast beef sandwich. I'm pretty sure we had terrible munchies. A couple of years later I came home late; everyone else in the house was asleep. I discovered a rather large piece of cold baguette in the fridge (my parents hoard bread as if it were gold). I tried it with butter and couldn't stop until I ate the whole piece. It was sinful and delicious.

Once I turned eighteen, I went off to college in Boston, and after college started working in the Hub of New England. Boston is a seafood paradise and in the early 70s chicken lobsters went for less than $1.50 a pound. Spaghetti with meat sauce, BLT sandwiches with fries, fried eggs over easy, black and white frappes, scallops, steamed clams, Breyers and later Häagen Dasz ice cream, cheap Chinese food complete with MSG—a kaleidoscope of flavors was waiting to be discovered. Fortunately my crowd at college was relatively athletic, and I started running bridge circuits. I went on to work for a major Boston corporation and my boss had a fancy for the occasional lunch at a French restaurant to relieve the monotony of the company cafeteria. Places like the St. Botolph offered my first exposure to roast duck, paté foie gras, Linzer torte, and espresso.

The corporation offered me a junior position at a subsidiary in Germany. I jumped at the chance and later met the man of my life there. While I don't drink beer, and there are many German foods that are not my cup of tea, I will not pass up the chance to take part in a traditional St. Martin's goose dinner, complete with dumplings, red cabbage, Brussels sprouts, roasted chestnuts and stuffing. As a German friend explained, the only way to digest a heavy meal like that is to ensure you drink a tannin-rich wine that will clear the way for the food. It may sound like Drano but believe me, infinitely more enjoyable than unclogging a drain.

Now as a senior citizen I have returned to my childhood home to spend several months a year in Miami. Miami has undergone a metamorphosis from a relatively sleepy town for retirees to a bursting cosmopolitan metropolis. The many immigrants from Cuba and other parts of the Caribbean, Central and South America have left a lasting culinary imprint here. If I think of Miracle Mile in Coral Gables, where I used to wander into the giant Woolworth's to buy a 45 single and where my mother remembers the excellent burgers with hand cut fries at the diner there, now this is the site of the equally giant Barnes and Noble with its own Starbucks. There are probably a hundred restaurants in downtown Coral Gables, and we all have our favorite haunts.

A familiar and popular place for my family is Graziano's Market. Not only is the Monday through Friday happy hour special—two empanadas plus a glass of Malbec or beer for $9.99—a real bargain, but also Graziano's has repeatedly won the best empanada in Miami award. The dough is flaky but not too thin, the meat version contains chopped olives, raisins, and hard boiled eggs, just like in

Argentina or Paraguay, and most important of all the empanada is baked, not fried as in many greasy imitations. Graziano's offers at least fifteen or twenty empanada variants, including spinach and tuna, plus many specialties featuring Argentine beef and some pasta dishes. Add to this the cases and cases of wine surrounding you as you eat, and you feel you are in an Italian enoteca, but with Argentine food and Miami atmosphere.

Cuban food is an important culinary part of contemporary Miami, and one of my personal favorites for coffee and snacks is Gilbert's. Our local store is in the strip mall at Red and Bird, next to the barbershop where my father and other nonagenarians are taken for a trim. We leave my father in the hands of the patient ladies who groom him and sneak out for a decaf cortadito and a mini medianoche. If you only drink decaf, like I do for medical reasons, you often notice that decaf coffee has a bitter aftertaste. Not at Gilbert's. The coffee taste is strong but smooth, the shot of milk and sugar make it irresistible. An excellent mid-morning companion is a mini medianoche, a tiny, delicate ham and cheese sandwich on a soft brioche-type roll with a hint of pickle. Two genteel bites and it's gone.

The latest opening that we have enjoyed is a new spot at the corner of Ponce and Valencia called Son Cubano. Cuban food with Asian flavors is the concept, as the smart young waiters have explained to us. They offer small plates, attractive for those of us keeping an eye on the waistline and the pocketbook. One favorite is taquitos, two small tacos filled with yellow fin tuna, marinated ginger, and a hint of wasabi. Another small plate features Cuban sliders, two mini burgers with Asian seasoning. My brother-in-law particularly enjoyed the masitas de puerco, spicy pork chunks, and my niece wants to go back again to eat the Cuban pizza, topped with ropa vieja. The restaurant often features live music, but the son music is rhythmic without being overpowering, so we were actually able to converse while dining.

With all these culinary seductions, the challenge for the future continues to be staying in shape. Off to the gym! And maybe tomorrow evening back to Graziano's.

PRIMO

By Beatriz A. La Rosa

He sits with legs spread out, his erect penis peeking from the leg of the tiny swimsuit he wears, a sly smile on his lips. It is resting impudently on his left thigh. His right hand is at the tiller. His eyes are on your face. You realize that you are too far from the beach to swim to safety. You hear your mother's voice in your head. Desobediente!

On a summer morning in 1955, you and your brother are at the beach. You are twelve; your brother is ten. He is the only boy in the family of five girls. He is also your favorite playmate. He has a sweet and inquiring personality, asking the questions you think but do not dare ask. His activities are much more fun than yours. He receives a pellet gun, a baseball bat and mitt for Christmas, and you get a lifelike rubber baby doll and a small sweeping broom with matching dustpan. He is kind, and he allows you to use his gun for target practice, which you do by shooting pellets at cans that he places too close to the side window of el Chino Luis' bodega.

Malcliados, cuidado! The old shriveled head of one of the Koreans who live in the back of the bodega shouts at you. In Cuba, we call all Asiatic people chinos.

Many times you get to play baseball with his friends on empty lots and streets paved with white sand.

Your first menstruation had been that December of 1954—the bloody mess scaring you since no adult had spoken to you about it. The extent of your sex education comes from the medieval Spanish nuns who run the school. The nuns walk the halls of the school dressed in their black wool habits—their hands hidden inside the sleeves—and black veils. Their eyes are alert, members of the Inquisition who in their inspection of the students are looking for that swaying Cuban hip and buttocks that betrays the sinner. You are sure one day they are all going to swoon from the Cuban heat.

During their lessons they preach purity of thought and action. Theie stories tell of those unfortunate women who have carnal thoughts and desires, their sins resulting in horrible deaths and eternal damnation in the fires of the Catholic Hell.

You live in a panic because you have dirty urges and desires and a pleasurable sensation "down there" when you think of boys—surely these thoughts fall into the category of things smutty and sinful. But in spite of your misgivings, nature takes its course and by summer, you have grown decent looking tits and your scrawny legs have become muscular and shapely.

The beach, your hometown, is in Cuba. Varadero is one of the most beautiful beaches in the Caribbean. Your family moved there when you were five, and they stay until you are fifteen. At fifteen, Cuban girls get a huge party and are "presented" to society. But because of the turmoil caused by the Cuban Revolution, you don't experience the ritual of being introduced to your peers as a marriageable woman.

That day you check the condition of the ocean early in the morning. The ocean can be seen through the balustrade of the back porch. This is an action repeated every morning during the summer. "The sea is smooth as silk," you call out to your brother and hurry up to have breakfast. You know you have to wait at least two hours before you get in the water. Otherwise you might suffer an embolia.

You are at the beach by about ten in the morning. By noon most of the bathers start leaving. You know that you and your brother should also go home for lunch. But it feels too good at the beach, and the water is perfect. This is the time when the wind picks up a little, and the brisote feels like fingers playing with your skin and hair. You decide to stay, disobeying the rule set by your father that everyone be seated at the table by twelve-thirty.

The beach is looking deserted. You and your brother stay. You are sitting on the sand, your legs in the water, every cell in your body awake, absorbing all the life that surrounds you.

You feel someone's gaze. Primo is looking at you. Something about this man is disturbing. You are uncomfortable when he is close to you. He has a strong, sinewy body and curly black hair bleached yellow by the sun. His legs are muscular and his skin a rich copper. His teeth are white, his smile contrasting with the burnished color of his face. He wears a very tiny swimsuit—maybe an Italian-style bikini—which the locals don't wear. The swimsuit rides low on his torso and the beginning of the groin area—that lovely composition of bone and muscle of the male anatomy. He is young and in great physical shape.

Primo reminds you of a picture of a Satyr, the mythical male figures with goat-like features and a permanent erection, which you have seen in the occasional art book that appeared in your home. The Satyr is depicted surrounded by ripe-looking naked young women. You hide from your mother when you look at the

Satyr, aware of the rising heat as you examine the male anatomy, sure that you are on the way to hell.

Primo is one of the locals. He is in his early twenties. Like Primo, most men in town earn their livings by fishing or working at the sugar mills during la Zafra, the sugar harvest. Because the harvest is seasonal work, most of the men fish or work doing odd jobs during the summer.

Primo somehow manages to buy a Sunfish. He rents the little boat to tourists and to the families who vacation in Varadero in the summers. He is also an escort of sorts, catering to the women tourists who invade during the winter season. He is very popular with the foreign women. You know—because you have heard the locals gossip that, well, these women ask Primo, "Besame Pescador." You and your sisters giggle and replay the "kiss the fisherman" scene, imitating the silly women who fall in love with Primo.

He is not the only good looking one doing this type of work. There are several who supplement their incomes this way. "Stay away from them," your mother warns.

You and your brother love Primo's Sunfish. It is so different from the one your father owns. Your father has a wooden fishing boat in Varadero with a sputtering engine—putt putt putt putt putt—and a mid-engine design. It is white with a blue stripe painted the length of the boat. The boat is no bigger than ten or twelve feet, and it stinks of fish and gasoline. The Sunfish, that is another story. Built in the United States, it is sleek, painted a bright lustrous red, so glamorous and so out of reach. Primo charges a lot of money for a ride, an amount that you could only have in your dreams. You keep looking at the Sunfish. The noon breeze kisses your face and creates a light chop on the water.

Primo smiles and calls out, "You two! Come over. I will take you sailing." You remember your mother's warning and know you shouldn't. But how and when would you be able to have this experience? Something that a few minutes ago was out of reach, impossible, is now being offered—and free. You clamber aboard, your brother sits at the bow, Primo at the tiller, and you in the middle.

The little sailboat glides through the waters, picking up speed. You leave behind the clear water of the shore and are now navigating the deeper turquoise water. You look ahead at your brother who is enjoying the soft rhythmic flap and whoosh of the hull as it rides the waves. Your brother's hands are in the water, tiny propellers creating the smallest of wakes. The water splashes your face and body, and the wind dries the water into a salty crust on your skin and swimsuit, the breeze cooling the heat of the sun. You wish you had a mango to suck on.

You realize the water is now the indigo blue of very deep water. The boat is so far and distant from the beach that the houses look like toys sitting on the sand. Why are we so far from shore? Looking for an answer, you look at Primo. And then you know. Primo has allowed his pinga to peep through the left leg of his bikini. A perfect tableau of sun and sea and a man's cock has been staged—just for you. And he is looking right into your eyes with a look that says that he is challenging you.

You are scared, embarrassed, and drawn to the sight of his cock. Your heart is beating loudly, and you feel the heat of shame flowing from your belly to your face. "You've really done it this time": you hear your mother in your head. Back and forth your eyes travel, forward to your brother, back towards Primo and his pinga. But your brother is oblivious to what is happening. He is absorbed with the water, with the breeze, with the blue sky that surrounds him like a mantle. The rocking of the boat is a lullaby sung by the most loving of mothers, content and at peace. You— you want to flee, but there is no place to go. The boat is narrow, and Primo starts moving his callused feet towards yours. He makes contact. His feet touch yours. You lean into the water, as far as you can without falling, to avoid this caress.

Primo finally heads back to shore. You are physically unharmed. But a feeling of guilt and shame persists. You cannot forget his mocking smile as he looked in your face. You go home, a bit sad and chastened. You tell no one about this incident.

You always had a lot of freedom during those growing years. But from that day forward, you avoid being alone on the beach, afraid not only of him but of the other men who, you are sure, know what happened because Primo told them. Some of the beauty and luster of that time was lost on that day.

You keep what happened a secret. Then one day, some fifty years later, you tell one of your sisters. She laughs.

"Primo showed his pinga to everyone!"

MY '55 CHEVY

By Thomas L. David

Many boys are intrigued by cars. It happened to me when I was about thirteen when U.S. auto makers were starting to feature bold designs. Gone was the thought that a car was just a streamlined box set on wheels. A design evolution began with the 1955 model year when the wrap-around windshield came on the scene in cars with white-walled tires and big chrome, often bullet-shaped bumpers. Chrome accented nearly every line. It was easy to fall in love with cars then. Pictures of autos built in the late fifties and early sixties still awe me, works of art with tail fins on long, wide bodies. Designs were so distinctive it was easy to distinguish one brand of car from another.

Distinctive designs disappeared in the seventies and eighties when car makers were pressed to provide better gas mileage. They took to the wind tunnel to devise shapes that minimized wind resistance and improved gas mileage. Since the wind tunnel doesn't lie, most cars started to look alike and they really do today. Safety concerns did away with distinctive bumper and front-end designs as pedestrians had to be protected. Beautiful chrome bumpers gave way to rounded, shock-absorbing, plastic integrated fenders.

I bought my first car, a '55 Chevy, in the summer of 1959 as I prepared for my junior year in college. It set me back about $700 when it had twenty some thousand miles on the odometer. The money came from my summer earnings from several years. I had had a summer job since age fourteen. My Chevy was a two-door sedan. It was 100% made in America. While others added *prestige* to their products claiming they were *imported*, Chevrolet took the opposite approach. Its commercials proudly featured American heritage including a jingle: "Baseball. Hot Dogs. Apple Pie and Chevrolet." Like most cars of that time it was two-toned, light blue with a white top. It had a six cylinder engine and a three speed manual transmission. Nothing in the bench-seated interior impressed; it was not Chevy's most expensive model and surely cost less than $2,000 new. It needed a radio which I obtained from a junk yard and installed myself. It never worked quite right. That modest set of wheels lasted about three years. In those days rust from salted, snowy roads and fifty thousand miles on the odometer soon put most cars to rest.

I was attending a college in Detroit at the time. Doing what college kids did, I invited four fraternity brothers to journey to Fort Lauderdale for the 1960 semester break, in my '55 Chevy, of course. It was crowded with bodies and luggage, but that was all part of the adventure. Not stopping for a motel, we drove day and night on the U.S. highway system to the Sunshine State. We took turns driving, and when it was Ray's turn, during the night, something happened that still makes me laugh. The charity in Ray's heart was bigger than the common sense in his head as he took sympathy with a sleazy looking hitchhiker. He stopped in the dark. I can't imagine where he thought another rider would fit, but as the hitchhiker tried to open the front door, Brooks, who was sitting in the front seat, awoke and had the answer. Compassion was not Brooks' strong suit. He screamed at Ray to get moving. He told the hitchhiker he was welcome to sit on the back bumper.

We stayed at a "basic" motel in Fort Lauderdale, each room equipped with a kitchenette just right for heating up pork and beans and hamburgers. There was a pool in the middle of the U-shaped building. It came complete with damsels sunning in their bathing suits. The expansive Fort Lauderdale beach was a main attraction as was the nearby and legendary Elbow Room, a Fort Lauderdale bar which still serves 'em up today. For one special evening we got dates and trekked to Miami Beach to see Jerry Lewis in a show at the Eden Roc Hotel, still a fixture in Miami Beach. Lewis had played the slapstick clown character in the TV Martin and Lewis Act that was famous in the fifties and sixties. And we were stunned. Instead of slapstick silliness Lewis gave a versatile performance, singing, dancing and telling great jokes, all in a two hour monologue without a break.

My '55 Chevy was a fine machine that served me well. It was adequately equipped for its time. What is more interesting, though, is the equipment it didn't have. Would you believe that my Chevy didn't have an oil filter? I added one, something critical for extending engine life. I also added a side-view mirror. Power-steering and power-brakes were absent, as were power-windows and seats. Seat belts and padded dashboards? Safety was not yet an issue. Air bags? They had not yet been dreamed of. Navigation system, back-up camera, heated back window, cup holders and heated seats? Not yet in marketing gurus' imaginations. Tinted windows, windshield washers, back-up lights, concealed radio antenna, permanently greased wheel bearings, anti-sway bars? Not yet on the scene. Stereo radio, smart key, bucket seats, anti-lock brakes? It took years before we saw them. Air conditioning? You might have had that in a Cadillac, but not in a Chevy. These advances in the automobile tell an interesting story. They are now thought of as necessities. They make our lives so much easier now. We are babied and coddled with things we really don't need for basic transportation.

Perhaps the biggest difference in today's cars is under the hood. Computers electronics have dramatically enhanced the power and efficiency of the internal combustion engine. My Chevy had a carburetor which mixed air and gasoline into a vapor that ignited in the cylinders to power the car. It started well as long as it wasn't too cold or too damp. Now electronic fuel-injection more efficiently meters the gasoline flow to the cylinders, adjusting the amount of fuel to match the engine's needs that vary depending on temperature and speed of the engine. Computer controlled variable valve timing alters the timing of valve lift by milliseconds adjusting the flow of the fuel mixture to the cylinders. It adds efficiency since the internal combustion engine needs different timing of fuel depending on the speed it is turning at. Also, rather than having just one intake valve and one for exhaust, multiple valves cause the fuel mixture to swirl, more efficiently burn and exit the cylinders. Together these computerized functions have resulted in smaller engines that create more power using less gasoline.

Computers metering the engine are only the beginning. I have read that auto manufacturers use more computer power than any other industry. Many cars carry more computer code than some jet fighters. A 2010 article in the *New York Times* estimated that more than 15% of the cost of a vehicle then was for computer electronics. That is nearly $5,000 per car. Even the most basic auto has 30 or more computer systems that control airbag deployment, power steering, variable valve timing, antilock braking, automatic transmission shifting intervals and on and on. And that was before the onslaught of computer systems that recently hit the market. They interpret data from radar sensors to give lane change warnings and can even activate brakes to avoid collisions.

A couple years ago when I was passing through an intersection, a truck, without warning, coming from the opposite direction, made a left turn in front of me. The collision totaled my car, setting off all the airbags. I emerged without injury, suffering only from the repulsive odor of the gas that inflated the airbags. The truck driver insisted that I had run a red light making a left turn into her. But technology came to the rescue. You probably don't know that all modern cars are required to have a computer that continuously records various operating conditions. In my case it saved the five seconds of information before the airbags went off. It disclosed that I was going 32 miles per hour in a 35 zone, and was going straight. Using that information and pictures of the remains of the vehicles, an expert's report concluded that not I, but the truck driver, was at fault. It saved me from insurance rate hikes.

Cars are now approaching perfection with all these electronic gadgets. Sometimes perfection can be a bit boring. My Chevy was far from perfect. And, like an oriental rug, an imperfection may be part of the charm. Typical of that time was a horn ring on the steering wheel which activated the horn when pressed. You realize, of course, that you couldn't just run an electric wire from the horn ring through the steering column to the horn. Such a wire would be twisted back and forth with every turn, thousands of times, and the wire would fail. There must have been a sliding electric contact in the steering wheel housing that was activated only when the horn ring was pressed. However well that mechanism may have been designed, it became a hit-and-miss operation as the car aged. The horn occasionally went off on its own. No problem. A little jiggling of the horn ring cured that. However, one cold winter night in Detroit, as I lay in bed on the seventh floor of a men's dormitory, I awoke to the sound of a car horn that sounded familiar. Yes, it was my Chevy. I threw on some clothes and raced down to my car. My tool kit had pliers which I used to disconnect the battery cable. It was only a temporary yet effective solution. You might think of an independently minded horn as a nuisance. No! My Chevy had character.

THE P.E. SEMESTER

By Kitty Winkler

I was a wimp. When other kids were playing softball in the back
yard, I was reading a book, trying out new nail polish or redecorating my room.

I shouldn't have used past tense. I was born a wimp, grew up
a wimp and still am a wimp. The only time I run fast is to go in
the other direction if someone mentions athletics. I squeaked by
when I was forced to endure junior high and high school physical
education and yearned for the day that I would no longer have to
dodge a flying softball, basketball or tennis ball. I longed to avoid
the embarrassing moments when I was the last person chosen as
teams were formed or worse yet, when my team's loss was totally
my fault.

I thought that going away to college would end all that mortification, but I was so wrong. When I went through Freshman
Orientation, I was aghast to learn that five P.E. courses would be required to graduate. Ridiculous, I thought. Surely, this outrageous

requirement would be rescinded by the time I reached my senior year, and I immediately dismissed it.

One P.E. course was required during freshman year. It was entitled Introduction to Physical Education, and included such horrors as volleyball, basketball, the Air Force exercise regimen, tennis and softball. All that this torture accomplished was to strengthen my resolve to never again enter a gym or appear on a playing field.

Time ticked by, and I learned that I would have to go an extra semester past what would have been my senior year because of credits that didn't transfer from the junior year I had spent in France. That didn't come as a surprise because I had been told in advance that not all of the credits earned there would be accepted in the United States. What did come as a very big and very nasty surprise was being called to my faculty advisor's office because of another glitch he had found in my meeting course requirements for graduation. The glitch turned out to be his discovery that I had only taken one of the five P.E. courses that were required for graduation.

"Oh Dr. Harrison," I said, "I completely forgot about that. Surely you agree that it is an unreasonable requirement."

A stony-faced stare met my eyes across the desk. "Miss Winkler, I believe you and every other student are informed early and often of the physical education requirement. It will not be waived no matter how much you appeal or I appeal on your behalf. You will have to stay an additional semester to get the needed P.E. credits."

"But I'm already staying an extra semester to make up for my French credits that didn't transfer," I whined, knowing even as I said it that it was irrelevant and would get me nowhere.

"Let's look at the schedule and see what courses you can take to meet the requirement, shall we?"

I learned that not only did I have to take four P.E. courses in one semester, they had to be in certain categories. One had to be a team sport, one had to be an individual sport, one had to be a dance, and one was an elective. I had already completed the Freshman requirement, thank goodness.

Dr. Harrison and I pored over the next year's schedule to figure out what courses I could take to meet the requirements. This was a tiny liberal arts university with few offerings in any category in a given semester, and it looked nearly impossible for me to get sufficient credits to meet the physical education requirement in a single semester. At last, we put together Field Sports for Women (team sport requirement), Archery (individual sport requirement), and Folk Dancing (dance requirement), but there was no course left for me to use as the elective I needed to complete the required five.

I am sure I looked near tears, and Dr. Harrison took pity on me. "Here's a Red Cross course," he said. "Maybe I can convince the Dean that in your special circumstance we can count that as a P.E. course."

He was as good as his word, and for the second semester of my post-senior year I was signed up for the four P.E. courses that would finally let me graduate if I could pass them. That thought sent a shudder down my spine. Could I possibly fail to graduate because I flunked a P.E. course?

The dreaded semester finally arrived, and I realized I would be spending it dressed in the white shorts and white shirt that were required for P.E. My first class was Archery, and I took heart. Although the bow was harder to work that I had imagined, I even managed to hit the target once in that first session of the class.

On I went to Folk Dancing. The instructor for that course, Milly Rhoads, was famous for being a hard ass. I worked diligently at my do-si-dos and all the other strange steps, but I discovered that the rhythm and beat of the recorded dance caller eluded me. Surely I could get the hang of this in the next few sessions.

The third course was Field Sports for Women. I arrived at the playing field, and almost turned around and fled. There was Milly

Rhoads again, blowing her whistle; and as I scanned my classmates, I saw that everyone but me was a P.E. major. They were bruisers! I was frightened of them in chance encounters on campus, never mind on the playing field. Teams were chosen. I was the last one selected, of course. That day's sport would be field hockey. The next disheartening discovery was that I was the only one in the class who had never played hockey and had no idea of the rules. Milly stared at me, and I could see the word "wimp" going through her head. I bravely tried to dribble the hockey puck down the field, but I kept finding that I was dribbling air, having left the puck several paces behind. It went from bad to worse that day, and I realized that I would have to study the game and do some out-of-class practice if I was ever going to pass this one.

I was relieved to be heading for Red Cross next. It wasn't even a real P.E. course; surely I could do well. The first good omen was that Milly Rhoads wasn't the instructor, Coach Newton, the men's basketball coach, was. The second warm feeling came when I realized the class was small; only eight of us were enrolled. We were issued Red Cross manuals, and the first session focused on the national standards we would have to meet to become certified in life saving. Life saving! This had never been my goal, but it was a course requirement and we learned we would have to pass a stringent national test at the end of the semester.

For that whole semester, I worked harder than I had ever done for academic courses. I studied rules in the library, I bartered help from classmates, I practiced moves until I nearly drove my roommate crazy, and still realized that the only course that was a shoo-in was Archery.

I was truly worried about Field Sports for Women. We had moved from hockey to volleyball to softball, and I couldn't do well at any of them. My body was covered with blue and purple bruises from head to toe, recording the many times I was punched and kicked by my muscular classmates. We had developed a growing following of students who came out to watch and laugh as I got pulverized and scorned by everyone in the class, including our coach. I was beginning to need the bandaging techniques that I was learning in Red Cross.

Speaking of Red Cross, I had unforeseen difficulty there too. Even though the class was small, seven of the eight of us were dedicated to being heroic life savers. The eighth, me, just wanted to get by. This meant that for most of our classes I was chosen to be the "victim" of the terrible accident that was going to require bandaging, Heimlich maneuvers, mouth-to-mouth resuscitation, or traction. I felt mummified and mauled after every session.

And Folk Dancing! As we galloped around the stage in the gym, I seemed constantly out of step with the caller.

My gouged ankles from my experiences with Field Sports were getting even deeper gouges from the prancing folk dancers. Milly Rhoads' expression turned sour every time she looked at me, and I gradually realized that this torturous semester was no picnic for her either.

Near panic set in as the semester wound to a close. If I failed anything (a strong possibility), how could I ever explain to my family and future employers that my education was prolonged by two added semesters of physical education?

I was right about archery; the instructor told us our final grades at our last session. I got an A! While that sounds remarkable, everyone in the class got an A except Rosemary Martin. Rosemary had failed to hit the target once in the whole semester (a woman after my own heart) and wound up with a B for her grade.

I did reasonably well on the national Red Cross exam. I had been the victim so many times that I knew most of the maneuvers, and the written part of the exam wasn't too tough. I pulled a B minus and was thrilled with that.

I couldn't bear to wait for grades to be sent home to know how I did in the other two courses, so I requested a conference with

Milly Rhoads, the dragon instructor of both Folk Dancing and Field Sports for Women. I told Milly my tale of woe about the extra semester, limited courses available, being a non-athlete (as if she hadn't noticed) and every pitiful factor I could drag up. My monologue was followed by deep silence from Milly and that same sour expression I had seen so many times on the playing field. Finally, she said, "Miss Winkler, I am going to give you the gift of a lifetime. Trust that it is not a gift for you alone. The thought of you appearing for another semester of one of my classes is more than I can bear. I am giving you a C-minus in both courses."

Hallelujah! Life is good.

REMEMBERING HANNAH

By Isabelle Whitfield

Hannah came to work for my maternal grandparents, John and Belle Robertson, when my mother was only a few days old. My grandmother, Miss Belle, and Hannah were the same age, both born in 1886. The beloved mistress and faithful servant grew up and grew old together in a small town in Alabama's Black Belt. Between them, there evolved an unshakable, mutually-devoted bond from experiencing the joys and sorrows of everyday life to-gether for over a half-century, except for Sundays. Sunday was Hannah's day off.

Though Hannah's life was seemingly pre-ordained by the time, place, and circumstances in which she lived, she became a much beloved and indispensable part of the Robertson family. To call her "the cook" or "housekeeper" would not do her justice. She was so much more.

Hannah and Miss Belle were both twenty years old when my mother, Louise, arrived. Hannah worked for my grandparents for fifty-two years, and my mother often said that she "never knew life without Hannah." She was there when my mother was first born, saw her through childhood, high school, and she packed her trunks to go off to college. She was there through two world wars, the dark days of the Great Depression, and welcomed Miss Louise's new husband to the family toward the end of World War II.

When my dear grandmother died in 1959, it may have been that Hannah felt she had no further purpose in life, no reason to go on without Miss Belle. She died less than two months later. Of course my mother was beyond grief-stricken to lose both her mother and Hannah so devastatingly close together.

But to remember happier times—an early memory of Hannah in my mind's eye is watching her sweep the front porch, then making her way down the sidewalk leading to the house, her strong arms sweeping vigorously from side to side with an old cornstalk broom, wearing a white apron over a simple print dress, with a red bandanna wrapped around her head. There are photos of Hannah holding me as a baby as she seemed to be glowing with pride that Miss Louise had produced a little girl, whom Hannah nicknamed "Little Bit." She also nicknamed my little brother "Ole I Will" because when he was told to do something, he invariably replied, "I will" but never did.

I remember Hannah in so many ways-----her punching holes in jar tops for us to use to catch lightening bugs, of her fixing a broken skate, of her soothing skinned knees or elbows, of her always knowing where everything was that we could not find in the house, of her coming for us at the "picture show" where we often stayed much too late watching the serials over and over, and then her marching us home down the hill after dark.

I particularly remember an incident when Hannah came to my rescue and saved me from a potentially sad fate.

When I was about four or five, I got into a bee's nest in a bush in the front yard and was the victim of angry swarming bees. Hannah heard me screaming, came running, and saved me from the painful bee stings by putting wet tobacco from my grandfather's cigars all over me. When I stopped screaming, she comforted me by saying that would "take the sting out," wiped away my tears, hugged me close and assured "Little Bit" that everything would be all right. I survived.

Of Hannah's myriad duties, which included everything related to housekeeping-----such as washing clothes and hanging them on the line to dry (I used to hand her the clothespins), ironing clothes, sweeping the house, dusting antiques, waxing the parquet floors, shelling pecans, feeding the cats, washing windows and dusting the window screens, planning the grocery list with Miss Belle, and, of course, cooking-----as well as watching my little brother and me and friends who came to play, our favorite part of Hannah's work involved what she did in the kitchen.

We never noticed as we licked chocolate cake batter from a bowl that Hannah never used a recipe. When my mother tried from time to time to pin her down on the ingredients for a special dish, Hannah would say, "I put in a smidgen of this" and "a pinch of that." How she made those hotcakes and waffles in the old waffle iron, the sweet potato casserole with browned marshmallows on top, her fried chicken, collard greens, black-eyed peas and cornbread, macaroni and cheese to die for, those memorable mayonnaise biscuits and butterbeans, the turkey hash after Thanksgiving, the homemade vanilla ice cream — will forever remain a mystery. I will remember her making fresh tomato sandwiches for us in the summertime after we arrived from the town swimming pool, and then letting us sit in the kitchen in our wet bathing suits to eat those juicy sandwiches and drink Cherry Kool-Aid to our heart's content. And I can still hear the tinkling of the small silver bell throughout the house and yard when a meal was ready. When we heard Hannah ringing the bell, we came running.

In those days in the Deep South, being a good cook did not have the same cachet for a wife that it seems to have today. What did confer prestige among the women in the community was not who *was* the best cook but who *had* the best cook — and Hannah's reputation was known around town as the best cook — hands down. She seemed very proud of her local fame and the compliments she received when it was Miss Belle's turn to host a meeting of the UDC (United Daughters of the Confederacy) and light refreshments, dainty sandwiches, and pastries were served, all made by Hannah.

On the rare occasions when we might misbehave, Hannah kept us in line. She would quote Miss Belle, who often said, "You raise cats and dogs, you rear children," and thus Hannah would proceed to "rear" us by making us mind our manners. She was a fair but tough disciplinarian.

Every spring, my grandmother's white Persian cats, as well as a few strays that wandered up, would invariably produce kittens. Once we actually saw a fascinating live birth of a litter of kittens and loved watching the mother cat feed her babies. We waited patiently for their little eyes to open and begin to explore the world around them. By then we had named them all. Thus we grew up with a multitude of feline companions, though they only lived outside as they were not allowed in the house.

But, when, from time to time, one of the cats or kittens died, Hannah always conducted a cat funeral service. The departed cat would be placed in a shoebox as a coffin and a grave would be dug in a far corner of the backyard that came to be known as the Cat Cemetery. Hannah assured us that the poor little creature's spirit had "risen from the dead" and our little friend was now purring contentedly in Cat Heaven. Then she would say a few appropriate words to send the cat on its way, finally closing by singing a gospel hymn, and we hummed along as best we could. Sometimes others attended the service----maybe one of our grandparents or our mother, but most of the time it was just Hannah and the children. Looking back, these solemn ceremonies may have helped us learn early how to cope with death, loss, and grief, and then move on.

Hannah was quite well-versed in the social codes of the day in segregated Alabama, and she enforced the rules strictly when various other "help" came to the Robertson home. It was the custom then that black folks were not to come to the front door. When selling vegetables, they came to the back door to offer fresh tomatoes, butterbeans, squash, okra, peaches, or watermelons. Hannah would find out what Miss Belle wanted and conduct the transaction. When extra help was needed for washing, ironing, or spring cleaning, Hannah would manage their duties as well. She often "got after" the black folks when she thought they were out of line or were not doing a good job.

But Hannah did not live to see the social upheaval of the civil rights movement of the 1960s in the South. She was understandably old-school, a product of her time, and believed that black folks had "their place." Paradoxically, she would probably have looked askance at the "uppity" black people creating such a "ruckus" as they marched through nearby Selma protesting for the right to vote. But I only knew Hannah when I was a child and was not aware that I lived in a segregated society. I suppose I just accepted life as it was, just as she seemed to, but I have often wondered what Hannah would have really thought had she lived to see the great social changes of that time. Would she have been upset at the way her people were "misbehaving" or would she have been secretly glad to see the progress toward equal rights on the horizon? She was so devoted and loyal to her white family that she may have thought it insulting and rude to see black folks "stirring up so much trouble." I do not know, but I wonder.

On Christmas Day when we gathered in the living room to open presents from Santa and exchange gifts, we always waited until Hannah finished the breakfast dishes and was ready to join us. We entreated, "Come on, Hannah, hurry up!" I remember vividly Hannah sitting in one of the Victorian chairs, presents piled high on her white-aproned lap with a big grin on her face.

My mother always said that Hannah had more common sense than anyone, although I am not sure that Hannah could read or write. She did say the most hilarious things sometimes, and she had a very simple but sensible way of looking at life. When told about the Great Wall of China and its being over two thousand years old, she replied thoughtfully, "It look like it be done fell down by now."

When the time came for Hannah to receive Social Security, my grandfather filled out the necessary forms for her. All she had to do was to sign her name. As much as she adored and trusted Mr. John, she stubbornly refused to sign. She finally sheepishly explained that her father, who had been a slave, had made her promise never to sign any papers given to her by a white man. She would not budge. Quite frustrated after days of trying to persuade her to sign the papers, he finally gave up, signed for her, and her checks began arriving.

On a cold February day in 1959, my dearest grandmother Belle passed away. I remember Hannah reminding my grieving mother to be sure to get that diamond wedding ring off Miss Belle's finger before she was buried. Hannah was, if anything, practical. When Hannah died soon after Miss Belle, in early April, my mother went to Hannah's funeral at the black Baptist Church. (We had already returned to school in Florida with our dad.) She persuaded an aunt to go with her and, of course, they were the only two white people among the mourners. My mother was comforted by the beautiful service for Hannah, and received heartfelt condolences from the congregation. She described the uplifting gospel singing that only black congregants seem able to perform, their voices rising in unison to send Hannah to her well-deserved rest.

But then the question arose: Where would Hannah be buried?

Customarily, the cemetery adjacent to the black Baptist church would be appropriate. But my mother had other ideas. She wanted Hannah to be buried near my grandmother Belle in the family plot so she could visit them together, bring flowers on special occasions of remembrance, and attend to their graves. However, no black person had ever been buried in the white cemetery. She argued that there was a small tombstone in another family plot that said "Our Black Momma," but was told by the cemetery authorities that it was only an honorary marker, that there was no actual grave there.

But my mother persisted. She somehow wangled a special dispensation from the mayor so that Hannah could be laid to rest with the only family she had known and loved for fifty-two years, a family who had loved her dearly and to whom she had been devoted.

Today there is a small granite headstone in the cemetery that says simply "Hannah" with her birth and death dates. She rests under a shady oak tree surrounded by white crepe myrtles in an arc around the family plot, which includes the remains of a great-great grandfather who fought in the Civil War. She was buried next to Miss Belle and Mr. John, and today Miss Louise rests there, too. It seems "altogether fitting and proper" that Hannah spend eternity with her beloved family, just as she spent her life with them, never leaving the black soil of Alabama.

When I go back to the home Hannah took care of for so long and so well, I reflect upon the enduring lessons Hannah taught us without our ever knowing it. She taught the value of hard work and discipline, of patience and perseverance, of love and kindness, of coping with life and death. I believe that Hannah's heart and soul dwell in all the rooms still, and her spirit will always linger in my childhood home of happy memories. For this I am grateful.

And sometimes I have a fleeting image of Hannah wearing her white apron and red bandanna, again sweeping the wide front sidewalk as she always did, sweeping rhythmically from side to side up to the green house, working her way back to the cherished home and family she looked after all of her life.

REPORT CARDS IN A DRAWER

By Ellen Leeds

B rown envelopes kept in my drawer. Never thrown away, or given away. I keep many of my possessions of days gone by, but these report cards tell a story. My story.

Skipping along the sidewalk to Clifton Avenue Grade School. Reddish Oxfords with short white socks. Blond, wild, curly hair, bandaged knees and plaid skirt with white blouse: running to the door. Dropped off by the side entrance especially made for the youngest of children, with a fence for them to play in and twirl around in the cool winter mornings. Clifton Avenue Grade School, Lakewood, New Jersey.

Kindergarten 1953-1954. Teacher Ruth Mary Davis. Principal Mrs. Ella M. Burdge. Inside a brown envelope, a report card showing two children with hands behind their backs, a gold stamp and two blue ribbons. My Kindergarten report card. All Ss given that year. Satisfactory progress: Social habits, Work habits, and Health habits all Ss listed and proudly signed by my mother.

1954-1955. Stella C. Brown first grade teacher. Allowed to be taken directly into the front door of the school now. First grade means more responsibilities. More independence. Now able to play in the large playground in back of the school. Now allowed to be with all the older children. No more confinement in the side entrance, enclosed playground.

November 10, 1954. "Ellen is doing well in the first grade. She prepares her work neatly. Her stories are well told," Stella C. Brown writes to my parents on the report card. "We're very proud of Ellen's report," my mom writes back.

Second report card from first grade, February 7, 1955. More time has passed and things get harder. "Ellen has shown progress in all of her work. She prepares her written work neatly, but sometimes has to be reminded not to waste time," writes Stella C. Brown. My mom doesn't respond.

Learning what to expect I want to do better. It isn't easy sitting in rows of desks, facing forward, not talking when I feel like it. March 30, 1955. "Dear Parents, Ellen does fine written work. She has shown improvement in reading. She should continue trying to increase her reading vocabulary. Her work habits are better," Stella C. Brown.

Summer is over. Freedom is again gone. I am feeling uneasy and sad to be returning to school. New teacher. Older now. Second grade. Walk into the class alone. Hair tied up in a ponytail. Sit in my seat, hands folded on top of my desk. I stare at the large black and white clock above the blackboard. Hazel Brower is the second grade teacher. "Ellen's class work is below average. She wastes time, talks too much and is inattentive in class. She is not working up to her ability. Her behavior needs improving," writes Hazel F. Brower. Four months into second grade and already a failure. School is no fun. The other kids are okay, but having to get up each day is a struggle.

January 24, 1956. "Ellen has shown improvement in her class work. Her behavior has improved, but she still talks unnecessarily," Hazel F. Brower writes.

March 23, 1956. "Her behavior could be improved-she still talks too much," Hazel F. Brower writes. "Her reading is below grade level but she is promoted to third grade." Summer is almost here.

I imagine a teacher who sees me and likes me. Grade three, taught by Ann Manning. A's and B's in English, in reading, penmanship, arithmetic and spelling. All Ss (satisfactory) in behavior. Had the summer transformed me? No comments written, only letters written into small boxes. I don't even remember Ms. Manning. She probably was wonderful. Third grade comes to an end.

Missing pieces of fourth, fifth, and then there was my beloved sixth grade teacher, whom I often think about. Mr. Introcaso, 1959-1960. What ever happened to him? Got the lowest possible grade in his class for math, E which was between 60-69, listed as failure. One quarter I received a D in English—hard to imagine. I loved this man. Remember his enthusiasm for teaching. After entering high school, I heard he was arrested for molesting a handicapped girl. Never believed it. Wanted to speak up on his behalf, but too young and scared. Always wondered what became of him?

Final, report card saved, seventh grade, 1960-1961, R. Gindoff teacher. New Principal, Joseph G. Mayer. (Heard he is still alive.) That year remains a mystery to me too. Look at the card and what does it reveal. Home Ec. D+. I mean, what would be the difference between a D and D+? Lots of Ds in spelling, and what is especially funny, A+ in physical education, the bane of my existence all through the school years that were to come. I truly hated each and every physical education class, especially in high school with those awful blue gym suits.

I'll put them back in the drawer again, those report cards of long ago. I made it through to college and beyond. I still can't spell very well. I don't like math, and definitely not domestic things, and of course it is true I talk a lot. I continue to write stories. "Your stories are well told," I've been told. I definitely see from exploring these report cards that some things just never change!

TO MICHELLE ON HER 23RD BIRTHDAY

By Elsa Goss Black

You were less than 36 hours old when the nurse first put you in my arms. As any new mother will tell you, and as I hope you discover for yourself someday, to look into the eyes of your newborn is to fall in love at first sight. It's a profound and primal connection, stronger than any other bond on earth.

For me, however, that sunny October day meant even more. It was a storybook ending, yes, but also a storybook beginning, an answer to many a prayer, to many first stars wished upon and to many candles lit all over the world. The years of yearning were finally over as I inhaled your magical, unmistakable baby smell and caressed your gorgeous face.

At long last, I had joined a club I'd often feared I'd never get to experience. I would never again walk into a Toys 'R Us like a stranger in a strange land, lost among the unfamiliar and bewildering paraphernalia of parenthood. I'd never again have that sinking feeling in my soul when I passed another woman pushing a stroller. My own infant was now cuddled in the crook of my left arm, my right hand counting tiny fingers and precious baby toes.

My miracle had arrived.

As Daddy once advised me, however, raising a baby is far more than putting a little white hat on a sweet head. How right he was! For one thing, I can count on the fingers of one hand the times you kept any hat on your head for more than three seconds. For another, there is the fact that becoming a parent means a life of long days and short years. This means that there are many times you think will never end, yet you mourn with all your heart when they do.

As with any mother and daughter, then, our journey since that first meeting has not always been smooth. In the many dark nights of my soul before your birth, I often vowed to God that if you came to me, I would never ask for anything else. But as they say, man plans and God laughs.

In His infinite wisdom, He presented me with a girl who seemed to know her own mind the second she drew her first breath. You were, and are, an indomitable and brilliant spirit, a strong-willed old soul who has always marched to her own drummer and made her own path. Not for nothing was your first sentence a defiant, determined, "I do it myself!"

I confess that I sometimes found it frustrating to have a daughter who wouldn't necessarily do things my way. Malleable you never were, that's for sure.

But witty and wise beyond your years you most certainly have always been.

I remain awed by the fact that you taught yourself to read before most of your peers even recognized a single word. Or that our first talk about sex came one morning when we drove past Mercy Hospital on Bayshore Drive. Snugly belted into your toddler car seat, you piped up from the back, "Mommy, there's a sign that says 'H' and that stands for hospital, where babies are born. So how are babies made, anyway?"

After I steered the car back onto the road, I began a very rudimentary facts of life conversation. Looking into the rear-view mirror, I saw you nodding sagely. A few minutes later, you said, "Well, I see. That's nice."

I've recalled that story more than once over the years and I'm not sure that anyone has ever believed me. But as the writer Dave Barry has written, "You can't make these things up." You were, and continue to be, just that inquisitive about the world around you, wanting to figure it all out in your own time and on your own terms.

I have come to admire that about you more than I can ever say. I am inordinately proud of the girl you were and the young woman you've become. Hugging you last May as you received your college diploma, I was overwhelmed by the amount of love and respect bubbling through me, just as I was four years before, when you won the Faculty Award at your Ransom Everglades high school graduation.

That award was a recognition of your steadfast determination and incredible academic achievements. You had ignored the head of school's admonition that you could not turn down your early admittance to Yale to attend the University of Southern California School of Dramatic Arts. Your reaction was a feisty, "Wanna bet?" and your teachers resoundingly supported you.

What a vote of confidence in your teenage judgment! I wish I had been able to react that positively at the time, but I have since learned that there are more important things in life than an Ivy League bumper sticker on your car. There is your child's happiness, which is paramount.

There's an adage that "a mother is only as happy as her least happy child." Because you are happy, so am I, my sweet Boo.

Nothing could ever mean more to me, so you can rest easy knowing that I will always have your back. You are smart, disciplined, hard-working, empathetic and kind, a spectacular young woman by any measure. I have every faith that you will continue to succeed in whatever you choose to do.

It's inevitable that I look back each year to that day when you and I were first introduced. In truth, however, I must admit that I had first seen you in your bassinet in the hospital nursery. Daddy and I had snuck up there to see if we could figure out which sleeping newborn was you. I gazed at each pink blanket and finally saw one small baby with an astonishing head of jet black hair.

"That one," I announced to Daddy with absolute certainty. "That's our girl." He shook his head, not quite believing my conviction that you were the daughter I had so longed for.

But updating the always relevant William Shakespeare, it is a wise mother that knows her own child. I knew you then and I know you now. You were, are, and always will be, the child meant for me, my beloved bashert, who grew not under my heart but in it.

And the tears staining this note are happy ones as I wish you the sweetest of all possible New Years and the most wonderful of all birthdays. I wish you all that you wish for yourself and hope that you believe, as I know for sure, that dreams can come true and miracles do happen.

THE SERENDIPITOUS ENDING OF THE ERRANT SUITCASE

By Sharon Wylie

And there the green Jaguar sat right on my doorstep! Let's go back to where it all started. This is the story of my time in Sri Lanka, not about the civil war which had been raging for 30 years, nor about the Kandy elephant festival, Parahara, which is the biggest Buddha celebration in the country, but it is the story of my survival for nearly three weeks without clothes, without shoes, without so much as a compact case. It sent all my coping strategies reeling.

Sri Lanka isn't a country that's well known to most travelers. It was formerly Ceylon, a country known for its tea. I didn't know exactly where to find it myself. But it was described as a teardrop on the bottom of India. After the travel books, the flight plans, the new roommate emails, departure day finally arrived.

A group of photographers was to meet in Colombo, the capital, on a Friday evening to have dinner and discuss the itinerary. Our American guide, Nevada, is a photographer who does assignments for *National Geographic*. After spending twenty-one hours in actual flying time, that is, not counting layovers, I arrived in Colombo at some point in the day, but I'd passed through nine times zones, so nothing felt real. The words *day* and *night* collapsed in on one another like a deflated balloon. But what knocked me back into real time was the discovery that my baggage had gone in another direction. "It will arrive on the next flight into Colombo. Don't worry. They always arrive, sometimes a little later," the Singhlese porter poured out in his best English. In retrospect, I feel there was a wink, wink, behind my back. So much for that soft bed with the cool sheets I had been visualizing. Instead I had the obligatory forms for missing luggage that needed to be filled out before I left the airport for the hotel.

I arrived at the hotel and introduced myself to my new room-mate secretly hoping after hearing my pitiable story she would offer me a pajama replacement. That was first on my missing wardrobe list. She was sympathetic and generously let me shuffle through her few belongings. She liked razzle-dazzle' sequins and glitter. So as not to wake up in the morning with a rash, I picked out a silky garment which became my permanent nightshirt. The next morning I assembled my grubby jeans and T-shirt to do yet one more day's labor. "This will be your final tour of duty. I'll get relief," I promised them. But they were denied their reprieve. The next flight came in with no sign of the misplaced suitcase. Then the next flight. And the next. My jeans were now standing at atten-tion on their own, but I had bought a new T-shirt with an elephant face on the front and an elephant rear on the back from the roam-ing street vendor. It was pretty hideous, but he was happy for the sale, and I was thrilled for the addition to my wardrobe. We rode a tuk-tuk, a modified golf cart, looking up and down the street for a western clothing store, but all that were available were saris and frilly blouses, not exactly hiking attire.

The next morning we drove to the military base to board a Y-12 Russian aircraft from the Sri Lankan Air Force and flew to the northern end of the country. We were some of the first visitors that area had had since the end of the thirty-year war. Tourists had been warned to stay clear of the fighting, the guns and the explosions. I tried to envision my luggage actually finding its way across the island to combat-torn Jaffna. "Of course, we will find you and deliver your luggage to you shortly" was the guarantee that whistled in the wind, always with a broad smile.

As one day peeled into another, I was graciously being offered this and that by the other participants in the journey, but there are some things you just don't share. I got the bus driver to make a special stop at a pharmacy, very possibly the only such establishment in Jaffna, so that I could buy toothpaste, the Sri Lankan brand was Clomate, and a deodorant called Rexona for Women, the fragrance being described as "passion-body responsive." I never realized you could lace passion into an anti-perspirant, but I felt absolute relief that it would mean a cleaner me.

My roommate was an Atlanta woman who spoke like a southern belle and wore a large rimmed hat, even in the jungle. She was my chief supplier. She had it all: a pair of scissors, stain remover, safety pins, a bit of lavender for under the pillow when we weren't sleeping well. Whatever bizarre request I made, she seemed able to fulfill it. She was like a magician pulling the unexpected out of her duffel, which oddly was lined with a black plastic garbage bag. "It serves two purposes: one to keep my clothes dry. Once my luggage was left on the tarmac for 24 hours during a heavy downpour and soaked everything inside. And the second reason is to keep out the bed bugs," also learned through experience. She tried not to bring home any pets from her travels anymore. She was a veteran traveler—just what I needed with my no-luggage status.

Meanwhile the refrain began. "It will arrive. We do not lose luggage," Air India sang through the phone on the occasions where we could get them to answer. Our guide, Manoj, who owns a travel agency in New Delhi, informed me that "no reputable travel group actually ever schedules flights on Air India anymore because the luggage often doesn't find its destination." Fine, why didn't someone happen to mention this in the inundation of pre-travel printed material sent to me?

When it became apparent that the day or two would be stretching into longer-time segments, I received offers from the others for items that I would need long-term. I accepted a visor for protection against the steamy sun from an Australian woman. When I got blisters walking on the hot sand around the temples, since we had to remove our shoes in respect for the Buddha, I received Neosporin, Band-Aids, and even an offer of moleskin from a nurse to soften the pain. My roomie gave up a pair of "chapel socks" which we used for our baby-soft feet, some too-large shirts and even a duffel bag to transport all my recent acquisitions. Several days into the trip Nevada mentioned that I looked about her size. She invited me to her room and pulled out from her suitcase several pairs of pants. My eyes luxuriated on the sight of those piles of laundered clothes. She let me take my pick. It was Nordstrom's! It was Saks! I tried on a pair of pants and *voilà!* They fit. And another. She gave me three. I felt thrice blessed. I could finally put aside those grimy jeans for something cooler and cleaner. It was like a shopping spree. She remarked that she had inadvertently packed many more pairs than she needed and didn't know why. Now she knew. She even threw in a few pair of fresh undies. I was reborn!

Manoj was persistent. He tried daily to track down the missing luggage and received continual promises of the next day's delivery, but the suitcase never materialized. We had reports of sightings in Kolkata— that hadn't even been part of my itinerary—and then later in Chennai. They had located it, apparently, but no one seemed to have the insight to move it any closer. Perhaps they were waiting for a spiritual sign from Buddha or Ganesha that would give them the go ahead. I had so wanted it to arrive by the time we got to Kandy, which was about midway through the trip. The only piece of camera equipment that I had put in the checked luggage, for good reason, was my tripod. I needed it for the lighted elephant parade. Now I felt that it would never arrive.

I began having fantasies about what I would do if it happened to turn up. I dreamed about walking into the hotel room and finding it sitting casually on the carpet or lounging on the bed. It was almost like anticipating the arrival of an old boyfriend. I became excited and a little delirious. What would I wear for the homecoming? What was my favorite outfit? Maybe I'd splurge and wear several in a day. Then I realized I had begun to forget what clothes I had packed and I had to ask myself the hard question. Would I ever see them again? Shirts that I had so carefully selected seemed like an ironic gesture. The piles I had made on the bed in anticipation seemed like an exercise in futility. I vowed I would never again bring anything I cared about, only those things that were one step away from the donation pile. My roommate packed only clothes that "could be washed in a bucket and hung up in a tent." Sounded like good advice now.

Because my stash was meager, I took up washing clothes in the sink nightly. The real joy would come when we stayed in a hotel more than one night, and there was laundry service. They weren't always the most modern. We would occasionally come back to the hotel and see our lingerie blowing in the wind. So this was the routine that worked for pretty much the rest of the trip. I would get occasional reports that the airline would be sending the suitcase in due haste, but I had lost faith. The others thought me marvelously calm. They toasted me at our farewell meal back in Colombo. "To

Sharon, who, being on the road for three weeks without luggage, really could've lost it and didn't." It was a distinction I could have cheerfully gone without, preferring to be a nobody with my own clothes.

I said a tearful farewell to my new friends still mourning the luggage I was leaving behind. I always thought in the end it would be at the airport waiting for me like a prodigal son to return home. I put in a final claim at the Sri Lanka airport and took off for New Delhi. Once in the Air India division of that airport, I requested a manager. The young men ignored my request as I'm sure they are instructed to do and made a cursory check of the contents of the luggage department. They continued to whisk around me as if they were too busy to acknowledge my existence. I requested and continued to request a manager. I was asked to sit and wait. I refused. I selected an annoying position where they were forced to walk around me.

Finally, a rotund man arrived. (You can always tell those in charge in this country because they have big bellies. It is an attractive feature to Indian women, as it was explained to me, because they know this person can afford to have plenty to eat.) He suggested I continue on my flight to New York City and do my checking there. "They will have far more resources." I glared at him with a thin veil of contempt. "I have a six-hour layover in New Delhi and have nothing better to do with it than search for my luggage." For the fifth time I described it: medium size, dark green, Jaguar brand. I planted my feet into the floor and stood firm. With a sigh of resignation, he told me to get my passport, put my other belongings under his desk, and follow him. We traveled to a part of the building even he had to have papers to enter. Our destination was a room in the lower floor filled with computers. He showed my last luggage papers to two men, and they conversed together both in English and in Hindi, so I was only privy to part of the conversation. But they did locate my luggage still in Chennai. They couldn't determine why it had never been sent on. So while they contemplated this absurdity, I requested they send an email to the airport in Chennai informing them I have left for home. "I'm returning to Miami now. News flash! There's no longer any reason to send it to Colombo."

At home in Miami the days dragged by. Emails were exchanged. They were sending it they promised. I was losing hope fast. One afternoon, I had a phone call with a thickly accented voice. But I understood the word luggage. "Do you have my luggage?" I exclaimed

"Si."

"Really? Where are you?" I could hardly form the words. I expected responses like New Delhi or Greenland.

"At your front door."

I dropped the phone and ran to open it.

And there the green Jaguar sat right on my doorstep.

WRITING BLUES

By Magdalena De Gasperi

I t is Sunday evening. There is a melancholy feel to the air; it is still humid, but the evenings are slowly getting cooler. I go for a short walk in my parents' neighborhood and watch the lizards scurry for their lives as my giant flip-flopped feet approach them. The time change added light in the morning but accelerates the languid dusk that now begins at five-thirty instead of an hour later. I had gone through my house and my parents' house seeking clocks and watches to adjust and feeling proud each time I completed what is basically a stupid task. Why is the correct time so important?

"Getting old is not for cowards" as the Germans say. I had driven to my parents' shortly after noon and had lunch with them; they had leftovers and I had made a Caprese salad plus avocado since the four huge avocados my sister brought me ripened all at once after a week of being granite rocks. We finished the lunch with Nespresso decaf cortaditos and some of the remaining

Belgian chocolates. My father retired for his usual two-hour nap—he is ninety-one. Now that he needs night care, his office has been turned into a small bedroom for the night nurse. His desk and papers have been banished to several corners of the house.

Some days ago I had started sorting through his papers and found many 35 mm slides. As a Sunday afternoon project I decided to look through the slides and found the slide projector in the music closet under the stairs. If the closet were any bigger, I thought as I tilted my head to prevent its banging against the low door, it could have housed Harry Potter before he went to Hogwarts. After searching on the Internet for instructions how to operate the projector and creating a screen by taping sheets of printing paper together, I clicked forward the first slide.

It was me around the age of three in a field near Boston, stroking a sheep. My first thought was, the closest I've been to a sheep since then is eating lamb chops. The following slides were jumbled in order. Many were of my sister and me in the mid-50s, with or without my mother. Some were of my two younger sisters, when we were in Boston. Others were of my sisters' children when they were small. Very few were of my father, who was the photographer and had carefully labeled most slides with subject and date. However, after being in little plastic shields for some fifty-odd years, many slides were damaged with mildew flecks. The mold seemed symbolic of a hazy future ahead – for me? for the slides? I viewed one full carousel with my mother and remembered there were several dozens of slides in other plastic shields, waiting to be sorted. I put everything away and took the remaining slides home.

In the last two years several friends and former colleagues have passed away at fairly young ages. Christian was seventy-one but his palsy was so horrible everyone at the funeral said it was a blessing and a release from his suffering. Barbara succumbed to her aggressive cancer at fifty-three and Jim was found lifeless in his hotel room in Italy. His wife wrote that his heart just stopped beating at age fifty-five. We watched his funeral per live stream. It was a first for me and worked really well until I lost the connection. I remember the last time I saw Jim in Germany. We drank red wine at two in the morning until he was relaxed enough to go to sleep. He seemed to live on overdrive, as if he had had a premonition.

My parents, on the other hand, have surpassed the average life expectancy. In both their families the mothers lived to be ninety-five and one hundred-and-two respectively. Reaching such old age is a blessing if one is reasonably fit. If not, it can be torturous. Yet the will to live does not diminish. My father claims he will die soon, but despite some significant health problems, his blood pressure is 120 to 80. He put away a large plate of ravioli today, plus dessert. Before I left them after watching the film *Gandhi* together with him and my mother, he had had his afternoon tea with toast.

I read some of the memoirs and essays submitted this week and last for our writing class. I want to join the common endeavor of writing, but am not inspired by politics or the past. My own present seems to dominate. I pull a book from the shelf for inspiration: a lovely, worn copy of Virginia Woolf's *The Common Reader* from 1935. I wonder, who gave me that? Woolf's essay "The Strange Elizabethans" seems to offer some consolation; writing of the intellectual Gabriel Harvey, she mentions one of his notes: "The present tense only to be regarded." Seems I'm not the only one stuck in the present. Gabriel Harvey also "lived to a very great age for an Elizabethan, to eighty-one or eighty-two." Woolf herself did not have the same luxury of longevity; having suffered from recurring bouts of depression, she drowned herself in the river Ouse in 1941, at the age of fifty-nine.

Thinking about my own situation, I may also have to face the challenge of filling a very long life with meaning. Our bodies are like old-timer cars, I once told the then-CMO of our multinational corporation. There aren't very many spare parts, and we have to put good fuel into our bodies. Unlike old-timer cars, though, we need to put in as much mileage as possible. From that perspective the Sunday was satisfactory, since I started the morning in the gym. My friend Virginia confirms my thoughts as she quotes the Elizabethan Harvey: "Health and the care of the body are of utmost importance."

The bigger challenge is arguably filling up the mind with the appropriate fuel. Reading regularly does not seem to be enough. Writing regularly is a challenge; sometimes, like today, it seems the motor is stalled, sputters as if it is about to go out. I hope that despite my parental obligations and also visitors from overseas this week, I can get back into the groove. Shakespeare's *The Tempest*, Latin American novellas, and the Miami Book Fair are on the horizon. I will take the advice of Gabriel Harvey as described by Virginia Woolf: "Make it your 'daily charge' to exercise, to laugh, to proceed boldly." Let the week begin!

THOUGHTS ON MY 50TH HIGH SCHOOL REUNION

By Ellen Leeds

Fifty years and it was there in front of me. I would confront at last my fear of going back where I was so unhappy. I hated high school. Returning to my fiftieth high school reunion was not an easy decision for me to make, for I would have to confront the demons that I left behind. I never attended any of the reunions held before this one, but somehow the number 50 loomed in my thoughts. Maybe this would be my last chance to come face to face with a part of me that always stayed stuck deep inside of me. I didn't have any of those cheerful memories of feeling a part of anything, or of cheering for the home team screaming out *Let's Go Piners* at football games. I always felt left out yet so much wanted to be included. I wanted to finally heal that young girl's pain still lurking in the shadows. Could I do it? Would I do it? For months I vacillated back and forth between sending in my deposit or finally forgetting it all and never looking back.

The check eventually was mailed and reservations made. My husband and I had ridden for three days up the eastern coast from Miami and arrived at Point Pleasant, New Jersey. The hotel was on the ocean, and when we turned the key into our room, it looked like a picture in a seaside beach advertisement flyer from the 1960s. A big box television sat on a brown wooden dresser. There was a small kitchenette to the right, an oversized dull green couch that a secondhand furniture store would have refused to take, a large bed with white sheets and a thin woolen blanket draped over the side, and finally to enhance this decor a small end table upon which sat a tiny lamp adorned with shells that lit the entire room. One thing that I couldn't fault it on was that it was immaculate.

The next evening was the beginning of the weekend's reunion events. We awoke the next morning, ate a nice breakfast at a restaurant overlooking the ocean, and then walked on the beach collecting shells which I hadn't done in decades even though I had lived in South Florida the majority of my adult life. We then took a stroll on the Point Pleasant boardwalk, bought some salt-water taffy, and I reminisced in thoughts of how many weekends as a child I would drive to this shore with my parents, eat steak sandwiches, go on the arcade rides, and watch the sea gulls dancing on the sand. It all flooded back.

Finally, the night arrived and I began preparing to go to the first event—a wine and cheese get- together. My yearbook was destroyed in Hurricane Andrew over twenty-five years ago, so I carried a copied one with me, hoping to ask for signatures for this new one. I dressed in a casual but nicely adorned striped shirt with sequin fall leaves, and zipped up my tight jeans for the opening reception. I worried that I might feel out of place and alone as I often did in high school. My husband was with me, and I told him if I felt too uncomfortable we would leave early. I hesitated walking over to the reception. I kept thinking, *Is this a mistake?* Finally, I decided it was time. I grabbed my yearbook, purse, looked again in the mirror for one final adjustment and slowly walked in to the large hotel ballroom where everyone was talking and mingling.

At first, not knowing what to do, I stood looking at the science-board-like display with faded pictures of classmates and names. Attached to the board two lists jumped out. The first, *Classmates Unable to Locate* and the second *Classmates Deceased* truly took me aback. I knew my high school friend, who took me to the prom, had died; but seeing his name there, the first on the list, saddened me. I was to discover later in the evening that he had died of AIDS. He was so bullied in high school and I wish he, like myself, had had an easier time in those younger years. Going down the list I began to appreciate having this opportunity to be at my 50th reunion, and not being a part of the *Classmates Deceased* list.

As I was standing there perusing the board, another former classmate came by and asked about someone who wasn't seen on either list. I looked at her name tag, not recalling her face, and struck up a conversation about Lakewood. I thumbed through my yearbook asking her to sign her picture and she obliged as did many others throughout the evening.

As I began meandering around the room, someone tapped me on the shoulder and said, "Aren't you Ellen Leeds? We were in the same kindergarten class together." That amazed me. In our little town everyone traveled from grade school to high school as one group. I was touched that I was indeed recognized and as the weekend progressed there were many such moments. I was soon to learn that I was recognized and I had brought back memories for many classmates. People had memories about me and my home, my family. I thought I was a ghost. I felt so very alone and depressed back then.

I wondered if I could have spoken to that young me that things might have been different back then. It might have sounded like this: "Hey you, Ellen, are you listening? Everyone is uncomfortable at our age. You weren't as fat as you thought you were. You will be remembered someday as a nice, friendly girl. Hey Ellen don't worry about falling in love or getting a part in the play, it will happen. Stop feeling so lonely. You have friends and will have many more in the future. Finally, and I want you to totally understand that everyone isn't starring at you all the time. Believe me, they all have their own issues."

I circulated around the ballroom and spoke to everyone that I could, accumulating as many signatures in my newly printed yearbook as possible. There was laughter, memories of skating on the lake in the winter time, bowling on Sundays, playing with my dolls, touching people's lives and I being touched by theirs. When my name tag eventually fell off my blouse, a woman actually stopped me to let me know that she had such fond memories of our girlhood together. We hugged. How after over fifty years did she recognize my face? I saw faces of long ago that I too remembered.

As I scanned the room, I spotted a grown man, but my mind flashed back to the boy he used to be with his briefcase walking through the hallways, and the girl who sang at our prom. I was able to have a serious conversation with her about our children who were adopted, a friend who went on outings in our pink Plymouth with my parents, now a grandmother—so many connections of threads that were important for me to tie together.

I wasn't the only one who came to find answers. As I paused to just soak it all in, a woman standing next to me said just what I had been thinking: "This was important for me to come today to get closure of those painful days. I never liked high school, and I wanted to come to put it all behind me." I looked at her and said, "Me, too." It seemed so childish, all this baggage I had carried with me all these years. She then went on to say, "I can't make the dinner tomorrow, but I am glad I came."

I didn't want the evening to end and was glad there would be one more night before my husband and I were to drive back to Miami. Tomorrow for the sit-down-dinner I would dress up and strut my stuff. I felt confident that it would be fine. More people arrived than had been there the evening before. All dressed in their finery, but no one could hide the fact that we were all pushing into our late 60s. Age is the leveler of time and memories. Yes, we could dye our hair, exercise, suck in the gut; but when you are at your 1966 high school reunion everyone knows the truth. I sat at a table with my husband and with that girl from the pink Plymouth, my dear friend and the only one I had kept in touch with over these many years. I then flitted from table to table getting signatures to fill my yearbook's pages, but more to connect with everyone. I was having the best time. I wouldn't have guessed that it would be so great. Here was that poor sullen young girl from long ago, taking pictures, laughing, sharing and being myself. Damn, why did it take so long for me to accept me?

I even was finally able to get closure about an old friend. A best friend at the time, who was someone I had hung out with for years in high school. As an adult I tried, for years, to reconnect with her but never could. A woman shared with me that that same girl and she had been friends for years as adults. Their husbands had traveled all over the world and then one day she didn't want to associate with her nor anyone who had lived in Lakewood, my hometown. She just dumped her for no good reason. Her words to me were, "All things have an end, even friends. I never looked back and neither should you." I was blown away. I had thought and thought about this woman, and was hoping to see her at this reunion to put it behind me; and now another former classmate put it all into the proper perspective. We have to look ahead and keep on trekking.

I posed for our group shot of about seventy classmates out of two hundred, and with my feisty self tried getting the group to give the old Piners' cheer. I then screamed out, "Give me a P, give me an I, give me an N…." Some followed along, and others laughed. I wasn't bothered anymore. I was being me, and knew it was okay.

At the end of the evening I got to sing the old sixties song "Soldier Boy" with the girl who had sung at our prom. Wow, that was fabulous even though I had forgotten most of the words. I know now that at 68 I can still take risks, still takes chances, and I would advise others like me to go to that reunion, it ain't so bad.

As I left the ballroom I took one more glance around. I had accomplished the mission to get closure, yet in that moment I thought I might just come back for new memories, at a future reunion, if they happen to hold one. Let's hope I'm alive to get the chance.

KEEPER OF THE FLAME

By Elsa Goss Black

I t doesn't come often, the silence, but when it does, it can be so loud. It can fill the house and flood my senses, moving with me from room to room, relentlessly reminding me that he is still gone.

I am who I always was, but something more—and so much less. A widow. Creed's widow. The initial fog of grief long lifted, the waves of sorrow crashing ever further from the shore, the aching loneliness still pays the occasional visit, an unwanted friend from the not-so-distant past.

Sometimes I can see it coming. There are natural triggers, certain seasons of the heart that summon it. Our anniversary, of course, especially as the years we could have celebrated mount. And it will arrive again at the end of this particular year, which will mark what would have been our 40th, our ruby anniversary. I already know the tears will come.

And so it was when our daughter graduated high school and then college, a cloud shadowing each otherwise sun-dappled occasion. Creed had been so proud of her and I cried as she received the diplomas and honors he didn't live to see. The same will hold true on the day she walks down the aisle, sometime, somewhere.

But those emotions are to be expected. Bittersweet but predictable, they can be prepared for, if not avoided or ignored.

Sometimes, though, the silence can still pounce unexpectedly when the dark of night looms large. I have learned not to take its wordless absence for granted. It will find me when it will.

And so it came after I recently wrote a long and highly opinionated piece against Donald Trump. At the urging of close friends, I posted it on Facebook and was elated by the positive reception and by many shares as it reverberated across the country online. I knew that it wouldn't be universally applauded, of course. But the cheering ended abruptly with the sudden presence of one high school acquaintance, who began posting diatribes against what I'd written and against every compliment I received.

His comments started tersely and slowly, then grew in length, speed and venom, like a particularly malevolent and vicious Hydra. As a journalist, I consider my shoulders to be broad and criticism of my opinions to be a badge of honor. As a First Amendment attorney, I consider freedom of speech to be nearly sacrosanct.

But I could soon feel that this was something different as the silence began to attack me from the unexpected wings. My dread began to rise and then, on my Facebook page, there it was, one perfectly pointed poisonous sword designed to bring me to my knees.

"Creed would be ashamed of your closed-mindedness."

The silence began to roar, tears at the ready. The charge wasn't true, would never have been true. Creed was a great journalist, a tireless supporter of The Reporters' Committee for Freedom of the Press and the International Center for Journalists. He would have been proud of what I wrote. But the barbed words still wounded me, making me feel as alone as ever despite the quick and fiery online support of friends and family.

This lunatic could not have hurt me, would not have dared, had Creed still been alive.

Wiping away the tears, however, I found my anxiety turning into anger, the lonely widow transforming into an angry avenger for the sake of her husband's memory. I deleted the comments, one nasty line after another, all 50 of the grenades thrown by an alt-right nut job. Finally, under the tutelage of a tech-savvy friend, I blocked the madman from my page and sent him back into oblivion.

Before I did, however, I wrote online that while I was a fierce defender of his right to express his opinion, I drew the line at his taking my Facebook page hostage as an outlet for his Fascist views.

"As I wrote before, have you, at long last, no sense of decency? You are beneath contempt for associating your venom with his memory: not on MY page and not on my watch."

And finally, "May God forgive you for bringing up Creed's name in the midst of your delusional rants. I know I won't."

And I don't. I won't. But I also know that his rage fueled mine, finally giving me the courage to fight the silence myself and to send it, too, back to oblivion. And for that, though I will never let him know, I am grateful. The silence is at bay, and when it finds me the next time, it will find a worthy foe.

PRINCESS CHRISTINE

By Kitty Winkler

The Watkins, whose estate backed up to our back yard, were
private people we seldom saw. They were a childless couple
who lived on a huge property. (It has since become a university
campus.) It featured a grand white brick house, a caretaker's cottage, a chapel, and a thickly wooded area where animals roamed.

I was four years old, my parents' first child. My brother was a
toddler and my sister had been born just a few months before. I
was the spoiled darling of parents who, after being childless for
the first five years of their marriage, had thought they couldn't
have children. The reality of having to share love and attention
with siblings hadn't quite dawned on me yet, and I thought I was
a princess.

My father had scheduled a meeting with Mr. Watkins to discuss
purchasing a tract of property that would expand our back yard.
My mother and I went along, and while the men were negotiating,
Mrs. Watkins served punch and cookies to my Mom and me and

showed us the enormous house. I was dressed in my prettiest blue velvet dress with white lace, and as we went from room to room in the house I was imagining what it would be like to live amidst all this grandeur. By the time we were on the wide staircase to the second floor, I had convinced myself that I was to the manor born.

The staircase ended in a large open area with corridors that ran to the left and right leading to bedrooms. Directly in front of us, against the wall was a long bench on which sat or stood an amazing collection of antique dolls. Mom quickly grabbed my hand and said, you can look, but don't touch. Obediently, I clasped my hands behind my back and approached the bench.

Mrs. Watkins showed us the dolls one by one. Only years later, when my Mom told me about it, did I realize what a valuable collection it was. All of the dolls were antiques from countries throughout the world. Some were dressed in native costumes, and many were in luxurious satin gowns with intricately coiffed hair. There was a male doll, probably from the turn of the century, who was dressed in a tuxedo, wearing a satin-lined cape and top hat. There were baby dolls, toddler dolls, child dolls, and adult dolls. One little boy in a sailor suit had a hoop that he was pushing with a stick.

How sad it seemed that the Watkins had no children to play with these beautiful dolls. My imagination was running wild; I had already made up a story about the elegant doll couple who stood together in a dancing position. I could have happily stayed all day, but much too soon, Dad was calling us, his business completed, ready to go home.

I pestered my Mom for days asking about when we could return to the Watkins. She made it quite clear that it had been a one-time visit, but I refused to believe it. Several weeks elapsed. One day the doorbell rang and the Watkins' caretaker stood on the porch holding a big box. Mrs. Watkins sent this for the little girl, he said.

Opening the box, I found a magnificent doll with light brown sausage curls and a dress of lavender satin brocade. She was perfect in every detail, from her silver slippers to her lace-trimmed pantaloons. Her age showed only in her beautiful face, which was crackled but in no way detracted from her beauty.

For me, it was a dream come true. Mom and Dad decided that it would be wrong to enforce a hands-off policy even though the doll was a precious antique, so I was allowed to play with Princess Christine—that's what I named her—to my heart's content.

Over time, the love and imagination I had invested in Princess Christine caused her to lose her luster. Her hair became matted and tangled, her dress got dirty and torn. But I treasured her to the very last when both arms had fallen off and her head cracked after she took a fall. Finally, my Princess had to be discarded, but the memories—among my first—are with me still.

ALL THAT GLITTERS...

By Joan Fisher

I spread the jewelry out across our king size bed. It looks like the detritus of a shipwreck, flotsam and jetsam of gold and silver and who knows what else. Piles of bracelets and clumps of rings festoon the bedspread like seashells and starfish on a beach. Our mothers died within months of each other, and they each left their jewelry behind. Retrieved from shoeboxes, Ziploc bags, and silk pouches, it is now arrayed like booty from a pirate ship for our perusal.

We each approach this task in our own way.

My husband, the clinician, is engrossed in examining a sparkly ring with his magnifying loupes. He is convinced that the stones are diamonds even though I keep telling him that it is unlikely. He prefers to visualize each item, inspecting workmanship and content. He analyzes each piece with his assay kits, a rare earth magnet and a diamond tester, separating the 14 karat gold from the metallic chaff, discerning the carbon from the cubic zircon. They are not diamonds.

I need to touch my mother's jewelry. Her bracelets and beads seem like an extension of her. I think of the celebrations that called for trips to the safe deposit box to retrieve strands of pearls and diamond earrings. I remember stories of how and when pieces were obtained: the gem-studded bracelets from my great-aunts, the good pearls from my father's mother. The not-so-perfect pearls with the exquisite diamond clasp from my maternal grandmother. I remember playing with the covered face of Mom's rose gold watch when I was a little girl. I liked to open and close the tiny lid and feel the cool scales of the wristband move beneath my fingers. We found the matching rose gold ring with a ruby crest that had also been a graduation gift. Finally, I touch the glittering diamond drop that we called the "rhinestone" because of its size and sparkle.

My husband's mother meticulously organized her jewelry in see-through cases. Most of her original jewels had been stolen during a car trip with her second husband, however the many gemstones and cloisonné pieces she had purchased on her travels through Asia survived. My mother kept inventories recorded on tiny slips of paper stashed in various desk and dresser drawers, and then she hid the jewelry where no one could find it.

"When I die, promise me you won't throw out any shoe boxes!" she used to warn me.

Mom was notorious for creativity in hiding her valuables. What robber would be interested in going through her footwear, her Band-Aid boxes, or the pockets of an old woolen suit?

We arrange the loot in strategic piles. The valuable, the sentimental, the fashion jewelry and the finer pieces are all clustered into glimmering clumps. I bark at my husband, admonishing him not to co-mingle! I am not ready to mix our mothers together. The light from my bedside lamp casts an eerie glow. The rest of the room seems to disappear, leaving the jumble of jewelry in the spotlight. I press my brothers to take whatever pieces catch their eyes.

"I only want the "rhinestone," I tell them, remembering the times when it came out of the vault for special occasions. I think of her getting ready to go out for a fancy evening in a cloud of Nina Ricci perfume. Dad in his tuxedo would fasten the delicate clasp and they would stand together, admiring themselves and the necklace in the mirror.

After hours of sorting and reminiscing, our backs hurt and our eyes are weary. I return the "good" jewelry to the silk pouches and velvet boxes. The rest gets tossed back into shoeboxes and plastic bags, like so much sea glass abandoned in a sandy pail. Even the costume jewelry requires too much emotional energy for me to deal with tonight. For now, I'll stash it all away someplace safe. Someplace a robber would never think to look.

EL ENAMORADO

By Beatriz La Rosa

A clatter of boots, a jangle of metal, and the raised voices of what sounds like a squad of men reaches the back porch. You stop the daydreaming. Stand up. Walk to the front of the house, to the door that opens to the street. A troupe of men dressed in olive green uniforms, dark beards hiding most of their faces, stands on the threshold. They carry semi-automatic rifles, and they are aiming their weapons at some unknown target. A few moments—how many you cannot say—go by before you grasp what is happening. Your eyes see, but your mind does not want to accept the reality of the scene.

The men are quite young, and are making an effort to look professional and menacing—virginal soldiers of a Revolutionary Army—come to arrest the enemy. The one who appears to be the leader, a man in his thirties, is also dressed in the olive green of Castro's troops, but he is clean shaven. This man. You recognize him. And you know that he is on the hunt, and the one being hunted is your father.

⚊╫╫⚊

"Tocas el piano con mucho sentimiento." The man walking by the front porch of your home in Varadero stops and addresses you. You are sitting on one of the yellow and green rocking chairs on the porch. The rockers are placed facing the street, situated so that you or anyone else in the household is able to see all that takes place on Segunda Avenida. Sitting comfortably and rocking back and forth, you read the latest comic book and watch life unfold around you.

Across from the house is the Hotel Pullman and a little to the right of it the building that houses La Cruz Roja. All the victims of drownings, car accidents, and those unfortunate beings run over by the tires of a bus after falling asleep under it are brought here. The police station is on the side street, to the right. This past summer—the summer of 1958—you saw the policemen in their blue uniforms bludgeon a man. The heavy thud of stick on flesh reached the porch, a low frequency sound that was both wet and obscene, and which seemed to slither from the station across the empty lot that separated your house from it, arriving, wriggling and ugly, at your feet.

From your seat at the theater that is your front porch, you see Playa, a habitual drunk, standing on a wood crate placed under the street light in the corner of Severo's bodega. Severo's bodega is to your left, and the corner under the streetlight is Varadero's own soapbox corner. Playa is the most famous of its orators. He seems to live his life shrouded in a cloud of alcohol and madness. This tall black man, wearing a shirt that is too long for him, declaims from the pulpit, his speeches full of fire, hell, and damnation. His nickname,

Playa, which is beach in Spanish, suits him posthumously when he is found drowned on the beach one morning. His body, resting on the sand close to the shore, was caressed by ocean waves, and was accompanied on this last trip by the little crabs that scurry on the sand.

You are fifteen this February of 1959. A month has passed since the date of January first when your life and the life of an entire nation changed forever. Fidel Castro descends from the mountains—a Cuban Jesus Christ plummeting from the Sierra Maestra rather than ascending to heaven from the Mount of Olives, having defeated the dictator, Fulgencio Batista. The Savior of the Cuban people leads the procession of his army from the easternmost provinces to the capital city of La Habana. The fervor of the crowds is ardent, and he parades with his black beard and beatific smile—his Popemobile an army truck—to the adoring chants of "Viva Fidel!" The Cuban people have been praying for change, and change is exactly what we are getting.

The man addressing you is in his early thirties. He is clean shaven. His hair is cut short and slicked back with brillantina, the Cuban version of Brylcreem. He is handsome, and his cotton pants and white shirt are ironed. He expresses himself well. He's an educated man. Mothers would like him.

Gracias.

You avert your eyes, flushed with the compliment.

He continues: Was that "Autumn Leaves" you are playing? It's one of my favorite songs.

Full of drama and feeling, this was a piece you thought you interpreted well and thus played in often—you did not get tortured by your siblings with the nickname Sarah Bernhardt for nothing—being prone to expressions of heightened emotion which were disproportionate to whatever it was you had reacted to. With downcast eyes, you check your feet and hope that you are wearing your nice shoes.

After this encounter, this young man, name unknown, sits every day for hours on one of the rocking chairs on the front porch of the Hotel Pullman, looking in the direction of your house. You are sure that he is in love with you. A ritual—him walking by your house at around six, you playing "Autumn Leaves" on the piano—starts from that day and continues for several weeks. Your message of love contained in the notes of the song, which in your mind you play for him. He sits and stares and walks by.

The attention from the handsome man, your enamorado, is a welcome distraction from the tense atmosphere prevailing in your home since the day your father disappeared. Two weeks before you meet your enamorado, you arrived from school to find a household sunken in a somber mood. Tia Margot, one of your father's sisters, is talking quietly to your mother.

The tia seldom visits your home, and you are surprised seeing her. Your mother is the recipient of criticism from her husband's sisters, who believe that we, the girls, have too much freedom. Women from a Buena familia don't bike alone or stay alone at the beach. The tias are also in the habit of measuring the amount of material of your and your sisters' swimsuits, alerting your mother when too much flesh is exposed.

Go with your sisters, your mother orders. Her look leaves no room for protest.

Your sisters—whose expressions remind you of wilted oleanders—are huddled in one of the bedrooms. Papi is gone. He had to leave Varadero in a hurry. A news article in this afternoon's *Alerta* accuses him of being an esbirro, a henchman, of Batista.

You sit on the bed, head between your hands. You don't believe the news. You know your father is not a killer. A man of peace, his hobbies are fishing and playing dominoes in the afternoon with the locals in the bodega across from la Cruz Roja. A man of simple tastes, he wears old shorts and shirts and goes barefoot most of the time. A fisherman, like all the other fishermen. His connection to the Batista regime is through a lifelong friendship with Pancho, a minister or something in the fallen regime's cabinet. And your father holds an administrative post in the regime which takes him to La Habana once a month.

But what you, your family, or his friends think does not matter. The accusations are serious. This is the time in Cuba when men are summarily tried by Revolutionary Tribunals where most of the accused are convicted in a matter of hours and where many are executed in front of a firing squad.

Paredon! Paredon! Paredone!

You remember what happened to the chief of police of Varadero, who thought people knew him well enough to know he was no murderer. He was executed days after he surrendered himself to the Fidelistas, the crowds clamoring for a tooth, a finger, a piece of him—a reliquary of sorts—from a man who days before had been their friend.

However, you, instead of worrying about your father, worry about what your classmates will think of you, managing to feel a shame which does not belong to you. Most of your friends are Fidelistas—the disappointment with the regime coming after the honeymoon—and you are afraid that you, a coward, will not have the courage to stand up and defend your father's honor. Instead, you feel the injustice of life, complaining to no one but yourself that your family seems to always be out of step.

You are not told where he is hiding. The atmosphere in your home is subdued and conversations are conspiratorial, hushed, and full of conjecture.

Your mother is now the head of the family and in charge of the administration of the farm, Santa Petrona. The day to day operation of the farm is done by Ramon, the overseer, who lives with his family in the house where your family used to live.

The time comes when your mother has to go to Santa Petrona to pay the workers and to deal with the administrator of the mill. She picks you from among the other siblings to go with her. That day, early in the morning, you leave Varadero in a rented taxi, proud that she has chosen you to accompany her. She is carrying a large sum of money, and she maintains a tight grip on her handbag during the trip to the finca, about a two-hour drive.

The first stop is at Tinguaro, the mill where the sugar cane is ground and refined. You admire her aplomb as she conducts business with the administrator. That day you feel like a heroine in *La Novela del Aire*, a popular soap opera that airs on the radio at eight at night, that you listen to with your mother and sisters. A sweet, haunting melody introduces the program, a music which many years later you recognize when listening to the live broadcast from the Metropolitan Opera House on Saturdays. A lost piece of your youth is recovered, identified, and catalogued. The beautiful tune that is the introduction of Octavian, the cavalier, in Strauss's opera *Der Rosenkavalier* has been returned to you.

You arrive at the farm in time for lunch. The laurel tree—its massive trunk and green canopy much like your life at the farm, mysterious and welcoming—is exactly the way you remember it. This tree sits at the center of the batey, a king whose power is derived, according to the Palo Monte religion, from the concentration of spirits that live in it.

You had hardly slept the night before, the anticipation of going back to this beloved place keeping you awake. It has been years since your last visit. The living red soil is odorous and warm, a friend you greet and who embraces you after a long absence. Angelita, Ramon's wife, has cooked a fricase de pollo. The chunks of farm-raised chicken—a luxury so sought after in later years—and potatoes, onions, pimento-stuffed olives, and capers swim in a broth rich with garlic, olive oil and wine. The white rice has been cooked with lard and is a little lumpy. You like your rice desgranado, and as you are about to complain, your mother's warning glance stops you. "No te atrevas."

One afternoon a disturbance coming from the front of the house brings you out of your daydreaming. You are sitting on the steps of the stairs leading to the yard at the back of the house. The yard is unkempt, with a leafy almond tree and some pink oleander and sea-grape bushes. In the summer the yard is saturated with the pungent smell of the ever present rotting bait and fishing nets of your father. Today the smells are coming from the kitchen which is nearby.

You gather a bunch of almonds which have fallen to the ground, their skins brown and dry. You split the almonds with a rock, looking for a clean break, so you make sure that you hit the almond at the seam, picking the nuts out of the shells with your nails, putting them inside a drinking glass; and when you have enough of them, eating them after you sprinkle them with a bit of sugar. The afternoon is peaceful, and the scent of the meal being prepared, the racket of the pots and pans, and the cook's voice as she hums the latest bolero are comforting. You are thinking of that man who has been circling you and your home, your enamorado. It is close to six, the time when he usually walks to listen to you play.

The commotion brings you to the front door where you see about eight or ten Barbudos at your doorstep, assault rifles ready. We are mostly women in this household—the one male in the group is my older sister's boyfriend—and we clump together. The soldiers take the women to the back porch and order my sister's fiancé to help them look for our father.

The Milicianos are thorough. In addition to looking in all the bedrooms, porches, kitchen, dining room and bathrooms, they look under the beds. Did they know he was a man over six feet tall who would have never fit under a bed? Did they have any common sense, or experience, in this sort of search? In spite of all the anguish we feel, we laugh and mock the stupidity of these men.

One of the men breaching the peace of your home is in his thirties. Clean shaven, he is a captain in Fidel's secret police and is leading this peloton of Barbudos disturbing the peace of your afternoon. He is the kind of man most mothers would want their daughters to marry. Your enamorado, the man in charge—from this day forward known to you and your siblings as "Captain Autumn Leaves"—has taken his mask off and has exchanged compliments and smiles for the olive green uniform of the Revolutionary Army.

SAMMY

By Thomas L. David

Hi. My name is Sammy. I don't know why I was given a boy's name since I am a female miniature Schnauzer. There is probably a good story behind it, but no one has filled me in. I like my name though and always run when I am called. I am all black and quite attractive I might add.

I was born in a town near Orlando to silver colored schnauzer parents. My three siblings are also silver. Obviously I am special, in more ways than my personality. My parents lived in a house with seven adopted children, humans that is, and a Great Dane. The mistress of the house works for a foster parents' organization. Apparently she adopts all the kids who can't find homes. Two of the seven kids, they came in all colors and sizes, were girls who were about six. They gave me and my siblings lots of love, playing with us and carrying us all around the house. They say human contact is good for dogs' adaptation to humans. I certainly am well adapted, though I bark a lot at new people.

My master, Tom, came to visit me when I was about six weeks old. I remember him saying how he liked black miniature schnauzers. No one explained why he came and I thought nothing of it; there were always lots of people in our house. A couple weeks later he came back with a lady named Ines. She smiled a lot when she held me and hugged me. I didn't know what was going on, but I liked the way she held me. Then they took me to their car and put me in a crate in the back seat and drove away. I didn't like that at all. Shortly after Ines took me from the crate and held me in her lap, all the way to Miami. That I liked.

Tom and Ines are my co-owners, but I live in Tom's house. I can't live with Ines because she lives in a condominium on Key Biscayne that doesn't allow dogs. Stupid humans! We visit her often though. Sometimes I even stay overnight with her. We take walks on Key Biscayne which is a nice change from Miami. I am real happy when we drive onto the causeway to Key Biscayne because I know I will soon get to see Ines. When we turn down her street I get so excited I can't stop squealing and barking. We sneak in the back door of the condominium and I race down the hall to Ines' door. Tom unlocks the door and I race through her condo until I find her.

I like Tom a lot. He feeds me, walks me and even gives me an occasional bone. But I must confess that I really love Ines. On Friday nights she usually comes to Tom's house to stay over. I can hear her car when it pulls in our driveway and I run to the front door to greet her. After a few moments with Ines I run back to Tom so he doesn't feel like I don't love him, but then it is right back to Ines. I like the high pitch of her voice. It makes me feel good. Tom doesn't allow me on beds or furniture. I usually honor that, except when he is not at home; he doesn't have to know that though. However, I am allowed on one recliner chair in the family room. It is soft and warm; one of my favorite places. When Tom and Ines watch the TV, Ines sits in the recliner and I sit right there with her. There is just enough room for the two of us.

I used to think Tom was pretty smart. Now I wonder. Sometimes before he goes out he runs upstairs, we live in a two-story house, to get his wallet or iphone and then comes down. Of course I follow him upstairs and down; it is part of my job description to stay close to my master. Then he will turn and go upstairs again for something else. I have even seen him do it three times. If it were me I would just get all the things with one trip.

Sometimes Ines sits in the recliner playing with her iPad. I don't like that. She should be paying attention to me. So I just sit on her IPad until she stops. Sometimes Tom and Ines hug and kiss. I am the one who needs the hugs. So I just push my way and snuggle between them. Then they laugh. I don't know what is so funny.

A special treat is when we visit the park across from Matheson Hammock. It is a big park that is not well known. Most people who visit there bring their dogs. We enter from Schoolhouse Road. Dogs are supposed to be kept on a leash. Tom lets me run free though. On special days when the mosquitos are not out we walk in the woods on the hikers' trails. That is heaven; all kinds of new smells, dead branches to jump over and lots of twists and turns. Tom walks kind of slow so I run ahead. I never let him get too far away though; I don't want him to get lost.

My favorite time of the year is Christmas. Tom invites his whole family and some friends for Christmas dinner. I like the people and love all the smells from the kitchen. Tom always cooks a prime rib roast. After everyone has eaten he trims the rib bones and for some reason puts them in that big stainless steel box in the kitchen. Later he gives me rib bones to chew. Each one has some meat on it and ooh that luscious marrow. I chew on those bones for days, drawing the marrow out of each end. When one bone completely dries out Tom gives me another. Maybe I love him too.

It's a pretty good life with Tom and Ines.

A TRUE STORY

By Paul Gustman

I was informed that my friend had died...when he told me so. He was even more surprised than I was to learn of his demise. The news was broken to him by a doctor's office secretary who informed him that his Medicare had been cancelled. "Why?" he asked. "It says here that you died on December 23, 2015." "But I'm here talking to you, breathing, with a pulse," he said. "But it says you're dead," she replied. And so it went.

He called Medicare and said, "I'm calling from the grave," and asked for help rejoining the living. The polite representative said that they had no choice but to cancel his health insurance since Social Security informed them of his "death." He would have to take it up with them.

He called Social Security for a phone conference or an expedited appointment—a wait of several weeks at the earliest. He came to the local Social Security office as a walk in, checked "other" as the reason for the visit, and sat. Three hours later he was called and told by the lady behind the bullet-proof glass that being dead was not one of the issues she could handle since his death "was verified" and he would have to wait again for the next clerk who handled "other" problems. "Verified how? Did they go to the morgue?" his question went unanswered.

Three hours later he saw another representative, who said the bureaucratic morass would be corrected in "a few days." *It was mentioned that Social Security makes public all personal information it has on file when someone dies.* That means that his Social Security number, mother's maiden name, and all other identifiers were now on the internet. Was this all a scam, a gateway to identity theft?

He waited for some notification from Social Security that the nightmare had been rectified. It never came. Two weeks later, after leaving multiple messages with Social Security, he returned to their office in South Dade, again waited three hours after checking "other." By now he was talking to any stranger who would listen, one of whom seemed attentive until, after many minutes, said, "Como?" Three hours more and he saw a supervisor, who informed him that during the previous visit they had missed a step in inputting data into the computer, and now my friend would come back to cyber-life.

He eventually was called by Mr. Johnson, a Social Security supervisor from Kansas City, who said that Medicare had been notified of the mistake, but mentioned that Social Security had four other computer systems and it would be another five to seven business days before all five would be updated. My friend did request that Mr. Johnson input the entire story in each system, since there was no chance he could ever contact Mr. Johnson again.

Two weeks later when Medicare confirmed that he was alive, someone charged $1,100 worth of Florida Panther's hockey tickets using his credit card and mother's maiden name. He changed personal information to *Grandmother's* maiden name, on all his credit cards. He received a condolence letter from his life insurance company, telling him how to file for death benefits.

Finally life returned to normal, until today, when he was told he couldn't vote. Since when does being dead disqualify a voter in Dade County?

IN THE PINK OF HEALTH

By Elsa Goss Black

O y, enough with the pink pumpkins already!
Early this morning, I was sitting in a waiting room at South Miami Hospital, waiting to see the man I refer to as my boob doctor. By that I don't mean a guy who lifts, implants or otherwise fashions a bodacious set of tatas. I mean a doctor who saves lives for a living. That is, if you're one of the lucky ones.

So far, I am, and thankfully I was there only for my annual check-up. But once you've entered the pink world of breast cancer, even as minimally as I have, you're never the same.

Especially when you have a mammogram and check-up during October, also known as Breast Cancer Awareness Month. It's an experience more frightening than any Halloween House of Horrors. No matter where you look, there are reminders that good news is never guaranteed.

There are pink goodie bags, pink lipsticks, pink nail polishes, pink emery boards and manicure sets, even pink bubble gum—all for sale. Four years ago, I was even treated to an MRI machine sporting a large pink ribbon decal. How I hated that marvel of technology, so gaily decorated despite the grim images it spit out.

The radiologist back then kindly, but matter-of-factly, told me I had a suspicious lump that needed to be seen by an oncologist. Why shouldn't he have been matter-of-fact, though? I wondered then, and still do, how many times a day he had to deliver news like that, news that no woman wants and so many receive.

I'm sure he's lost count by now.

For despite the millions of dollars raised for research, the stark fact is that one in eight women will still get breast cancer in their lifetimes. Trust me, this isn't a statistic to make a woman sleep better at night.

If only the lottery carried such odds.

As I say, though, I was and remain lucky, and maybe that's as close to winning the lottery as I'll ever get. If so, I'll take it.

My lump had been diagnosed by the man I was waiting for today. It was ductal carcinoma in situ (DCIS), then referred to as a Stage One tumor and now regarded by most oncologists as a pre-cancerous condition. He performed a simple lumpectomy, although even that procedure might not have been recommended under today's guidelines. But I listened to my doctor, whose feelings then, and now, echoed mine: "If in doubt, get it out." It all went so well that even though I got a nasty staph infection from the surgical staples, I still felt blessed. I still do.

And yet...

There were quarterly check-ups at first, then twice-a-year tests. Now I'm at the once-a-year call back again, just like most other women.

Except that I'm not. Even having the slightest brush with breast cancer, I'm not like every other woman anymore. I've joined a perpetual sisterhood of potential sorrow. No matter how many clean mammograms, breast ultrasounds and physical exams I have, the fear that the pink monster will reach out and grab me again remains, always and forever.

And I know I'm not the only one who feels that way.

Sitting amidst a roomful of women who have all traveled this pinkalicious path in one way or another, I felt the nerves kick in this morning and the hairs on the back of my neck stand up in the imagined chill around me.

As pleasant as the surroundings were designed to be, I surreptitiously looked around and sure enough, there was anxiety all over and the occasional abject terror in some woman's eyes. Just as I had observed each time I'd been in this reception area, there were worried silences and downward glances and sometimes soft, nervous laughter in the room. No pink butterflies, no bejeweled pink pumpkins, no looped pink ribbons, no pink flamingoes, not any pink decoration in the world—nice touches though they were— could lessen the palpable concern around me.

Each of us had already been among the "one in eight" and the only question left was where in our journey any of us would be by the time we left.

As had always been the case, there were also telltale pink scarves and turbans covering bald badges of courage ravaged by chemo and radiation. Any quick glance at these women was accompanied by a near-audible, "Oh, God, oh, please, not me. Not me, not me, not me."

That feeling was reinforced by the nurse who examined me before my doctor entered the room and cheerfully gave me an "all-clear." I'd not seen her before and she told me she was a temp, filling in for a nurse on maternity leave. She was also on the verge of tears, saying she loved the doctor and his staff but was totally unprepared for the drumbeat of sad news she'd heard every day of this rotation. She was counting the days until she could leave and quietly added that she hadn't had her own mammogram in two years. She had been scared by the women she'd seen and could hardly wait to schedule a breast exam on her first free day.

I told her that she should, that she absolutely had to, and that ignoring the possibility of breast cancer doesn't change your odds. You will either join our sorority or you won't. And if you do, you'll fight it every step of the way, for as long as you can.

I know that in my heart and soul. For among the whispered prayers and scars of battles being fought and battles already won, there was something else, something almost tangible, in that waiting area.

Along with all those damned pink doodads, there was hope, that thing with undoubtedly pink feathers. Coming amidst the uncertainty, there was still a ripple of resilience among all of us, a defiant determination.

Today, this morning, this moment, each of us is still here. Each of us believes in the color pink and the miracles it foretells and in all things bright and beautiful. What else, really, can you do?

Leaving the hospital and breathing in the welcome cool air and clear skies of a Miami autumn, I finally smiled and had one overriding thought.

What the hell? Bring on the pink pumpkins and have a great day.

PONCE DE LEON AND THE MIAMI METRO RAIL

By Magdalena De Gasperi

Here I was again on a glorious day walking down Ponce de Leon. It had rained briefly and there were a few puddles on the sidewalk that the sun had not yet dried. Walking on the street I felt the water spraying little drops onto the back of my pants. I had expected it to be rainy but apparently the brief shower had been it. The sun was warm and the humidity high as the water evaporated rapidly. I was wearing the new trail pants I had purchased and two pairs of socks: sock liners encasing each toe, like gloves, and then padded socks. The hiking boots were heavy and I felt professional, but warm.

I walked the first few blocks briskly. As I went by a cross street, I saw the street sign: Ponce de Leon. The plethora of Spanish and Italian street names in Coral Gables is something I took for granted as a child. Now as an adult who has visited Spain and Italy many times, it seems curious. Who was Ponce de Leon and what was his role in the settlement of Florida? I remembered something vaguely from grade school history.

After consulting Señor Google (biography.com), I learned the following: born in Spain in 1460, Spanish conquistador Juan Ponce de León led a European expedition for gold and in 1509 become the first governor of Puerto Rico. In March 1513, Ponce de León led an expedition of three ships and more than 200 men to Bimini from Puerto Rico. In a month's time, he and his men landed on the east coast of Florida. Not realizing he was on the mainland of North America, he thought he had landed on another island. He named the region Florida (meaning "flowery"), in reference to its lush floral vegetation and because he discovered it at Easter time, which Spaniards referred to as Pascua Florida ("feast of flowers").

The vision of the Spanish conquistadores in their heavy armor and sailing ships contrasts sharply with the mobility and lightweight clothing we enjoy today. Nevertheless, I felt very warm. I decided to make it to the next milestone: Nordstrom's at Merrick Park. There I wanted to try out the key feature of my new hiking pants: a zipper above the knee allowing me to transform them into shorts. I unzipped, but the dismembered pant legs could not be removed without removing my hiking boots. So I leaned on a giant planter enclosing an even bigger potted palm in front of Nordstrom's, removed the boots, removed the lower pants, retied the boots, and was off again. Walking in shorts felt great. Okay, with the hiking boots I felt a little like Heidi, but once I moved past Nordstrom's I forgot about my outfit.

After traversing the roundabout I took the walking trail that runs below the Miami Metro Rail. It was shadier than walking on the long stretch of Ponce de Leon along the University of Miami. In the shade the water had not yet evaporated, and as I walked through puddles, I felt tiny water droplets on my bare calves. The trail is long and offers few views of nature. On my left was the steel avalanche of U.S. 1, on my right cars whizzing by on Ponce. Straight ahead the heavy square pillars of the Metro Rail. Why don't people like Frank Gehry design public transportation? Three times the deafening roar overhead as the suburban train passed going northbound or southbound. Where have all the lizards gone? Can they hear that noise?

I thought about Ponce de Leon and what he and his men would have thought had they seen what happened to the Florida they thought they had discovered. Vast stretches of swamp land, thick overgrown vegetation, alligators, hundreds of bird species. In the north of Florida dozens of indigenous tribes who were wiped out by the diseases the conquistadores brought. The Spanish set up their missions and tried to convert the poor remaining heathens to Christianity. After some three hundred years Spain ceded Florida to the newly formed United States; it remained a territory until 1845, when it became the twenty-seventh state. Hence Florida has only been American for one hundred sixty years, after three hundred years of Spanish rule. Now with hundreds of thousands of Latinos in Miami, it seems as if Ponce de Leon has been justified in claiming this spot for Spain. The Spanish language rules again, at least in many parts of Miami.

The iron horse of the Metro Rail would have frightened both Ponce de Leon and the indigenous people of Florida. The heavy square pillars create an ugly industrial arcade sheltering the walking trail, and stretch on for miles. Finally I have to leave the shade and cross U.S. 1, continuing down Red Road to 80th street, today's meeting point, before taking a break and then returning along the same trail to Coral Gables. It would have been a lark to stand on the Metro Rail platform and watch people's reactions as Ponce de Leon entered the train in his heavy armor. He would have been glad that the trains are air-conditioned.

NOT ME!

By Thomas L. David

I t was in the 1980s at a simple party with seven or eight people, most of whom were unacquainted, discussing nothing important. I was invited by Marie, a nice lady who was a "friend." I had been divorced for a few years. Many years before, at a rather young age, I had married Ms. Right before experiencing the pleasures and travails of playing the field. It was a time to make up for that omission. Although divorce hadn't been easy, I did enjoy the exercise of meeting other women. We learn from life's experiences. In my case, a little proficiency for communicating with the fairer sex was finally penetrating my cranium. Marriage wasn't anywhere on the horizon; that was okay with me.

One of Marie's friends at the party—let's call her Betty—was petite and pretty. Ever alert, I quickly deduced from the conversation that Betty was quite intelligent. An intelligent woman is a turn-on, especially when lodged in a great body, like Betty's. Of course, I was immediately attracted to her mind. The aura of mental acuity was later confirmed; Betty had recently graduated from medical school and finished the residency thing. It was her second career and she was enjoying her new profession. Financial self-sufficiency. Another turn-on! As the evening wore on though, one sensed that Betty carried a little bitterness. Marie later confided that Betty now "hated" all men. She had endured more than one failed relationship.

By that time in my life I had more than once survived the rejection implicit in the word "no." Would my existence continue if I heard that word again? The need to explore Betty's mind prevailed, notwithstanding the possible hazard of another "no." Marie provided Betty's number and I called her for a date. To my surprise she said yes; we took in a movie or whatever. We dated a couple more times and were hitting it off quite well. Betty was bright and spirited, the first of her immigrant family to even go to college. Her first career in nursing didn't fulfill her abundant ambition; hence the stint in medical school. Quite a lady!

Life was good. Betty's bitterness toward the male sex seemed to have evaporated. She seemed like quite a catch. One day she invited me to lunch. After the usual pleasantries she demurely mentioned: "There is something I must tell you." Now any guy, even if it is his first day on Mother Earth, knows trouble is in the air, big time, when a woman says, "There is something I must tell you." Harmless communication does not need an introduction. Don't be concerned with, "Beware the ides of March." The prelude: "There is something I must tell you" is *the* omen of authentic peril. I sat up a bit in my chair.

"Tell me."

Now, please don't tell me you expected her to say, "I am pregnant." Did you? Well she did! I sat back a little taller in my chair. Appetite gone! We had not yet been intimate (I am not as cool as I hope to appear), but this was before the comfort or peril of DNA testing. Now this is a lawyer she was talking to. I knew enough about paternity lawsuits to send my worried mind racing. Was I now one of the men she hated? Had I been set up? Time to hire defense counsel?

Fortunately, Betty was not into hurting. But she was hurting. She said that she really liked me and thought we might even have what it takes to become an item. However, before we met she had given up on trying to find a mate. She wanted a baby and that mid-thirties clock was ticking. Now, many of us mope, whine or complain when life doesn't provide what we want. Not Betty, a woman of action. A few weeks before we met, she arranged a ski trip at a time when she was fertile. She auditioned (my word, not hers) some men (après ski?) until she found one that was good looking and intelligent. In her womanly way she arranged to receive one of his sperm. A little girl would soon be hers. Her skiing friend would never know.

Dating a woman, pregnant by another man, would hardly suit the aura of "Mr. Suave" to which, I confess, I at least partially aspired. She understood. It was a bummer but we agreed it best to part. As an aside, she mentioned she might call me in a year or so. A polite parting comment?

Talk about desperate. Had she been concerned about genital disease? How would Betty explain a father's absence to her daughter years later? Is it selfish to choose to raise a child without a father? What are the psychological implications to a child of not being able to identify her father? Would Betty later settle for some dead-beat guy as a mate, just to have a proxy father? Wow! The things us guys don't have to worry about?

To my surprise, about a year later Betty did call. She welcomed me into to her impeccable little Coconut Grove home and introduced her baby girl. Betty's knock-out figure had returned. She still had that keen mind. (You knew that was coming.) We spent little more time together. But raising another child? *Been there; done that* prevailed. Especially another guy's child! Reluctantly, we parted as friends, never to see Betty or her baby again.

FIRST KISS

By Kitty Winkler

I kept wondering when it would happen. According to my girl-friends, they had all been kissed; and here I was, no boyfriend, no hand holding, no kisses, and no story to tell. In fact, it had reached the point where every time it came up, I would look franti-cally for ways to change the subject. I suspected I wasn't alone in being unkissed. Surely I had more near misses than Evelyn, and I was almost positive that Margaret was lying when she talked about her many kissing experiences. She had too many stories of kiss-ing conquests, and the giveaway was that she never mentioned the name of the kisser. It was as if she feared we might check up on her.

The subject of kissing was coming up more and more since we entered the seventh grade, marking the start of junior high, and, in our minds, adulthood.

Our homeroom chats went something like this:

Joy: I had a date with Phil Saturday night. I didn't want to go out with him, but there was a great horror movie at the Uptown.

Me: You went out with Phil? Ugh!

Margaret: What's wrong with Phil? I went out with him too. But then he tried to kiss me, and I couldn't stand that.

Joy: Oh, Margaret, how awful! All that acne, and he tried to kiss you – you didn't let him, did you?

Margaret: What do you think? Of course not!

Joy: He didn't try to kiss me, but it was just our first date. I guess I'd better not go out with him again.

After my opening gambit, I had become a silent listener in this conversation. The minute the talk turned to kissing, I clammed up, knowing I was on shaky ground. I would gladly have kissed Phil, acne and all. I was that desperate to know what all the fuss was about.

A few days later, Martha came into homeroom wearing a boy's silver ring with a Roman gladiator's profile etched in its black stone. She was flaunting it, extending her hand and making swooping circles while struggling to hold all her books cradled in her other arm.

Oh, Martha! Evelyn squealed. Whose ring?

You noticed, Martha said. It's just something Tommy gave me.

Tommy! Joy said, I didn't know you were dating Tommy.

Oh yes, last night was our third date.

Did you let him kiss you? Evelyn whispered.

Of course, silly. It's okay on the third date.

Is he good? Evelyn asked.

The best! Martha said. You don't think I would take his ring if he wasn't, do you?

You haven't said anything, Kitty, Joy said, noticing my silence. Who do you think is the best kisser?

I was caught. I looked daggers at Joy for a minute, but quickly realized that wasn't going to get me out of this jam. Time to be creative—quickly.

Have you tried shaving your legs yet, Joy? I asked sweetly.

What? Joy said. Uh, no, not yet. I don't really need to yet because I'm blond.

That was an excuse, and Joy and I both knew it. Just a few weeks before, she told me she hadn't shaved her legs because her mother wouldn't let her. She got my point, and I didn't have to answer the kissing question this time.

After that, I became obsessed with how I was going to get this first kiss thing behind me. If I could have found a seventh-grade stranger, I would gladly have raced up to him, kissed him before he knew what hit him and have been done with it. The trouble was envisioning it happening with any of the boys I knew. I had gone to elementary school with most of them and couldn't get past thinking of them as the brats I knew them to be. It didn't help that I was six inches taller than most of them, having hit my growth spurt the summer before.

After a few weeks of torturing myself this way, I began to see the wisdom of finding a stranger to break the spell. The question was how to find an appropriate stranger, and how to work up to kissing him.

Nancy, a new girlfriend, who had come from a different elementary school, offered the opportunity. She invited me to a Halloween party at her church. The potential of the situation was intriguing. New people, in particular, new boys, would be there.

We would be in costume, which was almost as good as being anonymous. With any luck, in Nancy's part of town, the boys might have found an early hormone boost and be a few inches taller than the guys I knew.

I searched home and the stores for the most alluring costume I could find. The local drugstore had a magnificent pink eye mask with rhinestones sparkling at its upswept corners. My week's allowance went for it without a second thought. Then, a search of the attic revealed one of my mother's old formal gowns, a luscious pink confection with yards and yards of tulle skirt. I begged, and Mother yielded; it was as if she knew this Halloween was special.

When Mother dropped me off at Nancy's, Nancy greeted me at the door with, Oh, you look gorgeous! That increased the heady feeling that something great was going to happen tonight.

I quickly noted that Nancy would not be in competition. Dressed as a head of lettuce, no one could get closer than three feet from her without bumping the round chicken-wire cage that formed the foundation of her costume.

After coping with the logistics of getting Nancy and her costume into her father's car, we were finally on our way to the party. Mixed feelings of fear and anticipation battled inside of me, causing a damp sticky feeling in my armpits.

What's wrong with you? Nancy asked. You haven't said a word since we left home.

What? Uh, nothing. My mind had been completely focused on a daydreamed kiss, and Nancy's voice had come from far, far away.

To make up for my silence, I said, tell me about the kids who will be at the party, Nancy. Will I know any of them?

I don't think so, she said. They all go to school at Crescent Hill. I'm the only one who goes to Highland.

Really, I said, satisfied with her answer. This was the group of strangers I had hoped for; now all I had to do was find one of them who was kissable.

At the church, I jumped from the car, eager to get to the party. But then, I had to backtrack to help Nancy's father tug her out of the front seat. Her wire frame was wedged against the dashboard, and we had to bend it a bit to set Nancy free.

As I helped her straighten the chicken wire and the crepe paper lettuce leaves she had been sitting on, I wondered again why she had chosen such an unglamorous costume. The answer came to me. Nancy had no interest in the boys in this crowd, just as I had no interest in the boys I had grown up with. To her, this was a bunch of familiar playmates, completely lacking in romantic appeal.

With that revelation, I decided to confide in her. Just inside the entrance to the church, I blurted out my plan for the evening. I told Nancy all about my frustrations at never having experienced kissing when everyone else seemed to know all about it. To my relief, she was sympathetic.

I haven't been kissed either, she told me. I was beginning to think I was the only one left!

That confession led us to make a quick pact— she would help me find someone to kiss tonight if I would help her meet Gordon Brown, one of the brats I grew up with. I couldn't fathom why, but Nancy had developed a terrific crush on him.

We hurried to join the party already underway in the church's basement recreation room. We came into a room decorated with limp streamers of orange and black crepe paper. A few skeleton and pumpkin cutouts completed the decor. The costumes, though, seemed fantastic. Nancy introduced me to a pig (female), Dracula (too short), and Raggedy Ann (with real red hair) before she got around to introducing the pirate (who was perfect!) His name was Jimmy Robertson. He was blond, nice looking, and only a couple of inches shorter than me.

Nancy did her conversational best, and before long Jimmy and I were so caught up in our discussion of current movies, that we didn't even notice Nancy drifting away to another group. Jimmy was more than I had dared to hope for, and he was obviously as interested in me as I was in him. As we talked, I fantasized the kiss, and it seemed right. Now the challenge was to make it happen.

At the hamburger dinner, Jimmy sat on one side of me, and Nancy on the other. When Jimmy turned away to answer a question, Nancy poked me in the ribs.

Well? she asked meaningfully.

He's perfect, I whispered. Now how do I get him to kiss me?

You'll think of something, Nancy said.

After dinner, there were games— the traditional bobbing for apples and then a fairly bold one for the church setting, passing an apple from chin to chin without using hands. I was no more than an inch away from a kiss as Jimmy and I blushingly maneuvered the apple from my chin to his, but the presence of twenty watchers and the apple between us assured it wouldn't happen.

Finally, the games were winding down and we were only fifteen minutes away from the time that Nancy's father said he would pick us up. I was nearing panic. This might be my last chance for a kiss, and it seemed it was going to pass me by. As I entertained this gloomy thought, Jimmy abruptly said, Excuse me, I have to go for a drink of water. He took off down the hall to the water fountain.

It took me a minute to focus on the half-full glass of Coke he had left on the table where we had been sitting. Jimmy wasn't thirsty; he had been giving me a signal, I suddenly realized. I jumped up, and to no one in particular, said, excuse me, I need to go to the ladies' room.

I took off down the same dim hall and soon spotted Jimmy bent over the water fountain. For a dreadful moment, it crossed my mind that he might have actually wanted a drink of water; and I started to slip past him murmuring something about the ladies' room.

Wait a minute, he said and reached out to grab my arm as I went by. He rose up from the water fountain; and then it happened. Awkwardly and without preamble, he kissed me. It was over quickly, a funny messy kiss with the water from the drinking fountain making my face as wet as his. When it ended, neither of us knew what to say. Jimmy gave me a little hug and said we had better get back to the party, and that was that.

We went out once after that to a movie where Jimmy held my hand and kissed me again. Then we drifted apart, our romance thwarted by being in separate schools and too young to drive.

Of all the kisses since, I don't remember any in the same detail as that first one. I'll always have a special feeling for Jimmy—he carried me over the threshold to adulthood with that funny, first, watery kiss.

THE SECOND TIME AROUND

By Elsa Goss Black

A rt tells me he doesn't really want to celebrate his birthday, which is coming up soon. It's not a landmark birthday, so it's not as if he'd be expecting a big whoop-de-doo, anyway.

But it still has me scratching my head. How exactly do I mark the occasion? It's hard when a person says he doesn't want or need anything—and means it.

First off, I should point out that his reaction is vastly different from mine. I may not always like to count the years when my big day comes around, but I do like people to sit up and take notice. Frankly, in fact, I've almost never opened a card or unwrapped a gift I haven't loved. It doesn't matter if they're big or small, extravagant or not, shiny or dull. I pretty much love them all and when I say, "Oh, you shouldn't have," you should never, ever take me at my faux-modest words.

I really think you should have. All of you.

But enough, I suppose, about me. And that brings me to my second point. Who is this Art and why am I writing about him to begin with?

Well, Art is my companion of more than a year now, my new live-in partner and using a phrase I never thought I'd be using at this stage of life, my boyfriend. Does that sound as juvenile to you as it does to me? But what else to call him?

In fact, the lack of apt titles to describe our situation isn't new. A few decades ago, the radio laureate Charles Osgood did a deft rift on the love lines immortalized by Christopher Marlowe by penning the witty "My POSSLQ." It referred to the Census Bureau's use of that acronym to describe "Persons of Opposite Sex Sharing Living Quarters" and hilariously ended by observing: "You'll share my pad, my taxes, joint; You'll share my life—up to a point! And that you'll be so glad to do, because you'll be my POSSLQ."

Kind of gets you right there, doesn't it? Maybe that's why the term has gone out of general usage. I'm guessing it, along with the name of Charles Osgood, would hardly ring any bells with the vast majority of Americans today.

Be that as it may, however, our current domestic situation is not exactly unusual. You see it both with nonconforming, noncommittal young people and increasingly, among the older set, who aren't keen about losing Social Security pensions in the name of married love. Retirees may be delighted that couples of all races, colors, genders and all other possible persuasions can now get legally hitched, but when it comes to giving up a few government shekels themselves, they quickly back off.

It's a matter of "Not so fast, buckaroo!"

To put it another way, better to POSSLQ than to pay a steep price for a late in life walk down the aisle with, well, a walker.

I had to think about that the other night after we had dinner with one of Art's cousins, now happily ensconced in an over-55 community in Boynton Beach. At one point, she asked if we had thought about getting married, her husband adding sotto voce that they knew a number of couples who had gotten married "Jewishly, but not legally."

What's that, again?

How exactly do you get married Jewishly but not legally? Have a rabbi say a few baruchs over your bowed heads, then conspiratorially whispering mazel tov? And quietly break a few celebratory bagels afterwards with the secretly happy couple and a few close-mouthed friends and family?

As it turns out, and in a word, yes. That's pretty much how it works, along with not taking out a marriage license or otherwise informing the government in general, and the tax man specifically, that you two are anything other than, well, the same POSSLQs that you were before you said, "I don't."

Jeez. I don't know. Maybe it makes sense to just get married "Jewishly" after all. Or even Social Security benefits aside, not to get married at all.

Since there are no potential babies arriving by stork or otherwise, becoming Mr. and Mrs. in our golden years doesn't seem to carry the same weight or allure that it might have 20, 30 or even 40 years ago.

Besides, there's also a certain cachet around the whole idea of "living in sin." It's almost deliciously louche in its throwback to the Swinging 60s, a last hurrah to the hippie era left so long ago in the Boomer past. "Shacking up" is even more retro. It summons up shag rugs, shaken-but-not-stirred martinis and Sinatra toting his jacket nonchalantly over his shoulder, a rakishly-tilted fedora perched just-so over his bright blue eyes.

Yet married or not, that doesn't mean Art and I don't love each other deeply and treasure the twists of fate that first brought us together, because we truly do.

At this point, though, I need to let you in on some salient facts so you can fully appreciate how blessed we feel. Let me begin with the soon-to-be birthday boy.

After an early mistake of a marriage which still managed to produce two well-loved sons, Art fell madly for a woman much younger than he. Tragically and against all actuarial odds, she died, much too soon, from cancer. He was left living his worst nightmare as the deeply grieving, older and single father of his second family, a teenager and a nine-year-old.

How he managed to raise these two girls to adulthood and keep his sanity is beyond me. My own husband died after a long illness when our daughter was just entering her senior year of high school. Holding it together for both of us while shepherding her through the college application and acceptance process nearly did me in. I can't overstate my admiration for Art's own gimlet-eyed ability to steer his difficult course so successfully.

Nor can I overstate my relief that he didn't actively seek another woman in that period to deal with his loneliness or to help parent his daughters. Other men would have and plenty of other men do, whether it works out in the family's best interest or not. But Art was determined to fulfill what he saw as his sole responsibility: raising his heartbroken girls as he thought their adored mother would have wanted. Dating could, and very much did, wait.

That, my friends, is a man worth knowing.

Fortunately, my own backstory allowed me to understand that nugget of wisdom when I finally came across it. Prior to that, I had been raised to marry the proverbial Jewish doctor, lawyer or chief executive officer of his father's successful company. I had also been pointed in the direction of elementary education, so that I could "always go back to teaching" after my as-yet-unborn children were grown.

To my widowed mother's chagrin, though, I majored in journalism. Making matters worse, after graduation, I went to work for an urban newspaper and after breaking my engagement to my Jewish college sweetheart, ultimately married my editor, a divorced Methodist 26 years my senior. I'm still not sure which of those adjectives horrified her more.

But she ended up loving her son-in-law and even managed to make jokes about his being her contemporary, which was a good thing: our strong and loving marriage lasted until his death nearly 34 years later.

I can't call his death tragic, because he made it into his mid-80's, having led an active, varied and very illustrious life. In fact, it would be closer to the hard truth to observe that it wasn't that he died too soon, but rather that he lived too long.

He was in terrific health for his age—until he wasn't—and his mental, physical and emotional decline was incredibly painful for everyone, but most especially for him. He had long since planned his own funeral, but couldn't come to terms with the fact that life was robbing him of many of the joys that had made his own life so rich.

It was bitter and cruel, this final journey, and a horror for me, the beyond exhausted caretaker who became, after some years, a not-very-merry widow. People had tried to console me that I would finally be free, would be able to travel and to enjoy life again. Instead, the many years they told me were happily ahead loomed large and hollow. When the first fog of grief lifted, there was only an empty nest, floating anxiety and abiding fear.

So then, when, along with some job offers, came the surprising introduction to a retired widower, I jumped at it. Still grieving and unaware of it, I ignored every red flag staring me in the face and let my judgment be clouded by the fact that an unbidden romance had fallen into my lap.

How ironic, I thought, that at this stage of life I might have a relationship with a seemingly well-heeled Jewish doctor only two years older than I, just the sort of man I'd been raised to marry. And we knew so many of the same people, all Jewish, all traveling in more or less the same circles. A Venn Diagram valentine for the ages!

Perfect, yes? Well, let's just say that I planned, God laughed and Jesus wept. Let's also observe that the skeletons in this man's closet had skeletons, and closets, of their own. In fact, I think they all had tiny lockboxes, too.

I'll spare you any more grim details, not that this poor excuse of a human being deserves it, but because I do. I worked long and hard to learn from this colossal mistake, to stop feeling like a walking and wounded anecdote from "Smart Women, Foolish Choices."

It was painful, rendering me naturally leery of finding, much less getting involved with, anyone else. Finally, my stepdaughter-in-law, of all people, brightly told me over one Thanksgiving turkey that I needed to get myself online to find dates. Almost choking on my cranberry sauce, I blurted out, "Do I look like the kind of person who will meet someone online? I'll meet someone the old-fashioned way, on a blind date."

The whole family having met my old flame just once, and uniformly and instantly hating him and his teeny hands on the spot, she had every right to look me straight in the eye and ask, as she did, "So tell me, how's that working out for you?"

This wonderful and very smart cookie gave me a Christmas deadline to get my own dating profile online or risk having her do one for me. By January, I was getting online flirts, chatting on the phone with would-be suitors and actually beginning to date again.

I soon hated every minute of it, with all the phonies, jerks and abject idiots. Was there no end of retired men whose inflated egos far exceeded their actual grasps?

In the meantime, Art's kids had grown up and he began craving at least the occasional mature dinner partner, someone to go to a concert with or to take to a movie. He started to call on an old family friend, whom he soon sensed wanted more than friendship from him. Not wanting to hurt her, he, too, began to search online for someone to date.

It didn't go any better for him than it did for me. In his case, it was a straight two up and two down, where the women immediately began to diss their evil ex-husbands and once exhausting that subject, went on to the particulars of his bank account. He ended both dates before learning just how many zeroes at the end of his bank balance these ladies were seeking. It was only Art's reluctance to abandon all hope before his three strikes were up that he looked online once more.

And so it was that this wary widower spotted a woman whose online picture was a little out of the ordinary. Wearing no makeup or sexy Saturday night dress, she instead sported a huge straw beach hat, big sunglasses and an even bigger smile. She apparently stood out from the rest of the pack and he liked what he saw. He decided to roll the dice and send a message to her.

Reading his friendly flirt, she looked at his profile and liked what she saw, too. Unlike some of the pictures other admirers had posted, he was wearing a nice sports jacket rather than a down-to-there unbuttoned black shirt and heavy gold medallion resting on a hairy chest. Obviously intelligent, he still seemed to have his ego firmly in check and had a handsomely rugged face, a full head of silver hair and a dazzling smile. She flirted right back.

They—actually, we, Art and I—met in person soon after at a local Italian restaurant. I had just arrived at the hostess's stand when I sensed him walking in just behind me. Turning around, I saw the same flash of recognition on his face that I had on mine, immediately followed by equally appreciative smiles. Neither of us had played fast and loose with the truth by posting our high school graduation pictures online and, instead, we both looked exactly as advertised.

In today's dating world, that's no mean feat.

Moreover, while it wasn't love at first sight, not exactly, it was something warm, welcoming, almost familiar and totally comfortable. We talked for a long time during dinner and then for even longer after a jazz concert he had tickets to. When the clock struck very late, he escorted me back to my own car and we headed our separate ways—because my mama didn't raise no stupid girl and

I had refused to let a stranger, however good-looking, meet me at my front door.

Tellingly, other men had balked at my initial safety concerns. Not Art. He totally understood why I wouldn't want some unknown man to know where I lived. The fact that I had sufficiently let down my guard to go with him from the restaurant to the jazz concert—and only then because the concert was within walking distance of my house should a dating disaster strike—didn't strike him as odd.

He actually thought it was cute. And I was charmed by the fact that he did.

Not surprisingly, we wanted to see each other again and officially began dating the next weekend. In the 16 months since, we have grown closer and more certain that kismet had a part in our taking mutual chances and finding love again when the possibility seemed so remote.

Having each known a great love and heavy sorrow, we talked early on about whether what we were feeling this time around was real. Like the Velveteen Rabbit, though, our relationship soon revealed itself to be very real and fuzzy-wuzzy indeed. I realized this in spades at one point when I found myself asking, "What's that strange emotion I'm feeling?" and the answer came quickly. "It's happiness. Pure happiness."

And so it continues. Yes, folks, the man was and is worth knowing. He's my POSSLQ and so much more, today, tomorrow and for however long we have. He's my partner and my best friend, the one who makes me feel cherished, secure and sexy even at 65, the one who also makes me break out in great belly laughs every single day. How lucky are we? How lucky am I?

And as I wonder what exactly to give Art on his birthday, it occurs to me that I've already given him the most valuable gift at my disposal: my heart and soul.

Happy birthday, kiddo.

IS IT ALIVE?

By Thomas L. David

O ne of my hobbies is building furniture. Some friends upon hearing that respond, "Oh, you are a carpenter." More than miffed, I have to straighten them out. Carpenters are either ants or persons who rough cut lumber and nail or screw the pieces together to make something that is usually hidden behind a wall. Building furniture, fine furniture I hope, involves joining together carefully fashioned pieces of beautiful hardwood, using concealed joints to create a table, chair, cabinet or the like. When varnished or polished the result is a joy to look at and to use; it is not hidden behind a wall. I must explain to such friends that I am an artisan or at least a wannabe artisan, not a carpenter.

Building furniture is not unlike writing a book. The author revels in creating something tangible for others to enjoy. The right piece of furniture is a pleasure to use and to own. It can even be art. Museums attest to that, displaying many examples of fine furniture, most having been crafted centuries ago.

My arborist friend tells me there are thousands of varieties of trees in the world, many yielding beautiful wood. I have only worked with a dozen or so varieties. One of my favorites is American Cherry. It is forgiving compared to say oak or ebony, which are very brittle. Oak will crack at the slightest mistake; ebony is at the ready to inject a nasty sliver after anything but the smoothest cut.

Building furniture requires joining a number of wood pieces together after they have been cut to the required size and shape. A mortise and tenon joint is a basic method of joinery; it has been used for over a thousand years. Think of a tenon as a protrusion and the mortise as a receiving piece. If you put the forefinger of your right hand into the palm of your left hand and closed it your left hand would be the mortise and your right finger the tenon. Add a little glue to the surface of your tenon before you insert in the mortise it and you have two pieces that will stay together. Super glue will work with your fingers. Not advised though. Make the tenon two or three fingers wide and the joint will be even stronger. Early furniture makers used a chisel to dig out the mortise and a saw to cut the tenon into a smooth shape to snugly fit into the mortise. Now we have many machines that assist in fashioning pieces that will snugly fit, taking much less time and skill required of artisans hundreds of years ago. Good furniture will rarely include nails or screws. Joints relying on them will fail in a too short time, usually less than a generation.

If you hold a piece of wood in your hand, say about a foot long and an inch wide, it is like holding a bunch of microscopic straws. Wet that piece of wood on one end and blow on the other end and you will see bubbles on the wet end. This straw-like formation allows water to be drawn upward in a tree to feed the leaves in a process called capillary action, something you learned about in high school physics class.

Because of the way wood is constituted it doesn't die when a tree is cut down. When there is an increase in humidity the straw-like fibers absorb the moisture and expand. As the air dries the wood contracts. But it expands and contracts largely across the fibers and only negligibly along their length. It's like when you eat too much. You expand across the middle and don't grow taller. We call the side of wood that runs with the length of the straw-like fibers "with the grain" or the side grain and the ends "across the grain" or "end grain." How much will wood expand across the end grain? One estimate is that a red oak board eight inches wide will expand about a quarter inch from the driest to the dampest humidity. While you are unlikely to experience such an extreme in your home your will get enough from winter to summer to see gaps in joints that were not there when furniture was new.

This "alive" character of wood creates challenges for wood workers and explains why most furniture fails to hold its integrity through the decades. If you join the end grain side of a board to the side with the grain, the end grain piece will tend to expand and contract across its width as the humidity changes and the side with the grain will not. The repeated pressure from season to season can destroy the integrity of the joint and the furniture will fail.

The accomplished woodworker will design his joints so that wide end grain pieces will not adjoin the side grain or fashion a nice joint that allows movement. Just like a nice hug; when our sides, not our ends end touch. It takes a highly skilled artisan to fashion furniture whose joints will not fail over the years. So the next time you are in a museum appreciating furniture made hundreds of years ago don't say, "They don't make them like they used to." Instead say, "This piece was designed and made by a highly skilled artisan for a wealthy person who paid a fortune for it. Thousands of lesser pieces were made around the same time that broke apart in a few years and made good firewood."

Another joy of American cherry is what happens after its construction is completed. It starts as a rather light color but with time turns darker; it blushes to a reddish brown. And if you are lucky enough to have cherry wood with "figure" the color will vary, darker or lighter, depending on your angle to the light, much like a fine oriental rug.

So there you have it. Wood moves, it blushes, it shimmers with the light. It must be alive.

PLENTY OF NOTHIN'

By Elsa Goss Black

Date, Match.com, Senior Singles, Plenty of Fish. If you're a woman of a certain age looking to meet a man somewhere between early retirement and the funeral home, you know what I'm talking about.

If you don't have a clue, just thank your lucky stars and have a nice day. Because, trust me, if these names mean nothing to you, your day is already pretty damned good. In fact, your life is a frickin' bowl of sweet, ripe cherries waiting for the whipped cream on top.

For the rest of us, though, it's just one long parade of clown cars, one lousy honk after another.

I mean, if a man's profile picture has him sporting a wife-beater tee and a beer, you have to ask: what on earth is his SECOND-best photo? A shot of him playing bare chested pool boy at his over-55 condo association? Be still, my heart.

I grant you, looks aren't everything—or even the main thing. But still, expecting someone to be at least vaguely presentable is really not that high a bar. Except that it apparently is.

How else to account for the numerous selfies taken in front of bathroom mirrors, with both showers and toilets gleaming in the background? Or the prevalence of the Jewish Godfather look, black shirts unbuttoned to there and heavy gold Stars of David resting on white-haired concave chests?

And they say romance is dead!

How could that be true when "Jfree37" throws out this opening gambit: "I would give anything to have you in front of me now"? Or when "Interestinharry" from the booming metropolis of Hales Location, New Hampshire states flatly that "I believe that sex is the glue that binds a relationship"?

Who could resist? Well, apparently every woman in New England and down the Eastern seaboard, since he's now trolling for dates in South Florida. Would it surprise you to learn interestin' or not, Harry is now separated from his wife?

I didn't think so.

Even beyond those toe-curling lines, and I hope you don't think I mean that in a good way, there are the tell-tale clues in nearly every profile that there is something less than meets the unwary eye.

For instance, there was the guy from Delray Beach who wrote that his favorite hobby was "going for various types of target practice." Unsuspecting dates, perhaps? Or the guy from Pocatello, Idaho who loved to be "surriunded" [sic] by books. My own view is that maybe he ought to actually read one.

One of my favorite profiles was posted by a Jack of All Trades from Naples, a self-described teacher, businessman and retired "professional" soccer player who added that he loved watching TV news because he was also a former "jurnalist [sic]." I naturally wonder if he ever worked for Fox News.

But my absolute favorite was a man from Miami Beach, whom I went so far as to talk to on the phone. I don't know what got into me. Perhaps my head was turned by the fact that he actually lived in Dade County. After a few weeks of online searching, that alone seemed promising.

It wasn't. Let me just say that he suggested we meet for lunch at Shorty's. "That way," he noted brightly, "if it doesn't work out, I'll at least get a good barbecue sandwich out of it."

And I certainly hope he did.

THE BOYFRIEND

By Beatriz La Rosa

I was hired by Wainwright & Sons, Manufacturers' Representatives, in 1962. I was nineteen years old and had recently arrived in Miami from Cuba. I was a young, Catholic, Spanish-speaking, Cuban refugee who had responded to an ad in the Help Wanted section of *The Miami News*. The ad stated that a "secretary with good typing skills and who could take dictation" could apply. Since I had those qualifications—the ad said nothing of language skills—the following afternoon I took a bus to Coconut Grove for the interview with the owners of the firm.

Where do I get off to get to Oak Avenue? I asked the bus driver in a subdued, tentative voice, my thick Spanish accent betraying my nationality. I still wonder if that is why he let me off the bus ten blocks away from where I had to go. But I had a job at the end of the afternoon and would start with the Wainwrights in a week's time, with a salary of $50 a week.

The business was located in a white wood frame house on Oak Avenue. The front office, which was originally the Florida room of the house, had glass jalousie windows and a glass jalousie door. Ronnie, the office manager, and I, shared this space. From my desk, I was able to see, as I sat there daydreaming, the City of Miami Fire Station across the street. Sometimes the fire truck left on some emergency amid the clanging sounds of the bell and the screeching noise of the sirens. The firemen clung to the fire truck like monkeys to a banana tree.

In 1962, Oak Avenue was a quiet street of modest homes, where the lush subtropical vegetation of oaks, gumbo limbo and co-coplum trees insulated the houses from the heat of South Florida summers. Most of the owners in this section were elderly, white Miamians who would gradually leave the area as apartment buildings replaced the single family homes and loud Cuban refugees made "Miama" an uncomfortable place for them to live.

The black residents lived in another part of the Grove, and stayed put, maybe because they had nowhere else to go.

Three brothers owned the business. They were in charge of sales, and Ronnie, a young guy and recent graduate from UM, was the office manager, and my supervisor. The brothers, all nice white American men, spent most of their days calling on clients.

Ronnie's desk was next to the glass louvered door. I sat behind a modular desk, a sort of enclosure in the form of an L with a counter where the postage meter machine was placed. I faced Ronnie and the door when answering the telephone but would swivel to the right when I needed to type. I was responsible for answering the phone, taking messages, taking dictation and typing.

"You don't do nothing but mistakes," Ronnie said to me one day. "You need to get the name of the customers correctly."

"I tried, Ronnie, I tried," I answered, my face and ears red. I had trouble understanding the last names of the customers over the phone, and even though I asked them to spell them several times, I ended up with very different versions—Mr. Dungberg for Mr. Greenberg, for example.

I was frequently mortified those first few years in the United States. The Saturday morning I took the Florida driving test and passed with flying colors, the policeman kept asking me to "sign a cross" at the top of the form that verified I could now drive. I kept drawing a cross at the top of the page. I had seen in movies that people who did not know how to write sometimes signed with an X. *A Cross? Across?*

"Lady, please sign your name *across* the top!"

Ronnie had a perpetual runny nose; his shirttail was always out of his pants, which were creased, as though he had slept with them on. He spent late nights drinking at a South Miami bar named The Fox and dragged in his messed up, red-eyed and hungover frame late every morning. His person, his soul, and his clothes were in total disarray.

The days were quiet; the noise of the occasional automobile inserting itself and breaking the stupor of the hot summer afternoons. In 1962, The Grove was a peaceful place to be. No fancy Mayfair or Cocoplum shopping centers had been built, these buildings just a dream in some developer's brain. The shame of the politician's wife caught stealing at a fancy story in Mayfair, a mirage in the future. But there was downtown Coconut Grove, with the small shops and art galleries, the Hare Krishnas with their saffron colored robes, chanting and dancing on the sidewalks, and the drugstore on the main highway where I went every afternoon for coffee break.

The usual? The waiter asked as I sat atop the vinyl-covered banquette, making an effort to sit up with a straight back—lady like—struggling to keep my dangling legs closed—almost impossible—while the Grove-famous sculptor leered from across the counter.

Will you pose for me?

I answered him with the accustomed " No thank you," and concentrated on inhaling the butter-pecan ice cream with hot chocolate fudge which I always ordered and which was served in a sweaty glass cup. This was the most delicious indigenous United States concoction I had ever tasted, and I was addicted to it. The hot melted chocolate fudge stuck to my tongue and filled every crevice of my mouth; the cold sweetness of the ice cream and the crunch of the pecans a perfect match to the velvety chocolate.

At around five o'clock, the end of the day, two things happened in the office. First, the three brothers came to the front office where Ronnie and I sat, and second, all the firemen in the station lined up in perfect formation on the sidewalk across the street, looking at the office, waiting for my father to pick me up in our newly acquired, used Ford Fairlane.

My duty was to stamp the outgoing mail, and for this, I used the Pitney-Bowes hand cranked postal meter machine on the counter. The three brothers and Ronnie stood in the front office watching, transfixed, as I cranked. *Kachun – kachun* the machine went every time I pulled the lever down, and every time I pulled the lever, my boobs jiggled, Jello-like—or if you prefer the Spanish version, like *flan* not totally set—under my blouse. I did not figure this one out until much later. I thought they were being nice.

The guys at the fire station had a similar purpose in mind as they lined up on the sidewalk, their schedule matching my schedule. I was a voluptuous girl, who was in the habit of wearing tight skirts and low-cut blouses. And much to my chagrin, the nipples on my breasts insisted on showing themselves through the fabric of my shirts.

Ronnie left in 1963. He was hired by the FBI. Lord have mercy!

I was promoted to office manager. I was now by myself most of the time and was the only employee outside of the family. That is, not counting the black woman who cleaned the office every Thursday.

I had also gotten married that year.

"It must be three o'clock ," I thought one afternoon in 1964, an afternoon much like all the other afternoons. From where I sat, I saw that the men from the fire station across the street were already on the sidewalk.

I was about to leave on my usual trip to the drugstore when the front door opened. A man was in the doorway, a few feet from where I was. His figure was blurred—or maybe I saw him clearly and did not want to believe he was standing in front of me—a masculine shape silhouetted against the light filtering through the glass door.

The temperature in the room rose. My heart beat faster. My legs buckled.

"You!"

Three in the afternoon is a time of day laden with foreboding and premonitions. Awful things can happen to people at this time. And what is more awful than death? I have always felt the threat inherent in this oppressive hour, never able to lie down to rest, always attentive to the possibilities for evil that hide in every corner of every place I am ever in. The radio program in Cuba, "La Guantanamera," aired at three o'clock every afternoon, and I wonder if this ominous feeling is a residue of my obsession with it.

"La Guantanamera" was popular in Cuba when I was growing up. It opened with a trio of musicians playing the Tres, the Laud, and the Tiple, which are typical Cuban guitars. The men sang in verses, in the style of a Punto Guajro, a Cuban genre of music where poetry is sung. The verses told the stories, in detail, of the latest sucesos, or crimes of passion. The singers, much like the Greek Chorus in the ancient plays, repeated the lesson to be learned. I felt I was being warned.

I was kept awake at night by the suceso of the woman who doused her unfaithful husband with gasoline, lit a match, and set him on fire as he slept on the marital bed. Or the one of the woman who was stabbed multiple times by the jealous husband, her screams faithfully interpreted by the actress and raising the hairs on my head as I sat by the radio in the house in Varadero.

And the unfaithful wife, caught in the act with her lover, both shot by the cuckolded husband, the *pop pop pop* of the revolver and the howls of the victims—Ayyy, Ayyy, Ayayay, me matan—leaving the prison of the radio and resonating in the dead time of the afternoon.

I listened to it all, my ear stuck to the Zenith radio my family owned, the images of blood and guts seeping from the victims clear in my mind. But I had an amulet: the glass of water prescribed by Cuba's spiritual guide had been placed on top of the radio by one of the maids, and this water protected me from the evil I was a witness to. Clavelito, the spiritual guru of the people of Cuba—a lay man venerated and respected by Cubans and who also had a popular radio program—promised that this water cured illnesses, and protected people from all sorts of misfortune, if the person concentrated his thoughts on him. I did.

"Pon tu pensamiento en mi y veras que en este momento, mi fuerza de pensamiento, ejerce bien sobre ti."

At three o'clock in the afternoon, the time that Christ died on the cross and washed the sins of humanity, mine included, a ghost from the past stood before me.

Arturo. …

The Summer of 1958

Cuba, since March of 1952, has endured the dictatorship of Fulgencio Batista, a colonel in the Cuban army who seized power in a coup-de-etat on that year.

Opposition to his regime has grown by the summer of 1958.

His most effective foe, and the strongest opposition, comes from Fidel Castro, a Jesuit educated lawyer who leads Cuba's Revolutionary Army. The rebels, led by Castro and his brother, Raul, have landed in Cuba from Mexico in 1956 aboard the yacht

Granma. Two hundred men land. Days later, Batista's army annihilates most of the rebels, and the surviving men (sources cite maybe twenty or twenty-eight) escape to the Sierra Maestra mountains in the Oriente province of Cuba. Since that time, they have been gathering supporters and conducting guerrilla warfare on Batista's army.

In July of 1958, Fidel's men defeat a battalion of five-hundred of Batista's men in the battle called La Plata, in the mountains of the Sierra Maestra. The rebel army is on the offensive, and is descending from the mountains, conducting a four front offensive in Cuba's Eastern provinces.

Varadero, the city where I have been living since I was five years old, has been peaceful. Most of the fighting has taken place in the eastern provinces, larger cities, and the capital, La Habana. Varadero is a beach town, and families spend summers in one of the most beautiful beaches in Cuba. Varadero is a sanctuary in every sense of the word....

Varadero

In the summer of 1958, the year I meet Arturo and we become sweethearts, I am fifteen. He is much older, possibly twenty-two or twenty-three.

Varadero is a small town in the Matanzas province of Cuba. I live here year round. The population doubles during the summer months, when families from all over the island arrive in our small community. They are the summer residents and they are a cross section of the Cuban socio-economic make up. The very wealthy, the well-off professionals—doctors, attorneys—and the middle class families who don't own property but who usually rent for a month or two. The poor arrive on crammed buses very early Sunday and leave at sunset.

Most of the locals are fishermen or laborers. Some work in the service industry. Locals are mostly middle class or poor. We have four physicians, one dentist, four pharmacies, one priest, a first aid station—the Red Cross—two primary public schools housed in modest buildings, one parochial school, two churches, and a profuse number of small hotels and family- owned inns. We don't have a casa de putas, but we have a few whores who work independently.

In Cuba, there are two kinds of putas. The professionals who charge for their services and the other kind, which is any woman who has intercourse before marriage, who dresses like a slut, who generally likes men, and who does not conform to the norms imposed by a chauvinistic, male dominated culture.

"Betty, go get some eggs from the bodega. But don't ask the men if they have eggs."

My mother sends me to the bodega with the warning not to ask the men "if they have huevos" but to ask for posturas de gallina— egg layings—because in Cuba, huevos is the vernacular name for testicles.

Groceries are bought from the family owned bodegas. My family buys from El Chino Luis' bodega, across the side street from the house. Meat is bought from the carniceria. These suppliers—the meat market, the two bodegas, the ice man, the barber, the small shop that sells chicles and cigarettes, the Red Cross, the modest school building, the police station—stand in the perimeter of my home. When I sit outside, the ongoing tableau keeps me entertained for hours.

There is one big hotel, the Hotel Internacional, complete with a casino run by the American mafia. The hotel also has a swimming pool and the best nightclub in town.

There are two main avenues, Primera Avenida y Segunda Avenida. These are asphalted one-way streets. Primera Avenida runs south, Segunda runs north. Most of the side streets, at least in the oldest section—which is where my home is—are alleyways of packed sand, excellent for playing ball, which my brother and I often do. The streetlights are sparse, and their weak light only illuminates the area around them, creating a halo around the wooden poles. At night I see a sky bright with stars.

There is one cinema, and I go, together with my siblings, to the Sunday show during the school year, and more often during the summers. It shows mostly American films, and some European cinema. I am in love with Charlton Heston. It costs twenty-five cents to go.

"Is Arturo coming this afternoon?"

My younger brother Pablo and I are sitting on the front porch one August afternoon. I know it was August because the week before we were at the Club Nautico, celebrating the victory of the rowing team in the National Race, which took place that month. Arturo usually arrives at around five.

The afternoon is sweet. I am swollen with happiness after spending the morning at the beach swimming. A lunch of fresh snapper—caught by my father the previous night at El Pesquero—with fluffy white rice, fried green plantains, and slices of avocado, heightens the contentment I feel at being alive. We live a couple of blocks from the ocean, and a gentle breeze always blows our way.

Tomorrow will be the same. My two-piece flowered cotton swimsuit is drying atop the balustrade of the back porch. In the morning, I will wear it again. I hope it lasts the summer. It is stiff with encrusted salt and feels scratchy on the skin when I first put it on. It smells of the ocean.

"Cayo Confite, el Barrio de los Tibores, la Isla de los Mojones."

"What did you say?"

"You know, Cayo Confite, the Neighborhood of the Chamber pots, the Isle of Turds."

My brother is vocal, and he says things that I think but don't have the guts to say. We both giggle as he repeats what we locals call the neighborhood two blocks east from Segunda Avenida, the poorest section of town. The fetid smells of human waste and rotting brown seaweed—the same smell as rotting eggs—welcome visitors. The water on the side of Cayo Confite, the bay side, is an ugly brown color, a result of the rocky bottom and a rocky shore always covered with seaweed. Our side, the north side, is open water with multihued shades of blue, sandy bottoms, and crystalline water lapping on a white long sandy beach.

"Helados Guarina, Mango, Mamey, y Mantecado."

We hear the clanging bells of the cart and the ditty of the Helados Guarina vendor as it approaches our street. Every summer afternoon, at around four o'clock, the carrito appears, pushed by the vendor who is dressed in a crisp white uniform and who does not seem to mind the heat nor the effort it requires to make the cart advance. I have a mantecado, and my brother a mamey.

Cuban mantecado tastes of vanilla and eggs, and has a pale yellow color. I love the way it is packaged, in a round paper cup, with a tiny spoon attached to the back of the lid. I eat the ice cream slowly, allowing the rich flavors to inundate my palate. My brother has traces of the mamey ice cream in the wires of the braces he wears to correct crooked teeth.

He smiles a lot. He is a stick- thin thirteen-year-old who is so suntanned no one would believe his parents are white.

"Have you ever seen Mister Dupon? I ask my know- it-all brother.

Irenee DuPont, an heir to the E.I. DuPont de Nemours Company, owns a lot of property at the northern end of the peninsula, where he built a home and a golf course. I have no idea what golf is but that manicured expanse of green tells me that it is not accessible to me. I don't have a green lawn, as my house sits on top of the sidewalk, and the ground on the patio behind the back porch is mostly dirt with some motley spots of grass, an almond tree, seagrape bushes, and some spindly oleanders. That green, impeccable sea belonging to Mr. Dupon awakens something that I can never identify, a feeling of both shame and desire.

Mr. Dupon's home is called Xanadu. It sits on a rocky promontory on the north side and looks like a castle in a fairy tale. Inaccessible from the beach, it is surrounded by dienteperro, a coral rock as sharp as dog's teeth. The dienteperro keeps him away from us and us away from him.

Junco, the weight lifter and a croupier at the casino of the Hotel Internacional, is walking toward our house, wearing nothing else but the tiny shorts that reveal his perfect bodybuilder anatomy. He is chewing a raw piece of beef, a habit which he recommends and which, he claims, helps him maintain his amazing physique. He stops and talks to us.

"Hey, this guy in a motorcycle was run over by a car at the Curvita de Dupon. They say his brains were splattered all over the street. His body should be arriving at the Red Cross soon. "

As he announces the latest news, he struts his stuff, a cockerel with a cock. A sly half smile graces his face while he looks at me. He wants me to admire him and desire his pinga. He is really too old for me, a man in his thirties, so nothing is going to happen. But I have to admit that I like to look at him and imagine all the dirty things he would do to me.

Soon enough, we see the ambulance and the commotion at the Red Cross building. This is not the first time we are exposed to the dead. This past Easter, on Domingo de Resurreccion, we saw the bodies of at least five men who had drowned.

Still.

"Otro muerto."

I see the ambulance pull in carrying the body. Men unload the stretcher. The victim is on top. A white sheet covers him, tracing his supine form on the pallet. The crowd, which is now gathering in front of the Red Cross, sends forth a collective moan that reaches the porch. I think of the dead man. My angst is not because I feel sorry for him but because I become aware of the gossamer strings that hold my life on this earth. ...

Peninsula de Hicacos

The town of Varadero is located on the Peninsula de Hicacos. The peninsula is a narrow strip of land, 1.2 kilometers at its widest and about 20 kilometers in length, extending from the mainland in a northeasterly direction. Punta de Hicacos, its tip, is the northernmost point of the island of Cuba.

During the late 1800s, a few families from the neighboring city of Cardenas, an important port city, obtained permits to build their vacation homes in the section of town between 42nd and 48th Streets. My home is in this section of town, on Segunda Avenida,

Ours is a typical beach house, a wood frame house with covered wraparound porches and windows on every wall. The floors are tiled, and the banisters on the porch are painted a dark green. The tiles feel nice and cool on bare feet. Rocking chairs painted cream and green sit scattered on the porches. We are a middle class family, and our house is appropriately situated between the poorest section, Cayo Confite, and the prime real estate located on Primera Avenida, the avenue that borders the beach.

" Billetes de Loteria – premio gordo, Hoy!"

The old man who sells lottery tickets goes by. He is a gruff man, his graying hair shaved close to the head. His legs have been amputated well above the knee, and he sits on a square wood cart equipped with wheels at the bottom. His arms are strong and muscular, developed by the constant effort of using them to propel himself and his vehicle on the paved streets. Some kind of contraption is strapped to his hands—wood blocks that help him move his cart forward. He wears a necklace of lottery tickets.

"Cabrones, don't drop me," he yells at the band of kids who take him with them on snooping expeditions. The houses in Varadero are mostly wood frame, and there are plenty of cracks between the boards for this band of young delinquents to peep at women as they undress. Newlyweds staying in the old hotels get top billing though. Why pay a lot of money for those "live" shows in La

Habana when you can see them for free in Varadero? The boys raise the lottery vendor and his cart to the level necessary for him to get a good look. The only problem is that when they are caught and scrambling to leave the scene, the boys have a tendency to let go of him and the cart.

Most days I see the rich handsome young man—the one who drives the green Jaguar convertible—drive by. That car, I swear, glitters under the sun, and its resplendent rays pierce my heart.

"Santiago just drove by, and he is wearing one of those expensive Italian shirts."

Santiago's family owns the only dry cleaning shop in town. He is a friend and neighbor. He wants to belong to the jailaif, and emulates the wealthy residents of Varadero. And of course, of La Habana.

He dresses well and his manners are pretentious. He is a good looking young guy, curly blond hair, green eyes and fair skin. He is also Maricon, but we really don't care what his sexual preferences are. He is a regular at our house, a good friend, keeping us up to date on the latest gossip and fashion.

"Did you keep the Rotograbado for me? Santiago asks every Monday.

The *Diario de La Marina,* a conservative newspaper my family subscribes to, has a "social" section on Sundays, the Rotograbado. In it the photographs of the beautiful people of Cuba are published, capturing their images for posterity as they celebrate the important events in their life. The photos are finished in an elegant sepia color in glossy, superb quality paper. Weddings—the brides, according to the reviews "wearing the most beautiful dresses, designed by the most fashionable couturier" always look ravishing. The grandmother's jewelry is always an item that is mentioned and which attests to the pedigree of the family—the diamond brooch and earrings, or the cross around her neck, made with pearls and rubies. Debutante balls at the five exclusive social clubs, anniversaries, birthdays, baptisms, and any and all social occasions where the rich can glitter and shine, are featured on Sundays.

"Did you see the beautiful dress the Countess was wearing? And her son Jose Antonio is getting married."

Santiago knows everyone in these pages by name and comments on the affairs as if he had actually been a guest at them. You would think he belongs. Which is a contradiction because he sympathizes with the Revolution, and I have heard that his father is a Communist who left Generalisimo Franco's Spain because of his beliefs.

Santiago also reads *Bohemia*, the weekly magazine where men murdered by Batista's esbirros are featured. Two pages of photographs of the corpses of mostly young men, naked from the waist up, are always featured. Their wounds, in the black and white photographs, are black holes, small craters that violate the whiteness of their flesh. The dead are always positioned face up, bodies resting on a hard looking floor, or table, forlorn and abandoned. They look unloved and sad. Sometimes, the photo of a hangman, a well-dressed man with a thin moustache, is captured for posterity next to the body.

The pageant continues on the next page of the magazine, where a photo of an almost naked young woman, the Vedette of the moment, is displayed. Her voluptuous body overflows the page and a smile from very painted lips salutes the reader.

Santiago "borrows" the shirts that the rich guy—the one who drives the green Jaguar convertible—sends to the shop for dry cleaning. Santiago wears the shirts in the evenings and looks like a prince in them. His world and the rich guy's world are so far from one another that there is no chance of them running into each other.

"Do you think that guy ever imagined who wore his shirts? Santiago even drove through kawama wearing them," I ask my brother on one of those days when we look back to that time of our lives in Cuba.

Kawama is the most exclusive section of town and where the rich young guy lives.

Mansions with manicured lawns and carefully staged tropical landscapes sit by the bluest of oceans. Coconut palm trees, cocoplum, bougainvillea, hibiscuses, and oleanders dot the gardens and streets. Cream-colored Roll Royces, bottle-green Jaguars, and armored black Cadillacs roam its avenues, uniformed drivers at the helm. The old money and the new money—the wealth of the newly rich stolen from the coffers of the Cuban Republic, taken to the United States or Switzerland in suitcases overflowing with dollar bills—mingle here. Politicians and families of lineage share this beautiful spot, rejoicing in their good fortune and the privileged status that money and power bequeath.

When Arturo takes me on a ride around this section and if it happens to be merienda time, I see a bunch of mostly young women parading with beautifully attired young children in the perfect green areas of the neighborhood. These women are the nannies, the manejadoras, dressed in starched pastel-colored uniforms— pink, light blue, white—and they look like paper flowers against the blue summer sky. Tough looking men, dressed in military olive garb, guard the entrances to some of the mansions.

The Afternoon of the Billy Clubs

"CABRONES!" – "HIJOS DE PUTA!" – "ABUSADORES!"

The shouts reach the basement where the women's bathrooms of the Club Nautico de Varadero are located. I am hiding inside one of the stalls, cowering, wishing myself invisible, hoping that I am dreaming and I will soon wake up.

Pop pop pop pop pop pop.

I hear the crackling sound of gunfire and realize that I have to stay put. I don't know how long I have been inside the bathroom, and I am praying that the matones have been stopped and that I will not see those boots coming down the stairs. I am sickened by the smell of fear, my own, and by the sounds of violence. I don't want to die.

I hope my sister and cousin are safe.

I remember seeing them go upstairs, to the second level of the clubhouse, where the bedrooms are. I did not go with them. Blindly, in a panic, I took the first stairs I saw, the ones leading to the basement. I am here by myself. I have images of my friends being beaten and the memory of the dull sound—*thud thud thud thud*—of the clubs hitting human flesh. I am a coward. Me, the girl who admires courage above all else, is also the one who hides and runs at the first sign of trouble.

My aunt Nina, she is brave.

She predicted there would be trouble when she saw the truck full of Batista's henchmen going round the block. After several rounds of provocation by the soldiers, the young men leave the clubhouse and invade the street.

The melee starts. My friends are unarmed young men, civilians fighting trained soldiers. Insults are interchanged; the soldiers bludgeon the young men. Shots are fired. Some of the soldiers detach from the squad and start ascending the steps leading to the clubhouse, where I am hiding and where all the other women have sought refuge from the violence on the street.

My aunt stands at the center of the stairs.

"You cannot go any further! There are only young girls here." My aunt commands the soldiers to stop. They obey her, and turn back towards the street.

I always wondered how she managed to do that. Maybe the soldiers, uneducated men from humble origins, recognized her superior status, her right to be standing there. She, after all, is equipped with the innate authority inherited from generations of ancestors belonging to a privileged class in the Cuban social order.

"Esos son unos culicagaos." ("They are nobodies, those soldiers.")

"Where were you?" my sister asks. All the young women have left their hiding places and are congregating at the top of the stairs, on the front porch of the clubhouse.

"Don't cry." My cousin is sobbing as she tells me what happened on the street. She watches the ugly violence on the street from one of the upstairs window. I try to console her, but I too feel like crying, cheated once more of my complaisance by the unpredictability of it all.

No one is killed that afternoon. Some men are taken to jail, and later released. Some of them died later in the fight against Batista; some died even later in the fight against Fidel Castro.

No one wins.

That night, after dinner, I sat on one of the rocking chairs on the porch. The moon is full. I gaze at the sky with all the force of my being, awed by the mystery of life. The moonlight is blanketing the streets with a soft light, casting gentle shadows on the now deserted streets. In silence I receive the gifts of the infinite number of stars that choose to shine tonight, the perfume of the jasmine bush by the porch, the notes of Schumann's *Symphonic Studies* coming from my mother's hands playing the piano in the living room, and the muted voices of my family. I think of Arturo, my boyfriend, who will be arriving tomorrow. I imagine the future with him and remember the way his body felt against mine. I am comforted by the certitude that my life will be just the way my parents' life had been, in Cuba, surrounded by all the people and places familiar and loved. ...

Arturo

"This is for you," Arturo says as he hands me a package wrapped in tissue paper. It is August of 1958, and as usual, I am on the front porch of the house in Varadero. I have been waiting for him, paying attention to the sound of the motor of his Buick. I hear him before I can see him.

I tear the tissue wrapping the gift. It is a book covered in midnight blue leather. The leather is a little bumpy and similar in look and feel to the one covering my missal. He has brought me Somerset Maugham's short stories of British colonialists in the Far East. I love to read, and Arturo has been bringing me books ever since he became my boyfriend. I have graduated from the colorful comic books I buy from the bodega of *El* Chino to these tomes bound in supple leather, with pages of onion skin paper. I love the stories, and I also love the physical book. The leather cover, the weight of it, the soft crackle of the pages as I turn them.

"Let's go for a drive. Get your sister to chaperone."

I know what "going for a drive" means. Of course the chaperone is my younger sister, who hardly pays attention to what goes on during those drives.

I am getting moist with anticipation thinking of what is going to happen. Sometimes, even now, I believe that imagining what I desire is better than experiencing the reality of it, the physical manifestation of the idea. I hope death, under the same assumption, will not be as bad as I think it will be. Nonexistence could be bliss.

This afternoon we will drive to Dupon, and at the gate the guard will let us pass. The guard knows my family, and we always have access to the property as long as we stay away from the main house and the golf course. Arturo will park the car in an isolated spot. He and I will walk and hide under our shelter, the rim of a cave on the south side of the ocean, the ugly side. My sister will stay in the car while we go on our walk. We will reach the cave, he leading me, holding my hand, stepping carefully on the dienteperro we have to cross to get to it. Here, under the cover and sanction of the rocky canopy of the cave, surrounded by the briny odor of ocean and seaweed, he is going kiss me, insert his tongue in my mouth, put his hands inside my blouse, free my breasts from the constraint of the brassiere, suck and fondle my nipples, and press his warm, strong body against mine, his pelvis desperate against mine until I feel his hardness, until the heat rises in waves to my face, burning my skin, the sopping lubrication of my body dripping between my thighs and staining my panties.

The nuns at school—and my own mother—they say this is a sin. How can something that feels so good be a sin? I think that this is what seeing God must be like.

Arturo does not finger me. I believe he is afraid that if he does, there will be no going back for me.

"What's wrong?" my mother asks when I come home that evening, all flushed and still wet with desire for Arturo.

That night I go back to the porch to wait for him. He promised he would be back after dinner.

In the darkness, I watch for approaching headlights and listen for the engine of his car. I count many headlights, my heart racing every time one appears in the distance. I count them until midnight.

Enough. Come to bed. He is not coming.

I do not know until now that the headlights of a car could make a person very happy or very sad.

I should have known that Arturo does not always do what he promises. He has a habit of disappearing for a day or two. I know he drinks. I have smelled alcohol in his breath.

Maybe he went to El Kastillito.

El Kastillito is a popular night club near my house where all the men go to get drunk and find women. He goes there all the time. Or maybe he went back to La Habana. ...

End of Summer – 1958

The afternoon ends with the world bathed in a soft glow of pinks, yellows and violets. Dinner will be ready soon, and I can already smell the fish being fried in oil. My mouth waters thinking of the meal I will soon be eating. I hope Emilia, the cook, also fries some potatoes.

I am by myself, sitting on the steps of the front porch. I stand up, go through the wide open doors that lead into the living room, and carefully place an LP on the turntable of the record player my grandparents gave me as a Christmas gift. It is a humble phonograph, inexpensive, the kind that looks like a cardboard box. The needle has to be placed manually onto the record. I am very careful with this operation. I do not want to scratch it.

I am awed by the music I hear pouring from the gramophone. The most haunting melody I have ever heard permeates the space I inhabit, the magic of the music harmonizing with the dying day and the intense awareness of life I am feeling. It is the hymn to the "Evening Star" in the third act of Wagner's *Tannhauser.* I just purchased the LP with a couple of pesos I had saved, and this is the first time I hear this unearthly song.

Santiago, my neighbor, is walking towards the porch. He is sweaty, as if he has just finished working at the shop.

"I just heard the broadcast from Radio Rebelde," Santiago announces. "The broadcast was about La Ofensiva. Fidel's army defeated a battalion of five hundred men. Batista is losing. The Barbudos are coming down from the mountains. "

Radio Rebelde is the pirate radio station started by Fidel Castro in February of 1958. The broadcasts reach the Cuban population with messages from the Revolutionary Army. Santiago listens to the broadcasts all the time. He keeps my family informed. My father works for the Batista government. We are not allowed to listen to Radio Rebelde.

"A great victory for the Rebel Army, La Ofensiva." Santiago emphasizes how important this bit of news is. I understand his fervor. I sympathize with the rebels and most of my friends also do. But I am not active in any revolutionary activities and my family definitely is not. My parents still remember the Machadato, the Revolution of 1933, and the hard times they all suffered during that period.

"Vale mas malo conocido, que bueno por conocer. And there are rumors that Fidel is a Comunista" is the mantra repeated to me by my parents when I denounce the murders of young men by Batista's government, point out to them the poverty, the involvement of Batista with the U.S. mafia with the consequent gambling, prostitution and drugs, the corruption existing at all levels of the government, and the repressive measures of a dictatorship in the throes of death.

"Do you know Batista has Napalm and might use it to get the rebels out of the mountains?" Santiago continues his ranting about the political situation.

I have no idea what Napalm is. Santiago explains the devastation caused by these incendiary bombs. I am chilled by his account of this weapon that would become so familiar to me during the Vietnam War.

Events, objects, ideas—do they co-exist in space and time, bouncing in cosmic mirrors, reflected back and forth and traveling between the past, present, and future per saecula saeculorum? Napalm, a word I had never heard but a word that would reappear and have a meaning I could not even conceive of the first time I encountered it. How could I know that one day I would be in a place that was not Cuba, a citizen of a country involved in a war where three hundred and eighty-eight thousand tons of that word would be dropped in the country of Vietnam? Vietnam. A country located in a region so remote and different from the place I was born that it was used in my childhood to describe a far, far away place—La Cochinchina—the end of the world.

If that was a sign of things to come, how many more signs, auguries, premonitions did I receive and did not heed? Was Arturo's visit that day in a peaceful everyday afternoon in Coconut Grove a warning?

In August of 1958, I did not need a soothsayer to know that change was coming.

I wake up on January 1ˢᵗ 1959 to the news that the Rebel Army has triumphed. Days later, bearded young men dressed in olive colored uniforms parade through Primera and Segunda Avenidas. They ride in trucks, shouting and raising their weapons over their heads in a sign of conquest.

"FIDEL!" "FIDEL!" "FIDEL!"

They are on a victory procession on their way to La Habana to meet with Cuba's new Supreme Leader, Fidel Castro.

Soon after, my father is accused of crimes against the people of Cuba and goes into hiding. He and my mother leave the country. My family is scattered, broken. Six siblings who have been together for over fifteen years are divided, cut up, and distributed among relatives. Like Humpty Dumpty, we are never together again.

Arturo is still my boyfriend. …

Miami 1964

"Arturo was not good for you. Our aunts were right to make you break up with him."

Arturo's friend in Miami delivered the news to my sister. She has just told me.

"Arturo has been living in Puerto Rico. He had a girlfriend there for some time, but apparently she broke up with him. The day that this happened, he had been drinking. He went out looking for her. Someone told him she was at a bar that they both used to frequent. He went in, tried to talk to his ex-girlfriend, probably to convince her to come back to him. She was sitting at the counter with another man. The conversation evolved into a discussion. The other man tried to get Arturo to leave. Arturo took out the revolver he always carried with him, shot the woman and then shot himself. She is alive, but Arturo is dead."

Arturo.

When I looked at his face that afternoon in Coconut Grove, I hardly recognized the man I left in Cuba when I came to Miami in 1961. He was a shadow of who he was—but maybe it was me who had changed, who had become a different person than the one I was in Cuba. After all, the moment I boarded that Cubana de Aviacion aircraft and left everyone and everything behind, I was eviscerated. No more heart, no more entrails, just empty spaces where all those organs had been. A void that could never be filled took hold of me; the people and places I left disappearing from my life forever. I developed another set of lungs, another heart. And how else could I survive, when the oxygen I would breath from that day forward would be different, unfamiliar, foreign? My tongue and vocal chords mutated to be able to speak in a language that had no rrrrrrr, and where all the sounds were different. My Mother Tongue, its cadences and rhythms were swallowed by another tongue. The songs of my childhood, displaced by other songs, and the umbilical chord of my own language, severed.

I became a number in the Immigration and Naturalization files. A Refugee. A Foreigner. Forever.

I remembered Arturo. I remembered him well. He had brown eyes, an aquiline nose, thin lips, a warm, muscular body. Mostly, I remembered the way his body felt when he embraced me. The memory of him was imprinted—somewhere and everywhere—in my cells. I looked at him, at the expression of his face, or rather, the lack of expression, and realized that he, too, had changed.

Arturo had been apprehended by the Castro military police just before I left Cuba in 1961 for his involvement in counter-revolutionary activities. By that time, our relationship had ended and the last time I saw him was Easter Sunday of 1960. He spent three years in jail.

"Como pudiste hacerlo." ("How could you do it?")

"Why did you do it?" he repeated.

He stood in front of me, his words carrying a weight that burdened my heart. I was mute and numb. He had been my first love, had given me my first kiss. At that moment, nothing I said could change what was; make our lives the way it had been. I breathed his scent, remembering the way he tasted when he kissed me. He stood close to me, so close, that I could have raised my hand and caressed his face.

STOP ME IF YOU'VE HEARD THIS BEFORE

By Elsa Goss Black

"If I've said it once, I've said it a thousand times," our teacher shouted. "In fact," he went on, "I've said it until I'm blue in the face. There ought to be a law against using clichés! But you all turn a blind eye and a deaf ear to my pearls of wisdom and treat me like a dog, like a Jack of all trades and master of none!"

Our fearless leader began to look quite green around the gills as he announced that he would no longer whitewash the problem. "I've had it with your purple prose, and I am going to wipe the slate clean! From this red letter day forward, you will not pass this course with flying colors unless you learn to write your way out of a paper bag."

Apparently, his heart of gold had turned into a heart of stone because it was clear we were all in hot water until we straightened up and learned to fly right. He had certainly rattled our cages. But for crying out loud, he still wasn't about to put a line under it or otherwise zip his lip. With a face as dark as a rain cloud, he thundered, "Time is of the essence!"

We were struck dumb. Looking at us all with a hairy eyeball, our commander continued on, ranting that he was bone tired and bored to tears with our pieces setting his teeth on edge. "You're driving me right up a wall! I hereby order that my students will become their own teachers and learn to recognize a cliché in the blink of an eye, the drop of a hat, faster than a speeding bullet."

But how? That was the $64,000 question.

"Aha!" he gazed at us with twinkling eyes. "There is just one way to cure your Achilles heel."

We waited with bated breath. He intoned, "Now listen, my children. It's a tale as old as time that it takes one to know one. And though this be madness, yet there is method to it. Since the pen is mightier than the sword, I beseech you to bite the bullet and burn the midnight oil if you must. By hook or by crook, by the crack of dawn, you must go forth like a bat out of hell and weave every trite phrase you can find into a cock and bull story that will knock my socks off."

Bright-eyed and bushy tailed, I returned his gaze and thought, "Just keep your eyes peeled." Sly as a fox, I sat down at my computer and racked my brain. Why, our professor was dead right, I realized. "There's more than one way to skin a cat!"

Ever mindful that even a journey of a thousand miles begins with the first step, I began to type.

⇥⊦⊣⇤

At the end of the day, and to add insult to injury, I find myself all hands on deck, over a barrel and under the weather in a storm-tossed boat. I know the ropes and had thought all had been fine and dandy before I hit the high sea.

Minding each and every of my Ps and Qs, I was sure that I had dotted every *i* and crossed every *t*, as prepared as any apple-cheeked scout. After all, hadn't I been an old salt since I'd been knee-high to a grasshopper?

But that wasn't the way the cookie crumbled. Instead of plain sailing, instead of shooting fish in a barrel, I'm in another fine kettle of fish altogether. As luck would have it, I am far from sailing off into the sunset, neither sober as a judge nor fit as a fiddle. Amidst a gathering storm, I am now three sheets to the wind as it rains like cats and dogs. I don't know where I am or which way the wind is blowing. The shore may be only a stone's throw away, but you couldn't prove it by me.

All I know is that there's water, water, everywhere, and not a drop to drink. The deck would seem to be stacked against me.

But when all is said and done, I have only myself to blame for being between the devil and the deep blue sea. It's summertime when the livin' is easy, and I had been as nervous as a cat on a hot tin roof in the dawn's early light, all bent out of shape because time was ticking away. I wanted to take my job and shove it, take it easy and stop and smell the roses before I found myself pushing daisies instead.

I was beyond ready, willing and able to let the good times roll. All work and no play makes Jack a dull boy, and I needed to get out of Dodge this morning. Wanting to make hay while the sun was still shining, I decided not to put off till tomorrow what I could do today. I hauled ass and set sail.

But haste makes waste and as quick as a New York minute, I knew that I had gotten off on the wrong foot. I had jumped on board with both feet, and had thereby jumped the gun. I had to face the music: I was up the creek without a paddle, and only food for thought as I realized the fly in the ointment was that I had neither fish nor fowl to eat and nothing to wet my whistle.

Despite the best laid plans of mice and men, I was in both a pickle and a sticky wicket, in trouble with a capital T. Then it came to me like a bolt from the blue: it's not over till the fat lady sings. Knock on wood, I suddenly remembered what might be best thing since sliced bread: a cabinet full of bootleg hooch in the galley.

The long and the short of it was that necessity being the mother of invention, I was tickled pink that I could while away the lonely hours with demon rum till the cows came home or Twelve Good Men and True came by to save my bacon and tug me back to any old port in a storm.

And so I sit, the yardarm long gone over the mast and the hatches battened down. I'm twiddling my thumbs and whistling Dixie, bombed out of my gourd, the rum good to the last drop. I'm caught between a rock and a hard place, with only a smile for my umbrella, but I've still got nerves of steel and the luck of the Irish with me.

Damn the torpedoes and full speed ahead!

At heart, stone cold sober or drunk as a skunk, I remain a cock-eyed optimist who believes that you live and learn and that all's well that ends well. This day's been a nail biter, and the black night has proven that when it rains, it pours, but I think I still have the world on a string. I'll bet my bottom dollar that my ship's going to come in and that life will be just a bowl of cherries, come hell or high water, the good Lord willin' and the crick don't rise.

MY GRANDPARENTS' HOUSE

By Zooey Kaplowitz

My grandparents' house was more a schizophrenic experience than it was a home. Unlike the others in the neighborhood, it was not recessed from the street and did not have a genteel garden in front. They built the house soon after they arrived in the United States, and it expanded from there. It shared the yard with a large warehouse. Both were faced with stucco and painted the color of the sand on any public beach in New York. The entrance was a storefront, and the rear was a 1950s modern addition. Directly in front, inches from the curb, was an original and still functional Texaco gas pump. At the rear were the remains of what once was a small stable. A prolific peach tree stood in the neglected yard that separated the house and the stable. A cement walk separating the house and the warehouse brought you from the backyard to the sidewalk in front of the house.

You entered the house through a large storefront. The storefront had the charm and ambiance usually associated with an auto repair shop. Two large cluttered mahogany desks were placed against one wall. Black file cabinets were lined up against the other wall. Pinup calendars were placed anywhere there was space. There was an old couch and fruit crates to accommodate an overflow crowd.

This office was the domain of Charlie Schultz, my father's bookkeeper. His name was James Raymond Aloysius Gormley, but my father called him Charlie Schultz. Charlie was a corpulent Irishman with a bulbous nose and a flush complexion. He was always drunk and spent the greater part of his working day descending the steep staircase that took him from the office to the employee commode in the cellar. He didn't always catch all the steps, and when this happened, a loud thud was followed by the words, "Fuckin' lousy kikes."

Directly behind the office was the kitchen which was ugly and filthy, the place where the family would all congregate to read the Yiddish paper, *The Forward,* and listen to the Jewish columnist, *Valter Vinchell,* and watch my grandmother perform her culinary sorcery. She had her own way of doing things, even her own way of dressing. My grandmother was stuck in the fashion trend of her youth in Poland. She would wear a coarse dress accessorized by heavy cotton stockings, more than functional shoes, and a babushka the same hue as her colorful dress. Her cooking brought my mother and aunt to the kitchen to watch and learn. Her palette of seasonings consisted of salt, pepper, and paprika. The more than generous amounts of paprika always motived my Aunt Florence to say, "Momma, that bird looks better in death than it did in life." This was one of their private jokes. My grandmother and aunt had many private jokes. They excluded my mother from them which hurt her and led to arguments between my parents. Visits to my grandparents always led to arguments. Everyone argued for different reasons. My grandfather and father argued because my grandfather believed my father had stolen his business. My father and aunt argued because my aunt felt my father was my grandmother's favorite. My father and grandmother argued because he was angry that she was spending his money to support my aunt and her family.

These personal dynamics were very upsetting to me, so I would seek out my Uncle Stanford and Cousin Lana. They lived in the 1950s modern addition that was added to the original structure. Their quarters were stylishly furnished. My mother called their furniture "That ugly Scandinavian dreck!" She also said, "Your grandmother must have paid through the nose for that stuff." The pink walls and geometric designs were neat, but what I really liked were the African fertility goddesses with the big boobs. My aunt paid five hundred dollars for them. My grandfather said, "Such a bargain. You should have bought six."

My Uncle Stanford told me all about those goddesses and their boobs. I liked and still do like boob stories. He told me about a lot of things. He was smart. I thought everyone was strong when anyone would call him a schlemiel. It didn't bother me that he never made more than a nickel in his life, and he was a shnorrer. He answered all my questions. I had a lot questions which had to be answered fast before I came up with more. This frustrated and angered a lot of people. They didn't have the time for me. Uncle Sanford didn't work, so he had lots of time.

My grandparents' house became a puzzle to me. It was the only ugly stucco house that I ever saw that came with a storefront, a kitsch fifties addition, an adjacent warehouse with a stable in the back.

I was told my grandparents built the house shortly after coming to America. This impressed me, but I couldn't picture my grandparents climbing ladders armed with hammers and nails. I later found out that to a Jew "built" means paying someone to do it for you. My Uncle Sanford explained this to me. He went on to say, "Jews don't build things. That's why they were a nomadic tribe until forced into bondage by the Egyptians. Jews don't like manual labor. That's why they fled Egypt. That is also why your family never celebrated Passover. It reminded them of a time when they had manual dexterity."

"It costs money to have a house built. Where did they get the money from?" I asked my uncle. He did not know. He was the wrong person to ask. I then asked my cousin Lana because she knew everything about everything.

"Grandpa's daddy owned a kosher dairy restaurant in Kiev."

"Grandpa's daddy?" She was only two years older than I was but had this need to talk down to me. The whole family was condescending. I think it was built into my name, Melvin. I now call myself Mel, but it doesn't fool anyone. She told me that our great-grandfather was very rich and lived in a very fine home. He had a samovar and drank tea filtered through a sugar cube held clenched between his upper and lower front teeth. She demonstrated this for me. I believed that he may have had some money and lived in a nice house, but the bullshit about the sugar cube I'm sure was fabrication on her part. The girl was obsessed with tea. She was continually conscripting me into tea parties. Even today when I visit, I am immediately offered thirty-four herbal varieties to choose from.

She went on to say, "The restaurant was quite successful. It was patronized by the smarter Jews of Kiev. Artists and bankers ate side-by-side. The great Yiddish actor Boris Lemberger ate there before every evening performance. Not-so-smart Jews also dined there. Rag peddlers and fish peddlers were also welcome. Great-grandfather never turned away anyone with an appetite and the financial means to satisfy their hunger."

"If things were all that terrific in Russia, why did they come here?"

"I'm about to get to that, Melvin."

I really hated the way she said Melvin. She pronounced it as if the word schmuck was built into the intonation. "Do you know what the pogroms were?" I didn't know but nodded yes. "The frequency of the pogroms, the daily beatings of Jews and continual acts of vandalism upon their property wore heavily on great-grandfather's health." She had a great vocabulary for a kid. "Governmental edicts forced all Jewish businesses to be closed. The closing of the restaurant broke great-grandfather's heart and his spirit." She paused for dramatic effect. "He died weeks later in his sleep with a sugar cube clenched between his teeth." She paused again for dramatic effect. She was doing good until she tossed in the bullshit about the sugar cube. Her pause for dramatic effect ended. She began, "His parting words to Grandpa and his new bride, Grandma, was, "Go to America and open a dairy restaurant, and plant an orchard."

"How could he have partings words? He died in his sleep with a sugar cube in his mouth. What was he, a ventriloquist?"

"He gave them his parting words before he went to bed that night, Melvin." Another dramatic pause punctuated by the shake of her head and the shrug of her shoulder. "They came to America with a dream. It was very romantic," she sighed. "They were newly married. They were barely out of their teens, and they were going to open a dairy restaurant. They built this place to be their home and to house their wonderful dairy restaurant with a dining room where your father's office is now. They put a bathroom in the basement for the customers to use. The kitchen was behind the dining room. Grandma would do the cooking, and Grandpa would take care of the of the customers. Their living quarters would be above the kitchen and dining room. They also planted an orchard next to the house."

"So what happened to the dairy restaurant?" My cousin, who knew everything about everything, didn't know. I asked my mother, and she summed it up for me. It seems they opened the restaurant in an Irish Catholic neighborhood. It went bankrupt. This broke my grandfather's spirit. They had two children, my father and Florence. My grandfather had to find another trade. So he became a fruit peddler. This was demeaning to him, the son of a wealthy restaurateur, but he had no choice. They built a small stable in the back to house the horse that pulled the wagon. The orchard adjacent to the house was eventually lost to accommodate a warehouse for my father's expansion of the business. A lone peach tree was all that was left.

"It wasn't what they had dreamed of, but it was what they got," she said. My mother told crappy stories. She always let herself be burdened by the truth. My father was different. He lied all the time. That was the bond between us.

"Your grandfather won the money on the Sixty-four thousand dollar question! His topic was Jewish baseball players. And he pissed it all away on that stupid dairy restaurant."

I like that ending better.

MISPLACED

By Ellen Leeds

Him and Her

Where's my wallet? I had it and now it isn't here. I checked the car, and the den, but I don't see it.

He walks from room to room, cursing under his breath, angry that he has misplaced his wallet again.

Found it! It was in the bathroom, I don't know how it got there. I must have put it there when I washed my hands.

We can't go yet because I can't find my keys. They were up front when I came in the house. Someone must have moved them.

More cursing. Time goes by.

We are going to be late for our reservation. Why can't we ever get anywhere on time? How many times must I repeat myself? I want to leave on time and arrive on time. It's important to me.

I put them up front and someone moved them. I always put them in the same spot. They aren't here.

They both check under the couch cushions. He checks under the bed. She checks under the bed. Maybe the dog dragged them under the wall unit. Maybe he left them in the supermarket. No, not possible. He had them when he opened the front door when they entered their home earlier.

Here they are on my end table. I thought they were up front. One more thing, my glasses. If we go to the restaurant I need them to read the menu.

Can we leave? I'll read the menu for you. She has returned to the front door and is ready to go.

Her

She stands rigid. Next, she starts pacing. She glances at the clock. She looks down the hall and again looks at the clock.

I need to be on time, she reiterates. That possibility has come and gone.

I want to arrive relaxed.

She is on the verge of calling it off. What was something she had looked forward to is now crumbling. She comes to the conclusion that she does not want to go. She decides to table it for another time.

I don't want to go now! she screams. She feels her stomach contorting. She turns towards the bedroom to take off her clothes.

I absolutely do not want to leave the house. I am not interested in going anywhere, and certainly not with him.

Him

He thinks, again, I can't find my wallet. I know where I put it. I hate when she moves things. I am going to stay calm, and enjoy this evening.

How the hell did my wallet get to the bathroom? Yes, it's clear. When she gets impatient I can't think. If she would just stay calm, it would be ok. We don't always have to be at a restaurant before the doors open.

Why is she glaring at me? I know the keys are somewhere in the house. If she hadn't made it a point to rush home and get ready for this dinner so early, I would have been able to focus on what we were doing. Those keys are here. I remember coming in the house with them. I don't understand why we are always rushing everywhere. Oh, here they are on my end table. When I came into the bedroom to get the purse, she so desperately needed, I must have placed them there.

Where the hell is she going? I mean does she think I did this on purpose? I need those glasses. She'll order something I don't want if I can't see the menu. Let her go into the bedroom. I lost my appetite. I didn't like the restaurant she picked out anyway.

I don't want to go now. I absolutely do not want to leave the house. I am not interested in going anywhere, and certainly not with her.

Them

Minutes go by, then hours. He goes into the kitchen, passing her leaving the kitchen. Neither speaks.

Finally, he enters the bedroom. He walks directly to the bed where she is mindlessly watching the television. He speaks, I love you. Do you love me?

Yes, I love you. She turns away and resumes watching.

He leaves the room. She glances at him leaving.

She turns off the lights, pulls the covers over her and tries to sleep. She wonders if all is ok. A moment passes.

She listens.

She hears him screaming from the den. Do you know where my remote is?

PLANNING OUR EXITS: OR NOT!

By Eric Selby

I don't know how long that granite headstone stood there in the protestant cemetery in Derby Line, Vermont, without the two inhabitants stretched out before and below it. All that remained to be inscribed were the dates of their deaths.

Lloyd O. Selby 1917 —   Edith S. Selby 1916 —
I do know my Selby grandparents were still alive because when Grammy died in 1964, her grave next to what would eventually be my parents' (and, of course, space for Gramp next to her in 1969), I noted the irony that they didn't have a headstone whereas my parents did. My father, however, would soon make arrangements for a similar stone for them. He, the president of the local bank, took much pleasure in "making arrangements," quite possibly an off-shoot of

the many estates he settled and how often he found that people hadn't made "arrangements," placing those burdens on others.

He had, in fact, already had his obituary ready as well as my mother's, filed with the local newspaper as well as the state one ˎ and, I assume, had made adjusts along the way. This, of course, is a common practice.

Not only did my father plan his exit but he planned my mother's as well. He should have known that she would have to make adjustments. He had pre-paid the Converse Funeral Home in nearby Newport, Vermont, for everything including the two caskets which were top-of-the-line. He went for everything being offered including the flowers for the tops of the caskets: *Beloved husband (wife), father (mother), grandfather (grandmother)* in gold letters on a wide white ribbon surrounded by many white lilies. There would be two visiting hours, the hearse to and from the funeral and then to the cemetery—everything paid in full. And since their two adult children didn't come to visit often enough when they were alive, how could anyone trust they'd visit the deceased with appropriate for-the-season remembrances, those being flowers placed on the two graves at various times of the year but in winter an evergreen wreath and red bow prior to Christmas. This would start after my mother's death because he knew she'd be down there at his grave often.

I am not exaggerating.

Recently a woman, who may well be in her early eighties, talked with me about how her daughter doesn't wish to deal with her mother's will as well as other papers regarding the estate the daughter will be inheriting. The mother can't understand this aversion to dealing with the inevitable.

Which led me to thinking about this issue of planning for our exits, a topic I don't hear many people my age—I will soon be 76—discussing with each other.

My father even had more plans because he didn't trust my mother to make wise financial decisions—and he had plenty of evidence to support that distrust.

His death from bone cancer came slowly and painfully. A few months before he made his exit, he had their estate put into a trust, apparently with a bit of pomp and circumstance at their house with a couple of attorneys present, quite possibly to nudge my reluctant mother to sign the papers. Everything except the house itself went into the trust.

You need not feel sorry for Edith because she would be able to maintain the "lifestyle to which she had become accustomed" as a divorce attorney might put it. She tried once to break the trust without success. The house with its four bedrooms wasn't big enough for her. So she added to it, a little sunroom which I believe is where she died. She maintained two automobiles, trading them in every few years. She would live nearly two more decades.

But she wouldn't be taking up residence in that casket. She would be cremated, donating her organs to research. Or so she thought. (It seems she was to have had her two children sign papers prior to her death acknowledging that they were okay with this request. Jane and I never saw those papers.) Instead of having a funeral after she died, Edith Smith Selby gave herself one on her 90th birthday, a good way to check just how many people would attend—did attend! I gather many did, a big party with plenty of food. She also hired a person to write an extensive piece about her—a pre-death obituary with embellishments, printed in a tiny weekly published across the border in Rock Island, Quebec. She was, according to that article, the widow of Lloyd O. Selby and the grandmother of…. The six are named.

But where did these grandchildren come from anyway?

Ah, yes, the two children Edith had disowned.

My sister and I still laugh about our lack of an existence.

Do some people my age become obsessive about the details of their exits as my father obviously did, making sure that everything is under their control? My father was justifiably proud of his earnings, the first in his family to leave as much as he did. However, he couldn't stop my mother from being cremated although he probably wouldn't have cared.

I have told my children that I don't want an obituary or a memorial service. They can simply leave my ashes at the crematorium if they wish.

One of my many favorite *The New Yorker* cartoonists is Roz Chast whose memoir—most of it about her relationship to her parents who lived to be very elderly—is titled *Can't We Talk About Something More Pleasant?*

I suspect that is exactly why we avoid this final exit topic—it just isn't very pleasant, is it?

When the writers in this publication were discussing the cover for *Beyond My Window* and coming up with all types of possibilities for what would be beyond the window—planes flying, world-famous landmarks, a '55 Chevy, a lush tropical garden..., I mentioned maybe—I said this in jest at the time although in retrospect I rather like the idea since it would be so unexpected!—just enough gravestones beyond that window to represent each of us, maybe even with our first names as evidence of our absence from future OLLI classes and activities. You can only imagine the gasps and uncomfortable chuckles!

As you can see, that didn't happen for this cover.

YOU MEET THE NICEST PEOPLE...'

By Thomas L. David

A fool perhaps but I wanted to buy a motorcycle. In my mid-fifties, my friends said, "You're crazy"— or worse. Of course stubborn does not run in my genes. Call me curious! So I took the course that awarded the "motorcycle" designation on my driver's license and dove into the motorcycle magazines for some "learnin'." There are three types of motorcycles: sport bikes, the sleek multi-colored beauties you see the youngsters riding, often with a young lady perched on the back, derriere reaching for the sky on an upward sloping seat; trail bikes, set high over the wheels on suspensions with lots of "travel" to take the big bumps; and cruisers, a traditional category popularized by Harley Davidson.

Aristotle said that man is a rational animal, able to carry out carefully formulated projects and to formulate deliberative imagination. Rational? In my case it meant that I was able to rationalize, notwithstanding everyone's warnings, that I could safely enjoy a motorcycle. Part of the rationalization emanated from a magazine article citing statistics postulating that most motorcycle accidents occurred with riders juiced up on alcohol or drugs. Especially vulnerable were the youngsters who, acting as if immune to death, rode sport bikes at incredible speeds. At the time about six thousand dollars would buy you one that could top 150 mph. Their efficiency was due to advancements the Japanese made in the power of small engines, technology which has improved the efficiency of the cars we all drive today. Anyway, I fit safely among the old guys who take only coffee or soda before a ride. I must confess though, when I first started to ride, my pleasure quotient was at about 25% and my fear quotient at 75%. Those percentages reversed with time but began to revert in my later years as confidence in my coordination waned.

What is the allure of a motorcycle? Some mention the feeling of openness or freedom, being more in touch with nature. Another feature was best described by a young fellow in a letter to the editor of a biker magazine. Comparing them to a car, he said that in turns cars lean the wrong way. How true! Surely you have noticed when your car makes a sharp turn you are pulled by and have to fight the centrifugal force drawing you to the outer side of the turn. Bikers, however, love winding roads. One with their machines they lean into the curves instead of fighting lateral forces. They sway back and forth effortlessly following a winding road much like a ballerina floating around the stage. Well, maybe not exactly like a ballerina, but you get the idea. High speed race tracks mimic motorcycles by banking the turns, converting the turning momentum into just a slight pressure on the driver's seat.

My choice of motorcycle was a cruiser, but I didn't choose a Harley. It turns out that the Japanese produced a much better machine for less money. Though I would have loved to be part of the Harley in-crowd, my need for belonging usually stops when my intellect and pocketbook both object. My last motorcycle was a Honda Valkyrie, a monster of a bike slightly larger than the biggest

Harley. It boasted a more powerful engine, a smoother ride, way better brakes and better handling than a Harley. Complete with hard saddle bags for the overnight ride and plenty of chrome, it was my piece of biker heaven.

Harley's amazing success since the nineteen-eighties evolved from a marketing scheme that combined the appeal of "retro," the mystique of the rebel image and, from the biker perspective, a really pretty motorcycle. The Harley Davidson Company dates back some 100 years and was the last survivor of dozens of motorcycle makers, maybe more, who were active in the early half of the 20th Century. Buyers are attracted to bringing back something old and love to flirt with imitating the rebel image of motorcyclists popularized in movies. And a descendant of one of Harley founders has a unique talent for combining shapes and styles that indeed make Harleys prettier than other bikes. But the real attraction may be the sound from Harley's signature engine. It is an uneven gurgle of a roar, the reward for putting up with an engine which vibrates unmercifully. Harleys, like all other motorcycles, come from the factory with a mufflered exhaust system which is pretty quiet, much like cars. But most Harley owners like to show off their noise. Harley dealers, illegality notwithstanding, encourage buyers to pay for the option of a noisy muffler or straight pipes- no muffler at all. They remind me of my pre teen-age years when I attached balloons or playing cards to the front fork of my bicycle to rub against the spokes and make a "zoom-zoom" sound.

Harleys are still built with an engine configuration popular before World War II. It's a two-cylinder engine with the cylinders set at a 45° degree angle. That configuration is fine for tucking an engine into the confines between the rider's legs, but results in what engineers call an inherently "unbalanced" engine. It vibrates way more than say a straight two-cylinder engine, which is balanced in the sense that when one cylinder is moving up the other is countering its inertia by moving down in about the same plane. You can actually see the vibration in many Harleys when they idle. Harley now incorporates a "counter-balancing" mechanism in some of their bikes that cures most of the vibration, but many still suffer from shaking which quickly fatigues the rider and explains why most used Harleys have low mileage.

Though down deep I would have liked to own a Harley, despite its limitations, I have to chuckle at many Harley owners. They say their motorcycling demonstrates their uniqueness, their individuality. Then they proceed to buy a noisy muffler and wear black boots, jeans, a black leather vest and a mini helmet just like a couple million other Harley riders.

Through ten or more of my biker years I put more than fifty thousand miles on my bikes. The local destinations were many: riding with my biker friends for breakfast on Sunday mornings to a far-away "restaurant," usually of an ilk favored by truckers, Key Largo or even Key West to enjoy ocean views on the way, Holiday Park in Fort Lauderdale where they offer snacks and airboat tours, but the real attraction is the constant assemblage of dozens of bikers on almost every variety of machine, Alabama Jacks, in "downtown" Card Sound, for conch fritters and country music where the Elite wouldn't dare to meet, crossing the Everglades on Tamiami Trail where the sky seems higher than most anywhere else, "Robert is Here," on the way to Everglades National Park, an extensive fruit-stand where they serve every imaginable flavor of milkshake, and the Big Cypress Indian Reservation Museum, west of Fort Lauderdale, via what bikers have dubbed, "Snake Creek Road," one of the few really winding roads in South Florida. And then there is Harriet's, just south of Key Largo, for a delightful breakfast, pancakes as big as a dinner plate. There is not a male employee in the place. I thought about turning them in to the EEOC for sex discrimination, but the food was just too good to risk. You may have noticed one thing in common among the destinations. They were away from urban traffic and accessible mostly by secondary roads. At best, bikers and traffic don't mix. My group would often meet to start a ride before the traffic, early Sunday mornings, at the corner of Eight street and Krome Avenue; a place that might have been described as a "country store" a hundred years ago, although gas and diesel pumps now predominate.

My vacation bike trips took me far from home. One trip was to the Natchez Trace Parkway, a federally maintained road which commemorates and adjoins the course of the Old Natchez Trace, a trail commissioned by the early U.S. government that by the early 1800s was fully navigable by wagon. Like all parkways there are no buildings or signs, just the beauty of nature. The Trace made its way through heavily forested lands from Natchez, Louisiana to Nashville, Tennessee, a "trade route" in what was then the Southwest. The Trace was little more than a wide path cut through the woods for "itinerant preachers, highwaymen, traders, and peddlers regularly harassed by banditry," the Parkway brochure discloses. Though now overgrown, parts of the Trace have been preserved so tourists can get a feel for what traveling used to be. The Parkway has low speed limits and prohibits commercial traffic.

A similar parkway is the winding Skyline Drive in Northern Virginia. It, too prohibits commercial traffic and has a 35 MPH speed limit. I rode on it on my way to the Civil War battlefield at Gettysburg, Pa., where Lincoln declared, "Four score and twenty years ago..." It was a Zen-like passage through the woods, often with tranquil deer at roadside watching as I passed.

My best motorcycle ride ever was on the Blue Ridge Mountain Parkway. The Parkway ad best describes it:

The Blue Ridge Parkway isn't a road. Roads get you from "point A" to "point B." The Parkway entertains you from "point A" to "point B." It is a 469-mile cinematic experience, a masterpiece of the National Park collection, traveling from Shenandoah National Park to Great Smoky Mountains National Park with a sense of drama that ebbs and flows with the landscape. ..With protected peaks, wetlands, and trailheads around every sinuous curve, the Parkway is an avenue for exploration—a wildflower hunter's dream, a hiker's delight, a birder's paradise...

It winds through "pastoral landscapes of the Appalachian Highlands" of North Carolina and Virginia. It coils through the mountains and at one point circles over itself to match the escalating terrain. Nearly endless miles of curves courtesy of Mother Nature and no commercial traffic. Quaint? I pulled off once to find a gas station where you are trusted to fill your tank first and pay afterwards.

For those willing to rough it, a perfect destination is Two Wheels Only, a motorcycle resort on Wolf Pen Gap Road, smack dab in the middle of nowhere, Georgia. Most visitors camp out though a few very satisfactory rooms were available, if you don't mind sharing a bathroom. Like the name implies only two wheeled vehicles are allowed. What is the attraction? You approach it on the most winding set of roads I have ever seen. For bikers it is "twelve miles of smiles," followed by great dining. That means good hamburgers, chili and the like.

You may be surprised to learn that bikers get special treatment. Go to a concert, fair or almost any outdoor happening. While car drivers trek for hundreds of yards from their autos to the event, spots are usually reserved for motorcycles right up front. It makes sense. In the space for one car you can accommodate four or five motorcycles, often with two-up riders. When my group took vacation-rides we were often allowed to park our bikes in the front sidewalk area of motels, safely in the lighted view of night attendants. In February, visit the annual Seafood Festival in Everglades City, a tiny fishing village off Tamiami Trail near the west coast of Florida, and drive past all the parked cars to park your bike in the median right near the entrance.

In the mid-sixties when Honda came on the scene with their motorcycles their slogan was, "You meet the nicest people on a Honda." It is true. And not only for Hondas. Fill up at a gas station and more often than not car drivers, wide-eyed, stop you to inquire: How much did it cost? How do you keep the chrome so shiny? Where are you going? I have always wanted one but my wife...

Typical was an incident in South Carolina as I loaded "luggage" into the saddle bags of my bike outside a motel. A very average looking gent approached me, said some nice things about my bike and asked where I was headed. I answered Miami. He explained that he used to ride motorcycles. His cogent comments affirmed that. Bikers are always looking for the route less traveled by trucks and traffic, hopefully a winding road. He referred me to an alternate to my plan, a route a little longer but so much nicer than what the road a map suggested. His recommendation was a road that is part of the original U.S. highway system. The system is well maintained and was the backbone of travel in the U.S. before it was rendered semi-obsolete by the Interstate Highway System, now preferred by truckers and most everyone else. The reduced traffic on the old road system is just fine for bikers, though it has left many towns behind the times. A road with old, character rich small towns. Perfect.

Another special memory. Bikers throughout the Nation participate in "parades" where they bring toys or donations on their motorcycles to a central site for holiday gifts for poor children. In South Florida the granddaddy event happens in early December and is called the Toys in the Sun Run. Bikers from all over South Florida convene at a starting point in Broward County and parade, each with an unwrapped gift and a donation, to Markham Park where about a hundred vendors offer food, all kinds of motorcycle paraphernalia, and junk, to a reported thirty thousand bikers. You got that right. Blessed and led by the Broward County Sheriff, thirty thousand motorcycles parade on a route that includes part of I-95, which is closed for the event, in a ride that takes hours for all to finish. They all park together in an awesome mass of chrome and steel, leaving bike owners wondering how they will find theirs when they return. The most exciting part of it though is riding to the starting point. You leave home with a couple buddies but as you get closer other riders join in, and continue to join in, in front and behind until you're a part of a swarm of hundreds of motor- cycle lovers, all with charity in their hearts dutifully heading to the same place. It was exhilarating.

The time came to move on to another hobby, in my case build- ing furniture. So I sold my Valkyrie. I fondly recall the trips, espe- cially to the Carolinas. I now ride a Vespa, an old man's motorbike. It, too is an amazing machine with an automatic transmission, electronic fuel injection, great brakes, and wonderful maneuver- ability. Just right for short trips.

Thankfully, I survived an awesome motorcycle experience with me, wonderful memories and my bikes all happily intact.

TORTURE KEY

By Sharon Wylie

T orch Key is one of the many keys scattered along the stretch of highway beginning south of Florida City and halting abruptly at Key West. To my friend Carol and me it became ultimately known as Torture Key.

It all began innocently enough at a disco favored by an older crowd known as Studebakers. An old Studebaker was appropriately on display at the entrance, and if you couldn't identify that make of car, you were probably too young to be there. We tried to arrive by 6:00 for the free hors-d'oeurves. The music, of course, was from the sixties. Diamonds flickered across the wooden dance floor from the spinning disco light. One occasionally met someone special, but usually not. The crowd was made up mostly of divorces or soon to be.

On one occasion I did meet a cute someone who did spark my interest. We danced a few times learning the bare minimum of information one can gather in two songs. But as luck would have it, someone in my circle was able to identify him and knew him well enough to set something up. Oh, joy, I was going to see him again.

An arrangement was made for us: my friend Carol, her boy-friend Bob, and I were to reconnoiter at an island he was said to own. Adding to the mysterious tale of intrigue, he and his brothers were launching a yacht on a Sunday afternoon and I was invited to be Charley's date. To digress a moment, I'd like to add a word about Bob. He wasn't kind. He told Carol she dressed like an old lady. He was unashamedly cheap. In restaurants he ate off other's plates to avoid buying his own meal. He saw nothing wrong with picking away at your pile of French fries as he chatted. He invited a number of people to a party at his home on one occasion and then to everyone's dismay had not purchased either drinks or snacks. A guest made a quick beer run to try save the evening. On the way to the keys that fateful day so full of anticipation and expectation, we stopped at a gas station where he ordered me to buy the ice and had his date Carol pay half the gas. But Carol was madly in love with him. I tolerated him.

The Florida Keys are like beads in a necklace connected to one another by the Overseas Highway. But Torch Key drifts off by itself. We had to park and cross by motor boat. Putting across the inlet, I searched the horizon for a large home with a yacht preparing to be launched. We arrived at the dock and headed along the narrow path into the brush, not a colonnade of elegant palm trees. As we neared the noise and activity, it became evident there was not an air-conditioned island mansion from the porch of which we could drink mint julips, but rather a dilapidated house open to the elements and hardly habitable. We found Charley, not among a group of seafaring elite, but a gaggle of hippies foreheads tied with sweat-soaked bandanas attempting to push a paint-peeling vessel into the water, it's seaworthiness in question. Charley, the hitherfore object of my desire, emerged from his endeavor of separating the craft from dry land where it was probably more suited. It could hardly be termed a launching. He had folded his white T-shirt back over his head in a peculiar fashion revealing his dirt-splattered chest. He'd lost the luster of the disco lighting and the romance of any background music. The image popped like a pricked balloon. It was too raw and too real. He motioned us over and apologized for not meeting us at the dock. He and his crew had been working all morning to get the boat into the water. "Go to the house and get yourselves some refreshments."

We found a hostess of sorts among the array of people wandering about since very few were actually helping the boat to its perspective watery grave. We asked for a drink, anything to allay our thirst. Unfortunately, a small portion of a bottle of wine was all that was left. Unless these people had their own stash somewhere on the island, they would be in for a world of hurt when, if ever, they finished their grueling task. Carol and I split the remains. Knowing this was the last of our libation, we walked back to the dock to assess our miscalculations.

On the path we encountered a dead chicken swarmed by flies hanging from a tree perhaps in anticipation of an upcoming barbecue. "My god!" she exclaimed. "This is like a scene from Lord of the Flies. An island! Uncivilized riffraff!! A dead carcass! It's all here!" I was so happy she understood. We sat on the dock commiserating our predicament. Carol was as horrified as I, and as desperate, but not practical. "We need to call 911," she stated abruptly. It was the only solution she could come up with. Still residing with her mother, she hadn't developed all her adult skills yet. "Carol, even if we could find a phone, 911 won't come out to a forsaken island and rescue two women from a band of hooligans even with a murdered chicken dangling in a noose. Let's find the boatman and pay him to take us back to civilization." We agreed. Bob was nowhere in sight--probably somewhere happily participating in the fruitless disaster. Just as we were feeling sorriest for ourselves, the last of the wine I had been sipping and carefully preserving as the hot afternoon blanket of Florida heat enveloped us, was corrupted. A mangy dog appearing to be a resident of the property walked up as if to comfort us and in an instant slipped a big, sloppy tongue into my drink, the last liquid on the island. He took a thirsty slurp emitting a saliva spray. In resignation I threw the remaining liquid into the salty ocean. That was it! Where was our boatman, our Charon, to deliver us from this afternoon in the burning coals of Hades? We even had had our visit from the one-headed Ceberus.

Bob finally appeared from out of the shrubbery and realizing with our pestering that he was outnumbered conceded to return to the mainland. Carol and I paid the boatman his fare. "It's your financial obligation," Bob explained, "since I wasn't that keen on leaving." On the way home when we were safely in the air-conditioned car drinking cold bottles of Coke, she and I analyzed the absurdity of the situation in retrospect. We laughed uncontrollably, I think in a fit of hysteria. It culminated when she and I agreed, "This key shall henceforth be known as Torture Key!" Bob sat silently in the front seat finding no humor in it at all. No sense of the ironic. No appreciation for the literary flavor.

As a footnote, that was the last time I saw Charley. He was a major disappointment. In addition to his not being the owner of a yacht on his own private island, Bob had failed to mention the circumstances of his first wife and her demise. As the story went, she had fallen out of a moving car driven by her husband. Charley had been questioned in the death, but was ultimately released. I considered myself lucky to have escaped for the price of a bucket of ice and half the cost of a motorboat ride.

Carol ultimately wised up and dropped Bob when he suggested she put his name on the deed to her house. The last I heard of her she had sent for a mail-order Russian groom.

AND NOW ESSAYS

NOT A CROSS WORD

By Paul Gustman

Much of a crossword puzzle's popularity is mirrored in our lives. The Monday crossword puzzle in the *New York Times* is not unlike our early years. There is little to challenge us. We get credit for the basics—smiling, or just being a "good eater." If we sleep through the night, praise and possibly a younger sibling is heaped upon us.

Then comes Tuesday, a bit harder, not unlike the requirements upon entering school. Now we are measured by what we do, our ability to absorb letters, how they sound, how they combine to form word—the slightest difference in spelling changing the meaning as from no, to know, to now!

The progression is relentless. If you thought Wednesday was difficult, try Thursday's challenges, in which the puzzle must be fit between other commitments. You must run ever faster to prevent your world from becoming a series of unsolved problems.

As the week progresses, as your years accumulate, we get to Saturday, the most coldhearted of challenges. Those black boxes should be filled with uncontrollable clumps of gray, wiry hair, and the borders should resemble wrinkles drawn with stiff fingers, joints swollen by the years. You find you need help with the answers as you may in life—be it from a daughter, a son, a mate or a bottle of Aleve. Emergency aid from Google is available for the impossible fifteen letter words. Your success with Saturday's offering is measured by the number of times you must dip into the internet's well of wisdom.

Then comes Sunday, ostensibly the most difficult of all. In fact there is a reward for life experience, for having trod these paths for many years. The central opacity of the Sunday puzzle, like the mysteries of life often become clearer as the end of our week draws near.

Would that it were that predictable! The crosswords throw us curves, as does our daily existence. Some answers bend around corners requiring a change of direction, in games and in life. Having the flexibility to adapt is a winning attribute.

Puzzles occasionally challenge by violating the one box-one letter rule. Whole words may be inserted into a single box, not unlike a parent's requirement to jam multiple events into the same time slot. Sometimes resolving what seems to be unsolvable requires the help of someone who has been there before, often a grandparent.

Some crosswords have certain letters circled, the puzzle within the puzzle, spelling out a theme for the day—such as Independence Day for a July 4th puzzle. Each family also has a central thread. Unfortunately for some it is to survive the day. For others it is to take pleasure in the routine. Many are guided through the daily challenges by a quest for excellence, honesty, faith.

Finally there is the ultimate insouciance, the puzzle that doesn't confine itself to its borders. The rare one extends outside the lines, not unlike today's cyber-heroes who follow their creative urges and eschew the traditional path.

It would be nice if we could have the answers to yesterday's puzzle in today's existence and perhaps, in part, we do. Of course by the time we know how *that* school or *this* marriage turned out, it's too late to change anything. But nonetheless, it's nice to know that we did our best to solve the puzzles that life has presented to us and occasionally got it right.

READ ALOUD

By Paul Gustman

I want to read my writing aloud and so does everyone else in the class. Why?

Did we not spend hours in high school sitting in the last row, inhaling every molecule of anonymity, hoping against hope to avoid the notice of the French or history or English teacher when we felt ill- prepared? Why was then different than now?

For one thing we all volunteered to be in a writing seminar. Most have already established an expectation of acceptance and often outright praise for the product of our pens. There are a few that still require coaxing to take their first steps. The second and third steps flow more easily, often to the amazement of these new writers.

Why do we want to read aloud? Often it is for validation of our past. It brings acceptance to our choices if others would have done the same, or felt the same. It brings comfort to hear classmates express understanding or empathy for our life's decisions.

We are social creatures, pack animals at heart. We crave acceptance by our peers, which often results in an increase in our self-esteem. Is it not an extension of our parent's approval, one of the key building blocks of a confident adult? Conversely, most successful parents take pride and pleasure in seeing their offspring bloom.

In our family, it was the talent show. There were no instrument lessons in our house, so the audience was spared the squeaky violin strings or trumpet squeal suggesting animal sacrifice. To a gathering of my parents and unlucky aunts and uncles, we three kids would each sing—sometimes a version of an Ethel Merman show tune sung in a manner that would make Ethel question her career choices. But each performance was greeted with vigorous applause. I don't recall any snickering or expressions suggesting tooth extractions had taken place. There was a "winner" though I vaguely recall that each took a turn in the victory circle. I cannot remember the prize though it might have been as valuable as a quarter.

My first exposure to public speaking was a brave campaign speech in support of Sherry Marcus's run for sixth grade class president at PS 180 in Brooklyn. The speech was in the form of a song written by the candidate, with words replaced in the Davey Crockett theme song. I stood before the full auditorium and sang out several stanzas each noting the candidate's accomplishments followed by the refrain: "Sherry, Sherry Marcus, Runnin' for Pre-si-dent." The humiliation, to this day, was such that I marvel at my willingness to speak before more than two people.

My high school speech class coincided with a rush of testosterone. The saving grace was in the shape of Mrs. Grau, just a half dozen years older than I. For one speech, I sweated through an impassioned version of "The Gettysburg Address" making sure to show originality by emphasizing the word *People* in each sentence, i.e. "Government of the **PEOPLE,** by the **PEOPLE** and for the *PEOPLE*...." My grade was good but secondary to her approval, which was invaluable to this smitten teenager.

So with this inauspicious preamble, what would make me join a group of like-minded souls and vie for the ability to read aloud the product of my memory or imagination, or a bit of both? Writers tend to be interesting people and belonging to the group feels comfortable. They expand my social contacts at a time when our circle of friends had been set for many years. The writers are all talented in different ways, have had interesting lives, and I respect the work they produce. The corollary is that I value their approval of what I write.

Thus we come full circle. Is the class substituting for parental approval, made unavailable by the exigencies of time? Maybe, but there is self-generated pride when I do it right. I can usually tell. If not, my editors will, as Davey Crockett would say, "fix what needs afixin."

I AM

By Paul Gustman

I am bananas, that wonderful, sweet, soft, delicious fruit, so en-
dangered by some encroaching fungus. I'd better eat more.
They give me a sense of happiness, restoring my sugar and potas-
sium, sending my hunger on sabbatical.

I am the sweet potato casserole topped with marshmallows—
always browned on the outside and soft, flowing on the inside—
that my mother made each Thanksgiving. It remains my favorite,
even as I now teach my grandchildren to carve the turkey and taste
random pieces that fall to the side, always in the name of quality
control. Even the juicy stuffing, steaming from the mysterious cav-
ern of the bird, cannot compete. The forgotten cranberry sauce
was often discovered in the refrigerator—to my mother's horror—
as the dishes were cleared. The smell of Thanksgiving is impressed
upon my being.

I am the chopped meat—yes you heard that non-vegan, non-
kale admission—that fortifies shepherd's pie. (Who knew they ate

so well?) And tacos and hamburgers mixed with deeply browned onions and garlic and with an egg to complete the cholesterol conspiracy.

I am indeed a Nathan's hot dog, the thought of which still makes my mouth water and takes me back to the years when the perfect culmination of a day—at Steeplechase where we rode the life threatening horse ride or entered the park by going down a slide that always made my hands blister when I tried to stop myself mid-fall, or a day at Washington Baths playing squash 'til we could no longer hold the racket and swimming in the giant salt water pool, or even just going to the Boardwalk for Tuesday night fireworks—was the obligatory stop for a Nathan's hot dog, or two—or more. To this day that yellow and green sign above the picture of a steaming frank can make my car exit to the next Turnpike rest area even though we just stopped at the last one. The ghosts of my ancestors, each man dying prematurely of plumbing plugged with lipids, sleep well on my statin pillows.

I am any kind of cutlets, mostly chicken these days, as long as they are sautéed and covered with the delicious tomato sauce de jour. It reminds me of medical school days when two barely twenty somethings set up house and lived on the boxes of frozen veal cutlets delivered by my in-laws. "We're staying with you, so you shouldn't have to pay for this." Or, "You drove all the way to New York, so this is the least we can do." Cutlets got us through the lean years, and they conjure warm and special memories to this day.

I am the rack of lamb that my life-long friend and I cooked on one rained out Sunday. We looked up recipes, cooked an entire meal including a blueberry kuchen, had a million laughs and only one small food fight. Our wives were the coaches with helpful suggestions like "You might want to turn on the oven now." Each time our friends visit, the dynamic duo cooks at least one meal. Last time we learned to judge linguini readiness by throwing it against the wall, a practice greeted with frowns from our mentors.

And I am dessert, eclectic in flavor or texture as long as it is chocolate, or has apples or blueberries. Vanilla, or whipped cream may be tasted, tolerated, but not savored. The exception to the white dessert ban is rice pudding, with raisins if you please. I was introduced to this ambrosia when my uncle asked a pre-teen me to accompany him on a day trip to Tarrytown. I recall being enthralled by the adventure of going off without my sister and brother, a rare event. I didn't even mind the sales pitches for Hollywood Shoe Polish, delivered at stops along the way. Eating lunch out for me was not a common event. The diner we went to had tuna, ground fine and mixed with pieces of pickle. My uncle noted me staring at the giant goblets overflowing with rice pudding, just out of reach behind the refrigerated glass. "Give him one," my uncle said to the counter man. I finished every drop, and if the tapered bottom had permitted I probably would have licked it clean.

I am the foods. I am the memories, a sweet and nourishing part of who I am.

THE JOY OF EDITING

By Eric Selby

I would have titled this *Woe Is I* or "Comma Sutra" with a colon and then the title I have chosen. ("Comma Sutra: The Joy of Editing"). Except these two titles have already been used by Patricia T. O'Conner whose book is what I use most frequently whenever I have a doubt about something I am doing a final editing on. One is the title of the book (hence the *italics*) and the other one a chapter in it (hence the quotation marks).

I have literally thrown into the recycling bins a few self-published books, not necessarily because I thought the writing inferior but because those books quite obviously either hadn't been edited or, if so, then by someone who wasn't skilled enough to be doing so.

All of these books were self-published—or what some prefer to call independently published.

Of course I am aware that most self-published authors either can't afford to hire professional editors—of which I am definitely not one—or put trust into someone who may not have the necessary skills. Publishing houses in the United States use specific style manuals such as *The Elements of Style* by William Strunk, Jr., and E. B. White (yes, the author of *Charlotte's Web*). *The New York Times Manual of Style and Usage* is often the one used by journalists. Of course other countries have their own because they don't always have the same conventions. For example, in the United States, we place the comma before the end quote ("I saw that handsome man again," said Veronica) whereas books published in Great Britain and most of its Commonwealth use a single quote and place the comma outside ('I saw that handsome man again', said Veronica.)

These manuals, however, don't remain stagnant. I was surprised when I began to read Junot Diaz's Pulitzer Prize winning novel, *The Brief Wondrous Life of Oscar Wao*, a few years ago, to discover that non-English words were not in italics which had been the standard for years. (The family spoke *espanol*. Became: The family spoke espanol.) Then I read more fiction without the italics for foreign words. So I have encouraged the one person in our writing group who uses vocabulary that would be familiar to all Cubans to do the same. She is such a skilled writer that a reader can easily figure out, through context, what the words mean—or generally mean.

Language is constantly changing. So keeping up with what manuals now prescribe can be difficult for a non-professional like me. For example, when we go to Google—we capitalize it because it is a proper name—and then write a sentence using it as a verb, does the writer use lower or upper case (I Googled the information—or—I googled the information.)? So I am going to be consistent and use lower case.

Today much fiction and memoir, when employing conversations, no longer use quotation marks.

"Ruth, I really love that new hair style."

"Well, thank you, Rosa."

becomes

Ruth, I really love that new hair style.

Well, thank you, Rosa.

You, the reader, probably have a preference. However, I am beginning to like not having quotation marks. In editing these pieces, I didn't tamper with what the writers chose unless, of course, it was written like this:

Ruth, I really love that new hair style. Ruth doesn't reveal that she is wearing a wig. Well, thank you, Rosa.

So I would edit it to this:

Ruth, I really love that new hair style.

She doesn't reveal that she is wearing a wig when she responds, Well, thank you, Rosa.

Another favorite editing-type book is any of those by Lynne Truss who, like me, is appalled at the misuses of the apostrophe: *Apple's for sale* on a sign at a little bodega in Downtown Miami. Oh, really? So in addition to groceries, a person named Apple is for sale? A bodega that is also a house of ill repute! Hey, whatever you need to do to make a living!

Her most well-known is *Eats, Shoots & Leaves*. On the cover a panda is on a ladder with a paint brush covering over the comma. We bring our prior knowledge so we don't need to see any bamboo. With the comma in the title the panda is involved in three activities: eating, shooting, and leaving. What? Shooting? Ah, pooping maybe? Apparently this panda with the paint brush is the editor panda. So without the comma the panda eats the bamboo shoots and leaves. But that too isn't clear, is it? The leaves could still be a verb—walks away—or now a noun, meaning the panda eats both the shoots and the leaves of the bamboo.

All of the writers in this anthology have very unique voices which is not the case when one looks at the way far too many public school teachers teach writing. I cringe when a distant relative in a Vermont high school sends me his "themes."

Julia Alvarez is a famous author. First, she was born in the Dominican Republic. Therefore, she speaks Spanish. As a result, she knew about the girls in this novel called In the time of butterflies. Hence, the author could write so that a reader can understand. Furthermore, …. In conclusion,….
(I exaggerate. But not that much.)

Thankfully it has a conclusion because I don't want to read any more of it! I have told him I can no longer help him because apparently every paragraph has to have at least five transition words. I once told my Miami Dade College students this when they, having come from the local public schools with all this nonsense: "If you continue to write *In conclusion* before the last sentence—You don't think I can tell that the last sentence is a conclusion? sarcastic me asked!—then quite obviously I am too stupid to know where the introduction might be. So, of course, the first sentence would have to begin *In introduction*." Most got the point.

The one rule I stopped dealing with decades ago was the *lie* versus *lay* one as in: I lie down whereas I lay the book on the bed. The difference between reclining and placing. That part was fine. But then came this part: the past tense of *lie* (to recline) is *lay*. And from there one has to advance to *laid*. This was where most of the males wanted me to go. "Mr. Selby, please give us more examples of when someone uses laid" to be followed by the stage whisper of the kid next to him: "I want to get laid."

What a relief to be part of a group of well-educated, retired people—all of whom have a great sense of humor (yes, I know how to distinguish between *who* and *whom*)—and who have authentic voices. If one of them were to submit a piece without a name, I am quite certain I would know the writer by the narrative voice. Kitty isn't going to write about the insides of a car engine. Tom is. Isabelle isn't going to be lacing her southern pieces with espanol. Beatriz is when writing about Cuba. Paul did surprise us—and to the great delight of everyone—with one piece of fiction ("The

Pink Thong"). He sticks with memoir and essays which are rich with metaphors. Enough. You get the point.

But not all excellent writers do well with the last stage, the editing part. So what. *As long as they realize that the reader has to be considered; because when the reader isn't; than the reader will stop reading.* (Oops! Someone doesn't know how to use the semi-colon correctly. Well, another someone does—me. But I needed to make my point.)

Did you know that there are only two times when a writer needs a semi-colon, no matter how much a high school usage book or those English as a Second Language monsters might beat the poor semi-colon creature into a total avoidance by the writer. Patricia O'Conner takes care of that in less than one page (169). Between two independent clauses when there is no coordinating conjunction. (We were followed by a policeman; he wasn't looking very happy.) And substituting for a comma in a series of three or more when the comma has been used for another reason. (The girls walked to the post office, which was ten blocks away; took a bus from there to downtown, a rather shabby area of Miami; and were delighted to have found a lovely little restaurant for their late lunch.)

Then there is the ellipsis which one of our writers has fallen in love with.......! As you can see, it has absolutely no meaning in the prior sentence. An ellipsis (only three ..., and no more unless at the end of a sentence when you add the end point) has only one purpose: to indicate that something is omitted. Here is an example: The woman has been married to Frank, Joshua, Alfred, Jose, Donald, Maxwell.... (When she has had that many husbands, who is going to care about the additional ones! Or even the ones in the list!)

Fortunately most of these writers don't toss in clichés as apparently all politicians must so they don't have to speak truths: "*At the end of the day*, we will be passing this piece of legislation." (Since they don't seem to be passing anything anymore, it certainly isn't going to be at the end of the day unless, of course, it actually is.) Here are a few clichés that need to be nuked: *between a rock and the hard place, agree to disagree, by hook or by crook, easier said than done* (I could go on for pages but don't need to thanks to Elsa Goss Black's essay, "Stop Me If You've Heard This Before.")

Sometimes a misplaced modifying phrase or clause has been left as is because the reader will do the editing without realizing she is doing so. However one such as the following has to be corrected: *Born at the age of forty-five, the baby was a comfort to her mother.* I think babies are not born at the age of forty-five. Yet! *The baby was a comfort to her mother who bore the baby when she was forty-five.*

Which leads me to that *Yet!* You will discover that many writers use fragments.

And effectively so.

There will, of course, be places in this anthology of essays, memoirs, short fiction, and rhyming poems that the editor didn't catch even though he has reviewed every piece three times. Were this to have been published by, say, Simon and Schuster or HarperCollins (it does not have a break between the two proper names in case you thought you got me on that one!) among others, then there would have been at least three professional editors doing the editing before going to press.

Hopefully any misses here are not ones which will make you decide to toss this book into recycling.

AND NOW SHORT FICTION

THE PINK THONG

Assignment: Tell a story using the phrase "Pink Thong."
By Paul Gustman

David was not happy. The new slave girl had beaten all his clothing by the riverbed, using of all things beet root, leaving each piece with the humiliating color of red, and some the woman's color of pink! This he would not abide. David had long been the object of abuse and humor because of his small size. The sons of King Saul mocked him as a girl in disguise. Now with clothing only in the colors worn by women, his life would be unbearable. He would have to leave the home of the Israelites and head out into the desert.

He stormed down to the riverside in foul temper, holding the off-colored clothing and a switch in one hand. He saw a large dust cloud in a field off to the east and could not but explore its source. He crested a hill to find the Philistine army, with one warrior standing in front, alone, a sneer on his face. He was seven feet tall with muscles and scars fighting for space on his arms, legs and neck; a giant, spear in his right hand, broad sword in his left. David took in his size, his war wounds and his weapons, but it was the sneer that erupted bile from David's innards. Every taunt since childhood—every time he was disrespected, disregarded, mocked—was rooted in that sneer. A white-hot rage erupted in the guttural cry-yell-challenge that carried to the field of battle.

Every eye turned to David as he ran down the hill, a sole combatant against a giant, an army. The Israelites had begun to gather but none stepped forward to challenge the behemoth. From a hundred Philistine throats, laughter erupted, as this "champion" came forward, arms full of colorful laundry, to oppose Goliath, the invincible.

Not a sword on his belt or a dagger in his scabbard, David, face red with rage, marched to face a heavily armed combatant nearly twice his size. The only weapon at hand was the thin switch, insufficient to herd goats let alone do battle. "Think, think, think like the Hebrew fighters of old," he told himself, for surely his God would be with him.

The ground was littered with stones. That was something. He was an expert with a slingshot, having practiced for hours when left behind, as others pursued more physically demanding duties.

But where would he find a slingshot? Through the clouds a beam of light shone, landing on his pile of laundry—no, on one piece, the thong, the pink thong. He dropped the rest of the laundry and loaded a rock into the business end of the thong. Goliath was about to hurl his deadly spear, when he began laughing so hard, he missed by ten cubits. The giant regained his feet, drew his sword and in no rush, slowly strutted toward David.

David swung the thong in a wide circle above his head, the speed increasing with each rotation. Goliath, snickering at best, and occasionally doubling up with laughter—having to rest his sword upon his knee-- as all seven feet of muscle shook in spasms of mirth. Finally when only twenty cubits separated the two and each grasped the gravity of what lay ahead, David released the stone and the thong, and the rest is history. Goliath fell, mortally wounded, a strange pink garment dangling from his right ear.

For centuries beyond measure, on VP day—Victory over the Philistines—all Israelites proudly wore pink thongs to celebrate their deliverance from destruction.

MICKEY

By Zooey Kaplowitz

S unday morning meant breakfast at Canter's, at seven with
Mickey. This was the day when the goyim went to church and
the Yids made their pilgrimage from Boyle Heights in the east,
Santa Monica and Malibu on the west and the Hills of Beverly and
Hollywood in the north to Fairfax Avenue, the "Lower East Side"
of Los Angeles. It was the Mecca of every Jew who followed Horace
Greeley's dream. The avenue was lined with kosher butchers, bakers and halavah makers. Sunday was not the day of rest for these
merchants. Come Saturday and their doors were locked in honor
of the Sabbath. Sunday was the beginning of their business week
and their big *gelt* day.

Although I'd been on the coast for about twelve years, my body
was still operating on East coast time. I got to Canter's at about
six and found a space right in front of the joint. The flag was up
on my parking meter. An hour cost a penny. It was the best deal
in town. I deposited a nickel for five hours and started to walk to

the newsstand around the corner to get a shine. I walked quickly past Feldman's Quality Fruits and Vegetables. Old man Feldman and my father were boyhood friends in Poland and, like my father, Feldman was a royal pain in the ass. My father had the decency to stay in the Bronx.

At the newsstand I bought a copy of *Variety* and the Sunday edition of the *New York Daily News*. The headline read **Hitler Invades Poland**. I tossed the paper. If Mickey saw it, there would be no way to contain him. I kept the comics. They were safe, and I had to keep up with Dick Tracy and Fiorello LaGuardia.

Kenny did the shoe shines. He's been doing my shoes every Sunday morning at s6:10 for the past twelve years. He's the best and he knows it. Kenny was an old mick with a thick Boston accent. He came out West with D.W. Griffith as a production assistant. He was an apprentice to Billy Bitzer, Griffith's cameraman. He learned the trade when the trade was being learned. He shot a couple of silents himself until he got bitten by the booze and the broads.

"Hey, kid!" He's calling me kid for the past twelve years. I wondered how old I'd have to be for him to stop calling me kid.

"Hey, kid! There's only one way to deal with broads. Fuck them where you find them, and leave them where you fuck them." I found his advice to be a bit extreme, but it wouldn't have hurt Mickey to follow it once in a while.

I got to Canter's at seven. I found a table for two up front by the window so I could watch the door and keep myself busy watching the street when no one of interest was coming through the door. Nothing would be going on in the street for another two hours. At nine when the stores open, the tumult begins. Goldstein's Boys' and Men's Store is directly across from Canter's. Its sign says, *Specializing in Cadet and Husky sizes.* The store caters to short, fat, Bar Mitzvah boys and William Morris agents. I've brought my clothes there since I graduated from the mail room at the Morris Agency.

Mickey was my first client. He was carrying on a long distance affair with the French actress Dominique Dominique. At that time, she was the only person I'd ever met whose first name and last were the same. Their relationship consisted mostly of cablegrams. In the last one, she drops the bomb. She begins, *Dear Mickey, I don't know how to say this...."* (The usual bullshit: yadda, yadda, yadda.) *I met someone while I was vacationing in Bavaria. He is very nice, very sweet, and very attentive.* (The three *verys* that drive chicks wild.) *His name is Adolf, and he has been chancellor of Germany since 1931. I'm meeting him in Munich in two weeks for his party's rally. Pleased forward everything I left with you to my Paris apartment.*

Mickey was never the same after receiving the telegram.

Mickey was obsessed with getting Dominique Dominique back. He watched the NEWS reels hoping to see her in the Hitler entourage. He only saw Eva Braun. He awaited the release of her next picture. Two years went by and there were no new Dominique Dominique films. He sailed for Germany in May of 1938 to find her. He arrived in Berlin in July after spending a month in London catching the new shows. He saw a production of Hamlet. He thought it could be a vehicle for himself if they could cut the long, tedious speeches.

Berlin was hot in the summer, and the German army didn't help matters. He found the Storm Troopers rude and unpleasant and the German bureaucrats disrespectful of his status at the box office. He thought they needed to learn a lesson Hollywood style. Mickey was unable to get any information about the whereabouts of Dominique Dominique.

He set sail for the States in September, with plans to meet with Roosevelt in Washington. He had heard that the President had been a big fan of his from his early days at Republic Studios. Mickey made fifty cowboy quickies there, ten of them with Vera Ruba Ralston. The best one—and the only one that made Mickey a star—was *Posse at Hangman's Ridge*. Mickey portrayed the legendary sheriff, Wyatt Earp, in that movie. Roosevelt saw it fifteen times and screened it for his cabinet to teach them the value of courage under adversity. The President was also a great admirer of the late Wyatt Earp.

Mickey wanted to have Roosevelt send troops into Germany to retrieve Dominique Dominique. The Morris Agency sent me to Washington to negotiate with the President for Mickey. My Aunt Dora was the widow of Wyatt Earp. They had been married thirteen years. He died in Los Angeles in 1926. The whole family flew to the coast for the funeral. Tom Mix was one of the pall bearers. Mix sat shiva with the family for ten days.

When I met Roosevelt, he told me that he was a big fan of Mickey's and quoted dialogue word for word from some of Mickey's better films. He asked me many questions about Uncle Wyatt and Tom Mix. When I broached the subject of him sending troops into Germany, he became very serious and told us that if he could he would, but he couldn't deploy troops without an act of Congress. The country was against our involvement in this European drama. He suggested we rally the country behind Lend-Lease.

Mickey, when not making a movie, crisscrossed the country by car appearing in every town large enough to have a movie theater. He signed autographs, helped with raffles, and called bingo numbers on Saturday nights at local churches. He spoke to all, young and old. He drove home the message, "England is our friend. We must help them in their hour of need." I traveled with Mickey. We became close friends. He liked me because I could procure a corned beef sandwich anytime and anyplace. I negotiated three films for him. All of them told of the struggle for freedom. He was the hero in all these films as he promised he would be if Americans decided that they should play a role in Europe's struggle to eliminate Hitler. America was behind Mickey. When the time came they would be there to follow him into battle.

Mickey didn't show up until a little past ten. He looked terrific as usual. He wore a pair of brown tasseled loafers without socks, white flannel slacks, a light blue cashmere V-neck sweater and gray herringbone jacket. He was angry that I was sitting up front by the window. He asked to be seated immediately in the back so that everyone could see him as he walked self-consciously back to his table. I was starving. I ordered the Louis B. Meyer lox platter. Mickey ordered the Irving Thalberg over easy. Mickey was late because he had this idea for a sandwich. It consisted of roast beef, tongue and corned beef on a toasted open-faced Kaiser roll. One half would have Swiss cheese, coleslaw and Russian dressing on it. The other half would have sauerkraut and mustard. He wanted me to speak to old man Canter about putting it on the menu. It would be called Rachel and Rueben.

Old man Caner did not arrive until eleven A.M.. He was in his late eighties, a slight, proud, bald man. He entered the restaurant six paces behind his wife of sixty years. He always carried her purse. He walked from table to table politely asking for everyone's attention. President Roosevelt had a special message for the country. The restaurant began to fill with merchants and patrons from the street. Mickey thought they had come to see him. Old man Canter asked for silence as he turned on the radio. It was the voice of the President: "This day will live forever in infamy...." When the message was over, there was a silence in the restaurant and then a small voice could be heard. It was that of a small, fat 13-year-old boy in a brand new suit. He said, "We'll follow you, Mickey."

TECH SUPPORT

By Joan Fisher

S heldon closed the door behind him as he left Lillian's apartment. He hated to cut her off in mid-sentence, but his schedule was full and he had four more clients to service. He unrolled his shirtsleeves as he walked down the long hallway where the temperature hovered in the low sixties. The frigid air felt good. He had spent nearly 45 minutes in Lillian's stifling bedroom. His back ached from having to contort his body into the necessary positions, but he was satisfied with his performance this afternoon. And Lillian seemed sad to see him go.

He patted his pockets to make sure he had everything as he sauntered to the elevator. He pushed the up button and waited for the car to arrive. Sheldon looked down at the plush carpet lining the halls. The ornate pattern of flowers and swirls reminded him of 1001 Arabian nights. He looked up and gazed at a line of crystal chandeliers, hanging strategically every few feet. The faux candle lights created a lacey array of shadows on the moiré-covered walls, giving Shady Grove the ambiance of a bordello.

The elevator doors opened. Aggie and Maggie, two sisters who lived together on the third floor, greeted Sheldon warmly. While Aggie clamped her arthritic fingers around his forearm, Maggie tapped his foot with her cane.

"We've been waiting for you, Sheldon! When are you coming to see us?"

Sheldon pulled out his iphone and checked his schedule.

"Ladies, you are not on my schedule for today. Maybe next week."

A man can only do so much!

The sisters frowned and looked at each other. Then they turned to face Sheldon.

"Can't we make it worth your while?" Aggie asked. She looked as though she might stuff a few dollars into the elastic waist of his cargo pants.

"Sorry ladies, Mrs. Liebowitz is waiting for me," Sheldon apologized.

The elevator doors creaked open and Sheldon walked across the lobby and down the first hallway. The disappointed sisters watched his khaki-clad rump disappear into the shadows cast by the twinkling chandeliers. They both sighed softly. Maggie's phlegmy cough echoed off the metal walls of the elevator as the doors closed.

Sheldon Schwartz had never been popular. In high school his acne and dandruff had rendered him un-dateable. Guys ignored him and girls made him nervous. His lack of a social life provided him with plenty of time to hone his technology skills. By the time he entered college, he knew that he was going to major in computer sciences. On campus, he abandoned the video games he played in high school and wrote code for complex role-playing fantasies. By the time he graduated he had become a computer whiz. With his advanced skills, Sheldon was wooed by one of the Silicon Valley tech giants. His work was good but he kept to himself. He didn't join his colleagues for after-hours drinks nor did he participate in any of the company sponsored sports teams. When the financial crisis called for downsizing, Sheldon was one of the first to get a pink slip. He was told that he lacked team spirit. A vivacious brunette in human resources advised him to apply to a number of help centers where face-to-face human contact was not necessary. Sheldon tried not to stare at the colorful tattoos, which traveled over her left shoulder and meandered across her décolletage. He tried to ignore the meaningful glances she directed toward him over the top of his personnel folder. Sheldon's avatar might be a soldier of fortune who could have his way with captive females, but the real Sheldon was not capable of communication with a real woman.

After his unemployment benefits expired Sheldon had to return to Miami, jobless. He moved back home and into his old bedroom. He was miserable.

"Shelly, are you going to stay in your room all day?" his mother nagged.

"Uncle Sol has a nice girl for you to meet," his father offered with a feeble wink.

Sheldon did not act on any of the suggestions from his well-meaning parents. However, after a few weeks, his mother spoke to his aunt, who talked to her son, the accountant, who was cajoled into recruiting Sheldon to help with some IT problems at his office. With no other options on the horizon, he agreed to lend a hand in the business office of the Shady Grove Retirement Home. Sheldon updated their operating system, created a more efficient platform, streamlined the billing and cleaned up accounts receivable. He revamped the Shady Grove website and improved search engine optimization resulting in increased sales and revenue. His cousin, the accountant, was pleased and promptly put

Sheldon on the payroll. He was on the road to getting his own apartment.

Dulce Diaz, Shady Grove's Social Director, never missed an opportunity to stop by Sheldon's workstation. She liked to stand right behind him and peer over his shoulder, just near enough for the musky scent of her Shalimar cologne to initiate an allergy attack. Once Sheldon started sniffling and sneezing, Dulce would offer him tissues and invite him into her office for herbal tea. Sheldon, trapped in Dulce's domain, would break out in hives, start scratching and leave as soon as possible, pressing tissues to his nose. On one of these histamine-fueled encounters, Dulce, impressed with Sheldon's talents, asked if he might be interested in helping out one of the residents. Sheldon averted his eyes from Dulce's pouty lips and focused his gaze on the large framed certificate of occupancy just above her mane of ebony curls.

"Sheldon, Mrs. Liebowitz requested some special assistance. Can you stop by her unit and check on her? She's in 318."

Desperate to get away from Dulce and her pheromones, Sheldon agreed. He hitched up his baggy pants, grabbed his brief case and knocked on Mrs. Liebowitz's door. Sheldon quickly satisfied her needs. To show her appreciation, Mrs. Liebowitz insisted on slipping two twenties firmly behind his pocket protector. While he was sampling her chocolate babka she called her friend Heddy Wolowitz to brag about her satisfaction with the nice boy who had just "hooked her up". In minutes, Mrs. Wolowitz was banging on the door of 318.

"Hey sonny! Could you stop by my place? There's something wrong with my cup holder!"

By the end of the day, Sheldon had visited five other apartments, and had eaten eight rugelach and a dozen mandelbrot while attending to the needs of the ladies of Shady Grove. When they saw the money peeking out of his shirt pocket, each resident wanted to add her own "tip". He left the building that night with a wad of cash and a gassy stomach.

At dinner in the Renaissance Room the conversation was buzzing about Sheldon. The ladies who had spent time with him smiled mysteriously and cleaned their plates, their appetites suddenly stimulated. The uninitiated were begging for details. Who was the mystery man who left a trail of satisfied "customers" in his wake? The next morning Sheldon found a stack of "service" requests on his desk.

Sheldon could barely keep up with the demand for his attention. And it was so easy to satisfy the ladies of Shady Grove. Sheldon had become a very popular guy. Never had he been so desired, so wanted and so needed! It's true that he had put on a few pounds. The cookies and coffee cakes were hard to resist. And he had to be careful not to let any cinnamon streusel crumbs fall into the computers and printers he worked on. Sheldon delivered ultimate satisfaction as he adjusted DVD players and TV remotes, re-booted balky ISP's and installed virus protection programs. He set up apps for Skype and Face Time and up-dated Solitaire games and re-installed Adobe Flash. Sheldon had the magic touch. The grateful recipients of his technical prowess called him a life-saver, a god-send, a miracle worker! Such a nice boy!

Sheldon supplemented his salary with the gratuities he received from his satisfied customers. He was soon financially able to move into his own apartment on Brickell. He was enjoying his new waterfront view when he heard someone at his door. He saw a young woman through the peep hole.

"Hi. I'm Michelle, your next-door neighbor. Welcome to the building."

Sheldon looked into her sparkling blue eyes. She extended her soft, firm hand to introduce herself. Michelle smiled shyly and twirled a strand of blonde hair around her index finger.

"I was wondering. Do you by any chance know anything about computers? My wireless connection is down."

Sheldon followed Michelle into her apartment, admiring her from behind and breathing in the fresh scent of her shampoo. No sneezes. No hives.

"Everything's in the bedroom." Michelle led the way.

Sheldon followed her. "Yes, I think I may be able to help you."

LIGNITE

By Sharon Wylie

I t was summer. With my Aunt Julia we drive to the country to pay our yearly visit to my Uncle Ed and Aunt Ana. They don't live on a farm but in a little ramshackle town called Lignite. It's named after the type of coal mined there, which is not a particularly rich fuel, more of a poor man's coal. My uncle is a big, round man who wears dirty coveralls and flannel shirts. His black hair, with too much grease, sticks out in odds places, the result of an at-home haircut, I suspect, and he has a dark tint as if he were perpetually covered in coal dust. It has become embedded in his skin. My Aunt Ana stays in the background and speaks only when asked a question. Her only other input is an occasional little nervous laugh. My mom and Aunt Julia do most of the talking to Ed since he is their brother.

My cousin Myrtle Jean is several years older than I am. She suggests we walk up Main Street which runs in front of her house. There are no sidewalks and only occasional pickup trucks bumping by, so we walk on the dirt road kicking up dust as we pass empty stores like graveyard mausoleums. We meet an occasional person who greets us, "Howdee, Myrtle Jean." Two men drinking in front of the Blind Duck Tavern watch us and raise their glasses. No one is in a hurry. My cousin always has a new boyfriend, usually from school, but sometimes they are just guys temporarily working in the coal fields even though she knows they're too old for her. She talks about how cute they are and how they like her and how she wants to go off with one of them and leave this town. We go back to her house having walked the whole street down and back and play with the new kittens. There are cats running everywhere in and out of the house, and no one seems to care if the doors stay open.

We enter the house through the kitchen where a cabinet door hangs by one hinge. A few random cans are exposed—pork and beans and sauerkraut, a box of Cherrios. Our arrival must have interrupted a meal of sauerkraut and hot dogs, the remains of which are still on the table. The air is thick with the smell of cooked cabbage. Half empty glasses sit about. Water apparently is the beverage of choice. One of the cats, gray and full-grown but skinny, has jumped onto the table and is joyfully dining on a partially eaten hot dog. Our movement into the room doesn't startle him, and he continues to gnaw with even more vigor in spite of the interruption. A smaller cat, bearing a physical resemblance and most undoubtedly kin to the larger cat, is watching and waiting for a moment when it can make an unchallenged leap onto the table top rich with strewn food on mismatched plates. A broom whose straw base spreads in all directions from overuse leaned in the corner standing as a threat to whisk anything off the floor including a small feline if anyone had an urge to move it. The single window is covered with a piece of drab yellow calico obviously with the intent of adding a spot of brightness to the room encased in shadows. But it is sadly ineffective. A string swinging from the ceiling is attached to a fixture with a single uncovered light bulb.

It is a pull cord meant to bring light onto the murky scene, but any amount of tugging would not bring forth even a single ray of illumination.

"Do you want to go up to my room and escape my little brothers?" Myrtle Jean queries. Her brothers, Larry and Harry, are playing with my brother, pretending to drive some rusted farm machinery. She grabs a flashlight from an invisible drawer. "I know where all the steps are, but anybody else might trip and fall." I am appreciative of her concern. She is anxious to take me on an adventure, but a safe one. We cross to a staircase which is barely visible in the dark. Not set at an angle like most stairs, it is more like climbing a ladder. "Watch the broken step," warns my cousin. She shines her light down into the dusk revealing a hole where a stair used to exist. A black spider with long legs disturbed by the sudden flash scurries into a darker part of the woodwork where she can continue her endless weaving. "My daddy built this second floor," announces Myrtle Jean proudly. "He said the family was just growing too fast, but we couldn't afford to move to a bigger place. Oops, another loose board on the step here. Be careful," she admonishes. A downward beam follows this prediction. My uncle Ed did have more children than the usual family—five in all. My mom says it is because his wife is a Catholic. The smaller cat apparently having grown tired of waiting for its rival to give up his masterly hold on the table top follows us up the stairs. A soft mew breaks our silence and announces his arrival in the darkness.

Two unpainted doors greet us on the second floor. "This here's mine." She indicates the one to the right and presses open a door covered with a wild display of hearts cut from blue striped contact paper similar to the style I had noticed on a couple of the shelves in the kitchen. They are randomly placed, like a shower of disharmony in an attempt to bring style and romance into her corner of the world where there was very little. The kitten dashes in front of us happy for the company. Once inside her room, I notice the heart theme continues with more of the shapes having been pasted on her window. Several pages had been ripped from movie magazines and tacked on the shadowy walls too dark to reveal the subjects. There is no other form of decoration, other than her and her sister's clothes hanging on a rope strung from nails across the room. Two beds on opposite walls from one another were each covered with a faded chenille bedspread, one yellow the other blue. There was still a trace of the design which had once existed when the fibers had stood raised above the cotton backing, but are now colorless and hardly discernible. Again the sole means of light other than the few rays stealing through the window past the plastic-coated hearts is a single hanging light bulb.

We are no sooner inside the room when she sticks her head back out of the door and checks out the hallway. She closes the door even though it doesn't fit completely and gives it a shoulder push which compresses it another couple inches but still gapes. Once done, she tugs the string on the light. This one works. "Guess what I have!" She raises her eyebrows as if to magnify the surprise. She walks to the bed with the shabby blue bedspread and flings it back to the mattress. I notice she had only one threadbare sheet, not two, but, heck, this way it would be a lot easier to make the bed.

CAUGHT!:
LIGNITE, PART 2

By Sharon Wylie

Myrtle Jean rips back the sheet and lifts the thin mattress. She reaches her hand underneath and pulls out a pack of Lucky Strikes—a little flat either because of the weight of the mattress on them or there aren't many left.

"Where did you get those?" *Why would anyone ever want cigarettes?* I'm thinking.

"I took them from my father's pocket. Here, try one. They're fun." She pulls out a book of matches marked with the bar's name on the cover, The Blind Duck. She rips one from the line of little blue and red heads and then produces a small light by scraping the match along the edge. She puts it up to the end of the cigarette, leans her head back like they do in the movies, and takes a big drag followed by a big cough.

I don't really want to do this. "I'll just try yours," I tell her not wanting to be a spoil sport. But she doesn't want me to miss out. "No, no, here's your own." She was so proud of her secret stash. She lights one for me, and I take a small drag; it burns all the way down my throat. Not for me. She continues to take in deep breaths while I just suck on it a little so she doesn't notice I'm not excited about this adventure.

"What's going on in here?" The door flies open and Myrtle Jean's sister stands in the doorway. Mary Ellen is older and bigger. She isn't much taller because she has a short neck. It sort of sinks into her shoulders and her head can't look straight ahead but angled up toward the ceiling. She looks like she's constantly shrugging her shoulders. She's been like this since she was a little girl. The doctor dropped her when she was born. She can sure still yell though.

"Get out of my room now!" Myrtle Jean screams back. The kitten leaps straight up and off the bed to run for a dark corner to hide. From a safe place it follows the action. She drops her cigarette to the floor and steps on it to put it out. She keeps her foot solidly planted as if she can force the evidence down through the floor boards.

"It's my room, too. Where did you get those cigarettes? I'm telling Dad. They're his, aren't they?" She doesn't really wait for an answer to one question before she hurls out another. I slink sideways to the valentine window and slip my contentious cigarette out the open two-inch crack. I'm out of Mary Ellen's range of sight because she can't really turn her head from side to side anyway and has to look mostly straight ahead. When she does turn her head, she has to turn her shoulders also. Myrtle Jean and Mary Ellen are so involved in their screaming match they don't notice me moving around. Mary Ellen is very angry, and I suspect she is a little jealous of her little sister because I think the boys don't pay as much attention to her because of her neck. Quicker than I thought she could move, Mary Ellen reaches out and snatches the pack of cigarettes. "I'm using this as evidence. Open the window and air this place out. And then expect to get into trouble." She has become the adult. She tries to slam the door on the way out for effect, but the door still doesn't close all the way even with the extra force. Instead of a bang it's more of a whoosh sound. I know this must be the highlight of Mary Ellen's day.

"Bitch," is Myrtle Jean's parting words.

It isn't long before we hear heavy pounding coming up the stairs. Uncle Ed throws open the door and demands, "Come downstairs and bring the pack of cigarettes with you!" The gray ghost in the corner of the room flicks his paw into the air as if to protest against the new actor that has intruded onto the scene. Her father pulls Myrtle Jean downstairs and announces publicly her punishment. She will smoke all the rest of the cigarettes in the pack. Good thing we were able to dispose of a few when we did. Myrtle throws a look at her sister. The boys gather to watch the spectacle. My mother says, "Now, Ed."

"All kids do this," Aunt Julia chimes in. I wonder if they smell liquor on his breath like I do. Myrtle Jean's mother, Aunt Ana, slips from the background and is about to protest. Her mouth opens to speak, but instead of her voice it is her husband's that booms out. "She's got to learn. She can't sneak around like this and steal! That's the worst of it!" Mary Ellen has a smug look on her face. Her father has covered all her little sister's sins.

Myrtle Jean bravely faces her punishment. Her father lights the first cigarette. She's not taking the big movie-star drags like she did in her room but only little puffs. She finishes that one, then another. She goes through four more before the pack is empty. She isn't looking so good. Her face is pale and she sits down on a weathered old chair someone has left outside. As soon as she's finished, she runs into the house and up the stairs giving Mary Ellen a shove on the way. The kitten follows. The boys laugh and continue their game of pretending to drive on the rusted farm machinery. It's time to leave. I climb the darkened stairs to say good-bye to my cousin. Her face is flat on the pillow, and when she lifts it, I see her cheeks are red and tear-stained. "I really do hate them all—every last one of them!"

SHELDON

By Zooey Kaplowitz

I n 1936 my brother Sheldon became the first Jew at DeWitt Clinton High School in the Bronx to win a tennis scholarship to a goyish college. "School's a gravy train, Izzie." He had a great time. He attended a public school. Public schools have extracurricular activities and girls. I studied at a Yeshiva. It was gruesome. If Dickens had Jewish ancestry, Oliver Twist would have been forced to study Talmud. Everyone calls me Izzie. My real name is Israel. My parents gave me the name in hopes that someday a country would be named after me. Sheldon was my big brother. He came bursting out of our mother four weeks premature. Ninety minutes later, they pulled me out by my feet. I grew up in the shadow of Sheldon, and still live there.

Sheldon could be a real no-goodnick. My Talmud teacher's name was Shlomo Goldfarb. He was a strict and demanding old man. He would not let anyone get away with anything, with the exception of Sheldon. He caught my brother stealing prayer shawls from the synagogue and threatened to have him arrested. My brother was going to sell them to Benny Pearl, the ragman. My brother cried and pleaded with Mr. Goldfarb not to call the police: "I was not stealing them. I just wanted to take them home to my house so that I could feel closer to God. I was going to return them." Goldfarb bought this, and afterwards every time a religious article was stolen from the synagogue Goldfarb would declare, "There should be a thousand such thieves." Sheldon was a hard act to follow.

Only family called him Sheldon. A big anti-Semite two years his senior called him Sheldon once. Sheldon went out that night with his Louisville slugger. The big Irish kid was laid out for a month with a fractured skull. The police report read "assailant unknown." No kid ever called him Sheldon again. He had them call him Curly. There was no reason for him to be called Curly. He had very fine straight hair, but he got a kick from every kid in the neighborhood and school having to call him Curly.

In the old neighborhood all the kids called him Sheldon. We left the old neighborhood when my father started making real dough from his real dough. I always get a kick out of saying that even though everyone always looked at me like I was schmuck when I did. My father began his career as an apprentice of Yonah Shimmel versus the renowned knish baker. He worked for the great Mr. Shimmel for five years. He took the art of knish baking seriously and through grit, determination, and a brother named Moish who was an associate of Meyer Lansky was able to become half owner of a very popular kosher restaurant. It was known for twenty-seven varieties of pareve and meat knishes. The most popular being the potato prune.

The restaurant was located east of Greenwich Village in the heart of the Yiddish Theater District. Moish was the silent partner. My father was the working partner. The restaurant bore my uncle's name, and housed my father's love of good food. My father looked like a man who loved good food. As a kid, he was very short and gregarious. The old ladies used to tell him, "Don't worry. As soon as you're bar mitzvahed you will shoot right up." Then years after that event on his wedding day he was still only four feet eight. Although he never shot up, he did spread out. He tipped the scale at four hundred pounds and earned the nickname Yummy. I never saw the old man without a turkey leg in his hand. His motto was: "I never came across anything that could be eaten that I didn't like," embroidered on cotton and placed on the wall above our kitchen table. Uncle Moish was another story. Moish grew to be five feet four but preferred kicking ass to eating. Moish was a tough kid. His nose was broken five times before the age of ten. A man of few words. When he spoke, it was through the side of his mouth. My uncle dressed like a dandy. His shirts were made of Irish linen, and his suits and shoes were imported from Italy. He was a man meticulous about his appearance. He was only seen once with a hair out of place, and that was when he was found floating face up in the East River with eight bullets in his chest. This made him even more silent as a partner.

Moish was buried in Mount Hope Cemetery in Yonkers. His plot was located on the side of a hill. It overlooked the Saw Mill River. My father sat Shiva for him on a milk box for six days. He mourned and said Kaddish for him for a year. He bought an expensive tombstone to commemorate Moish's life, and at the unveiling of that tombstone he announced to friends and family the first of many expansions of the business. The restaurant was being built up for me. He had bigger dreams for Sheldon.

The name of the restaurant was changed from Moish's Dairy Restaurant to Yummy's Famous Dairy Restaurant and grew to occupy half of a city block. It was cavernous. The décor was utilitarian. The tables were made of chrome with stained red Formica tops. The chairs were chrome and upholstered in various shades of red vinyl. Saw dust was on the floor and therefore often on the clothing of patrons. Open pickle barrels were spread throughout the place for the indulgence of the customers. The waiters were old Jewish men hired on the basis of their flatulence and lack of civility. Their job was to get the customer in and out as fast as possible in as rude a way as possible.

The customers loved being so patronized.

The busboys were young Yiddish theater hopefuls. There were greenhorns, new to America and did not speak much English. Their job was to clear the tables, entertain the customers, and aggravate the old waiters. These two factions were in constant battle in both Yiddish and broken English. And, of course, the customers loved this because Jews like good theater.

While all of this was going on, my father was, with turkey leg in hand, behind the counter, at the register, supervising the cooks, overseeing the bakers, and at every table kibitzing with the customers. Business was always good, and we got through the Depression very comfortably. Sheldon wanted for nothing. And I too wanted for nothing.

My father was getting very rich, and wanted Sheldon to have higher class friends. "A smart Jewish kid with the brains to go places shouldn't be wasting his time with a couple of Wop hoodlums," he would say, adding, "Shelly's a good kid. And he wouldn't have gotten in trouble with the police if it weren't for those god damned greaseballs putting ideas in this head."

My father wanted to move to Westchester County and live in a fancy gentile neighborhood. That was not acceptable to my mother. No Jews meant no Mah Jong. So we moved into a very stylish building on the Grand Concourse. The move pissed Sheldon off. To spite my parents he still hung out with his two friends, Auggie and Anthony (pronounced through the nose as Antny). Even after moving to the Bronx, he saw them whenever he felt restless, exhausted his allowance, and needed money. The building we moved into was posh, and my mother furnished our apartment with great expense and very little taste. She covered everything in plastic. The first time the living room furniture was used was when we sat Shiva for her. In order to sit comfortably and eat you would have to leave the house as she followed everyone around with a broom and a dustpan. She had a monumental fear of embarrassment. What would the maid think if she were to arrive in the morning and find a mess in the house? She would get up at six a.m. and clear before the maid arrived at nine. And then spend the rest of the day cooking for the woman so she wouldn't tell people that she wasn't generous. My mother was as obsessed with the house as my father was with his business. He was seldom in the house, and she was seldom out of it. My brother was left to his own devices. I didn't have time for any.

The move did not affect me. I was to continue studying at the Yeshiva. I would ride down with my father in the morning, and work the cash register until it was time to go to school. After school I would return to the restaurant at five where my father would sit me at the center table, and for four hours I did English and Hebrew homework. After that I worked the cash register again and then rode home with him at midnight. It was not as bad as it sounds. I got to like it there. I got to spend a lot of time with a lot of terrific people. I made friends with young actors from the Yiddish theater, and students from New York University and the New School of Social Research.

Sheldon did really well in high school. He was captain of the tennis team and a member of the chess club, the debating team, and the National Honor Society. He was president of his class all four years and starred in every drama club production except *Charlie's Aunt*. He refused to do that part because he didn't want the "dumb Micks" seeing him with a dress on. He hated every Irish kid in school and in the neighborhood. He didn't play football because he didn't want them piling up on him. He didn't play baseball because he didn't want them throwing fast balls at him. He waged a one man war against anti-Semitic Irish youth. If one ever bothered a Jewish kid, Sheldon was after him.

These Irish kids were not prepared for Sheldon. They fought with their fists. Sheldon would never do that. He was afraid of getting hurt. His good looks were precious to him. Sheldon went after them with a baseball bat and on many occasions in the company of Auggie and Anthony. The police report always read "assailants unknown."

Sheldon graduated at the top of his class, and we were all very proud of him as he gave the Valedictorian address. He not only did well in high school, but he was also a legend in the neighborhood. There was a triangular vest pocket park two blocks from our house called Poe Park. In the center, there was a cottage Edgar Alan Poe once lived in.

Sheldon shtupped every girl in the neighborhood who looked good, had a small nose and wore a parochial school uniform in that cottage. He was quite the ladies' man.

The girls all thought Sheldon was dream stuff. He was tall with dark hair and looked great in cashmere—and bound for success. My parents bragged that he would become a rich and famous attorney. He was labeled "hunk of the heartbeat" by the girls at the candy store. I was the twerp, kid brother of that "hunk of the heartbeat." He grew to six feet. No one knew that could ever have happened in our family. It defied genetics. I was more like my parents, peaking at five feet and never more than 115 pounds.

Then Sheldon went to Dartmouth College in New Hampshire. When I finished high school, I worked for my father during the day and attended the New School at night. Sheldon did well at Dartmouth and got to play some terrific tennis and was popular with the rich chicks at a nearby finishing school. The allowance he received from our father did not cover nightclubs in Boston. At the end of his third semester, he had to either leave school or face arrest, conviction, and possibly ten years in prison for mail fraud.

He had been stealing other students' checks sent from their parents—and cashing them.

"The goyum were always creating problems for a decent Jewish boy trying to get ahead in life" is how my parents excused Sheldon.

After his sudden departure from Dartmouth, he went to work in the deli during the day. At night he, Auggie and Anthony worked for Mr. Lansky as thugs, their job was to attend Nazi Bundt meetings and break them up with the help of their Louisville Sluggers. He also began to take acting classes with the old Russian lady who played the gypsy in the Wolf Man movies.

After the bombing of Pearl Harbor and the patriotic fervor created by it, everyone was rushing to fight in the war. Even big movie stars enlisted, but Sheldon felt he could do more for his country by not fighting. He wanted to fill the gap in Hollywood left by the male stars going to war. His boss, Mr. Lansky, had become quite successful in circles that could fix things. He arranged to have Sheldon given a deferment by the local draft board.

Sheldon left for Hollywood. Mr. Seigel was there waiting for him. Mr. Lansky had sent him there eight months prior to see if there was any action. Mr. Seigel knew a few people at the studios and introduced my brother, now being called Sonny Jerome. They liked him for his charm and good looks.

Sheldon's career lasted from 1942 to 1945. He was in every fan magazine and with almost every starlet, but only for the duration. When the war was over, the real stars came home, and there was no need for Sheldon and the screen or in those fan magazines.

He made twenty films, none of them memorable. A few film buffs remembered him. At the height of his popularity he wanted to join a restricted country club in LA, a club that didn't allow actors. "But I'm not an actor," he told them, adding, "I have ten films to prove it!" This was a story falsely attributed to Victor Mature.

So out came the baseball bat. And he was once again working for Mr. Lansky and Mr. Seigel who was killed in 1953. Sheldon was found dead a week later in a cheap motel off Hollywood Boulevard, a bullet to his head. The police report read "assailant unknown."

My father said, "It was a gentile who got killed, they would find out who did it," always blaming the goyum. "It was all their fault. He was a smart boy. The world should have been his." They continued, blaming what happened to him at Dartmouth on the goyum.

My parents are dead. I am married, living in Scarsdale with two sons whom I don't have time to be with. I keep remembrances of Sheldon such as his baseball bat. I framed reviews of his movies. All of them hanging behind the counter in the deli. The old timers who still come to the deli talk about him: "those god-damned lousy goyum."

THE SPOT

By Ellen Leeds Kaplowitz

M r. Henkins spent half his time reading the newspapers that arrived from the surrounding townships, the other half trying to get kids out of his small but popular business called The Spot. Often entering The Spot could be treacherous with stacks of bikes piled in front of its doorway. The Spot was a magnet for kids because each week the newest comics were displayed on its racks, and every candy was ready for the taking. Woodlake was easily traveled by bikes, and The Spot was one of the favorite locations for kids to rid themselves of their weekly allowances.

Teens loved it as well, for there were rows upon rows of the latest movie and teen publications. Magazines where they could sing along with the words of any popular hit from American Bandstand. Magazines that had covers which told which teen idols were dating whom? Any possible gum—bubble or spearmint only two examples—and maybe run into friends hanging out peering through the many racks as they leafed through the pages. *Teen Life*,

16 Magazine, Teen Screen, and the nefarious *True Confessions* were but a few.

Mr. Henkins had been the proprietor for decades and before that his parents. He rented one of the apartments upstairs to Mr. Twitters, and he lived with his wife in the other one. When the kids were away in school, older folks would stop by on their way to work to buy the daily news and gossip.

Those who needed to get in touch with someone might use the pay phone located in the back of the tiny establishment. Sometimes as many as fifteen people would be standing along the walls of The Spot to read, eat, and some even to buy something from the hundreds of weekly publications available.

There were floor-to-ceiling racks. Something for everyone: food, health, history, sports, women's issues, fashion, daily, monthly, young, old, and in between. Newspapers in English, Yiddish, and even in Polish for Miss Polusky who arrived not too long ago to assist with the new influx of immigrants to Woodlake. Considering the size of Woodlake, one might wonder if there were enough people to purchase this array of material. Yet Mr. Henkins felt it necessary to have it here.

Mr. Henkins secretly wished that the children who frequented The Spot would purchase their treats and be gone. After locking up each evening, there were candy wrappers everywhere and sticky fingerprints on the walls. He'd wash off the smudges but then they'd reappear. It made his life difficult. After all, these children were the beloved urchins of their parents, and weren't going away.

Mrs. Henkins used to take charge of the children. It had been his wife's job as they pointed to the penny candies in the jars lining the counter, or reached for the Little LuLu comics if they couldn't get them; but her recent illness left him alone, now in charge of everyone and everything.

"Hey, Mr. Henkins, can you help me with this zipper, it's stuck," Joey shouted from the bathroom. Wasn't it enough that he picked up after them every day? Wasn't it enough that these unruly kids seemed to have no appreciation of his property? And now he was expected to assist one in his own store bathroom? He pretended not to hear. Joey was seven, so how could he not open his own zipper? Mr. Henkins continued reading the Woodlake high school football scores when again Joey blurted out this time much louder, "Mr. Henkins help, help!"

Mr. Henkins looked around and waited for someone else to go to the little boy's rescue, but no one seemed to have heard, or perhaps they purposely tuned him out. Mr. Henkins shook his head and reluctantly walked towards the bathroom. Joey was sitting on the floor with his shirt tail somehow wedged in the rungs of his zipper. Mr. Henkins wanted to yell at the boy, but laughter came tumbling out of his mouth. "How did you manage to do that Joey?" he chuckled.

Joey, in tears at this point, just hugged Mr. Henkins who lifted him up and after freeing him from his predicament; carried him to the front of the store and soothed him with a large lollipop. "Now, Joey, stop that crying. You are a big boy." Joey sniffed a little, rubbed his nose on Mr. Henkins' shirt, hugged Mr. Henkins and left.

Without watching him leave Mr. Henkins turned to the children leaning against the walls and screamed in his booming voice, as everyone temporarily faced him, and snapped to attention, "How many times must I tell you if you aren't buying anything, GET OUT, GET OUT NOW!"

And they were gone.

So Mr. Henkins, smiling, took up the newspaper he'd been reading.

VAGABOND

By Zooey Kaplowitz

I got my first television job in 1972. It was on a half hour show about high school students and teachers called "Room 222." This show is still being aired on cable—and in far-off lands. Three weeks ago, I received a residual check from that show. The gross amount was thirty-two cents. Fortunately they only withheld three cents for social security, taxes, and all the other bullshit. So I was still left with twenty-nine cents. As of three days ago, I still hadn't cashed the check because I was nervous about walking around with all that money.

That day I received a letter from the Room 222 people. They had made a mistake. Accompanying the letter was a check for forty-one cents. The gross amount was forty-eight cents. That added up to seventy cents. I was left with the question, "What should I do with this money?" Should I spend it or should I save it? Seventy-five cents doesn't sound like much to most people. It couldn't buy a house in Beverly Hills but another one hundred and twenty-three thousand checks like thee would give me a down-payment toward a little place in Echo Park, 1.3 square miles of steep hills, overgrown yards and California bungalows worn by time and untouched by gentrification. Raymond Chandler wrote *The Big Sleep* on a converted service porch of one of these houses. And a lot of the movie *Chinatown* was shot there, but I'm not a saver and my life at that moment sucked. The money was burning a hole in my pocket and I liked to live my life vicariously on the edge. So I went to see a movie.

"McArthur Park" is a song recorded by Richard Harris in 1968. It is famous for the line "Someone left the cake out in the rain, and I don't think I can make it...." Figure that line out. McArthur Park is also that—a park!—on the frontier of downtown Los Angeles. Across from the park, in view of only the junkies and rummies who live there is a small, slim, dull gray building in the shadow of a large bank building. This little building is the mecca for college students who can't get dates and the film buffs they grew up to be. It is the Vagabond, built in 1918. It was one of the first picture houses of the not-so-post Nickelodeon era of silent films. Great silent films like *Wind*, *Sunrise* and *Wings* were screened there. In the Vagabond's hay day in 1928, Clara Bow, the "It Girl," was a fixture there. She was a woman who really liked sex. She said of Gary Cooper, "He's hung like a horse, and can go all night." In the projection booth, one night, one at a time, Clara Bow seduced the entire University of Southern California football team and the projectionist.

This is true!

I read it in Kenneth Anger's book *Hollywood-Babylon* and if you stay in your seat, after the audience has left, you can let your mind go, and conjure up the ghost of Clara Bow moaning, "Don't stop! Don't stop! Oh, please don't stop! Yes! Yes! Yes! Oh, Christ yes...."

I also read something else about the Vagabond in Kenneth Anger's book. One night while a Mary Miles Minter double-bill was playing at the theater, the body of William Desmond Taylor was discovered in a trash can behind the theater. Taylor was the director of the film and the lover of both fifteen-year-old Minter as well as her mother. He had been shot three times in the chest. The navy blue Rogers Peet jacket he wore with the family crest embroidered on the top pocket was covered with blood and reeked of a French perfume called Noir, worn by both Minter and her mother. They were under suspicion for a while. The case was never solved.

The Vagabond is now an air-conditioned run-down semi-inner-city art house. The lobby is deco with gothic overtones. The once comfortable overstuffed red and black seats are worn, patched and mostly broken with arms that rattle. The dusty organ is still in mint condition and silently occupies its same place up front, screen right, but the old Nickelodeon feel has been replaced by oppression. The walls of this demi-picture palace are covered on both sides with full-wall murals. They play films for only two nights. This was the second evening for the adaption of Alexander Solzhenitsyn's *One Day in the Life of Ivan Denisovitch*. I didn't want to miss it. My policy was to see every film screened in Los Angeles, present and past. The film and the book are about an innocent Russian soldier convicted of treason who was sent to a camp in Siberia to freeze, starve, and to work like a mule. What better way to see this film of Stalinist inhumanity than to be wedged between monster murals of Czarist inhumanity on a broken seat that put my butt on five different levels and having no knee room. Years and gravity created a theater where the members of the audience would have to be under four feet tall to sit comfortably. None of my friends ever wanted to go to the Vagabond because they were too tall for the seats. But my low level of gravity made the seats a custom fit.

It was a week away from Christmas and cold. There are no big seasonal changes in the Los Angeles weather, but there are extreme changes in the temperature during the course of a winter day. The early morning before nine is chilly. The days are very warm while the evenings and nights go from cold to colder. I was always dressed for the warm day, unprepared for the cold at night. Winter evenings have always depressed me, maybe a primal need to hibernate.

It hardly ever rains in southern California, but when it does it pours. I hadn't had an audition in two months. Then one day I had four, three for commercials. I was completely wrong for the one in which they wanted a wasp Ivy League type, not a short corpulent schlep. The guy pulls into a gas station on his motorcycle. The attendant is so anxious to serve him that he squeegies the mask of his helmet. I had no idea what to do, so I just followed him with my eyes as he squeegeed. They asked me if I could ride a motorcycle. I said I could. But, of course, I couldn't. What to hell. I wasn't going to get the commercial anyway.

The fourth was for the film *One Flew Over the Cuckoo's Nest*. My agent told me they were looking for a kooky kid, and I got it mixed up with *The Time of the Cuckoo* and thought I was being set up for a silly comedy. I wore Bass Weejuns, no socks, khaki pants and an Izod-type short sleeve shirt for the ad about the guy on the motorcycle. I was determined not to screw it up.

So I got to the *Cuckoo*'s *Nest* one at four. The waiting room was full of unknowns, unknowns being actors who worked a lot, make good money, but are not household names. I was a nothing, three levels below a nobody and couldn't even get a job waiting tables. I was discouraged with a knot in my stomach. I didn't do interviews well. The two producers and the director were seated around a table with a chair for me at it, an actor-friendly interview. They introduced themselves. Michael Douglas I recognized. He was on *The Streets of San Francisco* and one of the producers. Saul Zaentz was the other one, a very sweet man. Then the third man introduced himself. When he spoke his name, the knot really tightened in my stomach. This was Milos. He pronounced it *Milosh* Forman. I told him I loved the way he directed *Closely Watched Trains.* He told me that he didn't direct it.

You see, I didn't know there was more than one director in Eastern Europe. Naturally I felt like a shmuck. He told me he'd directed *Loves of a Blonde* and *Taking Off* which I had seen and loved. He used a lot of offbeat nobodies like me. I figured there were going to be great parts in it and that I was probably going to blow the meeting. They asked if I'd read the book. I hadn't. Then Michael Douglas said I was the first actor to come in who wasn't acting crazy. But I blew it and became suicidal. I should have spent that seventy cents on a pre-paid funeral plan. This was the perfect night for a film set in a Siberian work camp.

I arrived at the theater at eight. It was cold. I was dressed for spring break in Fort Lauderdale because I hadn't been able to go home. I didn't want to miss the beginning of the film—I was running late—but then there was a long line to get in. The women all looked like Annie Hall and the guys like Francis Ford Coppola. I couldn't grow a good beard, so I went back and forth between a Woody Allen and a roman Polanski look.

The Vagabond had a policy of only hiring the handicapped. The kid who ripped the ticket was spastic. He had no talent for his job. When finally seated, I had missed the opening credits. I was upset. And cold. They had the damned air-conditioning on. So when I went to the lobby to ask the manager why, he said—can you believe this one?—that the theater wasn't heated.

While there, next to the concession stand, I who was on a diet, found everything so tempting. I hadn't eaten all day. I was once a fat kid who was not a fat adult.

It was in my junior year of high school, after seeing *The Wild One* that I decided to become an actor. And that day, standing next to that concession stand, freezing, I vowed I'd look like Marlon Brando—the young version!

So back in my seat, freezing, I was watching a film about a guy freezing. I was hungry as hell watching a film about a guy who rarely was given food. There it was, my condition right there on the screen. Every time Ivan was given a scrap of meat, I wanted to grab it from him. So I stayed through the film even when I wanted to leave. This was a bad neighborhood, and I didn't want to end up in a trash can like William Desmond Taylor. So I tried letting my mind drift in the direction of Clara Bow, but that only made me aroused. I was so horny. I didn't need a third condition. The movie was so long. I tried going to sleep. But then I fell off the broken seat.

The murals were no help. What consolation could I get from a baby carriage barreling down the steps or a student getting smashed in the head with a rifle butt? These were not fun murals. I had the thought I'd need to get rescued from the film by a dog sled.

I was told watching for water to boil is endless. Well, try watching it freeze!

Then a scene came that changed everything. Ivan stuffed his clothes with newspaper to keep warm. I ran to the lobby to get a newspaper, finding one in the bathroom. It smelled of urine, but it felt warm as I stuffed it under my shirt. Soon after getting back to my seat, the theater emptied and the murals free of human figures. The newspaper warmed my soul while the urine smell stuffed up my sense. I fell into a deep sleep on the broken chair, discovered by an usher. My joints were frozen—or so I thought— and I was on the verge of frostbite for sure. But I had made it through the film

When I arrived home, I showered for what seemed like hours to rid myself of the urine odor. I ate almost everything in the refrigerator. When I checked in with my service, there were two messages.

The first was from Bill Traylor. I was studying acting with him. He was a friend of Michael Douglass. The second message was from my commercial agent. I actually landed the commercial about the guy who pulls into a gas station on his motorcycle. And I still couldn't ride one. Surely I was going to die.

They were interested in me for the role of Billy Bibbet, a part that could put me on the map.

I was going to die riding that motorcycle into a gas pump in the Simi Valley before I even got a call-back—and I didn't have a pre-paid funeral plan.

THOSE GOLDEN YEARS

By Eric Selby

They had relocated from Long Island to Coral Gables, Florida, when Del, after forty years as a Wall Street investment banker, retired. That was ten years ago. Louise, his wife of nearly fifty years, has occupied herself in their 1930s Mediterranean-style home, decorating and redecorating and, on Mondays, supervising the two Cuban gardeners—her Spanish essentially that of adding an *o* or an *a* to English words although she is proud of having learned *aqui ahora* which comes out as *akwee a whore a*. These young men had not, of course, been the ones who transformed the ugliness of what had existed when the property was purchased into the *ravaging*—that's what most in her garden club members have said anyway—tropical wonder that a top-of-the-line landscape architect designed and then had professionals execute. Louise had thought that, by now, her name would emerge as a candidate for president of the club—a new one was elected annually, giving more leadership opportunities—especially since the last two haven't belonged as long as Louise has. She'd never be presumptuous enough to suggest that it was her turn. Besides, how would she feel if the secret ballot revealed that she'd not won?

Buried beneath her public rhetoric is her private disdain for most of the gardens she sees in Coral Gables where dead fronds lie on unraked lawns which, on the whole, are more bare ground than anything else. She hasn't commented on a few of the members' gardens they think are so lovely. They are not! Not at all!

Their health, on the whole, has remained steadfast although each has a small collection of pill containers. Sometimes, when his Simvastatin runs out, Del has been known to borrow for a while from Louise's supply. Upon discovering that her month's supply has lasted but three weeks, she scolds him and makes yet another call to the doctor who, in turn, assures her, one of his many Medicare patients, that he will renew the prescription. "You know, Mrs. Cate, it is good for a year," he always says. "You don't have to call each time."

Unlike Del (Louise loves her return address name: Mrs. Delbert Geoffrey McArthur Cate III—the Southampton Cates, of course!), Louise is diligent about prescriptions and all medical appointments, of which she has an ample supply. She sees a podiatrist, a gynecologist (she had a successful hysterectomy years before they moved to Florida but takes no chances), a cardiologist as a preventative measure, two dentists because of the need for second opinions, an audiologist, an ophthalmologist and, of course, Dr. González, who seems to be everyone's GP in her circle. However, Louise trusts nothing he says. After all, he's a Cuban. Del, on the other hand, has no issues with "that humorous doc. He's one hell of a golfer!" Louise reads up on ailments, notes the latest drugs being advertised on TV and becomes easily annoyed because her husband does not.

At the moment, however, Louise is talking to their daughter who lives in Santa Barbara and is married, unhappily. She has two children to whom Louise is always delighted to wave "bye-bye" after their annual week at Christmas (although they haven't come for the last two), children who seem unable to say a proper thank you for gifts of garments that seem more suitable than the things they arrive in. Thankfully, they are now matriculating at a couple of community colleges and apparently have begun to do something called adding tats to their bodies, whatever tats are. Louise is afraid to ask. Often the mother-daughter conversation, a daily occurrence, is about those two and just what disappointments they are to both mother and grandmother.

Del is in the kitchen pouring gin into a glass pitcher. He has already dumped in a dozen or so ice cubes, a complete tray. He will use more vermouth than Louise likes. But she is busy in the library on the phone. He will join her, carrying a tray bearing two stemmed Waterford glasses into which he has placed olives speared by toothpicks (two for him, three for her), the Waterford pitcher of martinis and the usual little plate of thin, unsalted wheat crackers and a soy "cheese" from some place Louise calls a boutique market. (She once shopped at Publix and immediately wrote it off! "You should see the types of people who shop and work there! Oh, my!") It is supposed to taste like Swiss but clearly does not—in Del's unspoken opinion. Louise allows no cheeses in the house, one of many efforts on her part to lengthen their lives even more.

"For the life of me I have no idea why they do it," Louise says into the phone. The conversation, Del observes, has apparently moved on from the one about what types of drugs her grandchildren could be consuming and something about what they are doing with decorating their bodies. Louise knows only about marijuana and cocaine. Her daughter—his daughter too, of course, even though they rarely talk any more—no longer tries to educate her mother about all the others out there that she knows full well "those two" are taking, the children who "take after their father who is nothing but an alcoholic and a womanizer like this horrid president we have now. And how loathsome to drink beer instead of cocktails!" Louise sighs deeply whenever the conversation turns in the direction of the son-in-law—and it always does because he loves to "rake the bastard over the coals." Louise laces clichés into her speech all the time now, sitting as she does for two or more hours before CNN listening to Washington politicians.

Louise is sitting in the needlepoint Chippendale chair next to the Chippendale table, well polished, upon which the telephone has rested for nearly ten years. (Of course she has another she carries around in whichever Gucci handbag she selects to go with whichever outfit she selects, called a smartphone that she knows almost nothing about how to use and has it only because she might need to call for medical help while out and about.) Once Louise settles on a room arrangement—and doing so has, at times, taken years—that arrangement does not change, including this telephone from the early years of dialing. She will start her martini here and later, when the conversation ends, she will move to one of the two matching Queen Anne upholstered chairs across the room, each at a slight angle with a cherry Queen Anne table between them. It has delicate legs and feet. This is where the tray Del is carrying will go. Louise likes facing the wall with the leather-bound books she has purchased in various antique boutiques, books that will never be read. Louise does look at the cartoons in *The New Yorker.* She doesn't realize that Del reads almost everything, taking the most recently discarded one to his club where he likes spending the day. At least that is where he says he goes, and Louise has no reason to believe otherwise.

Del's club, where he plays a round every other day, is one that Louise approves of although she hasn't found some of his golfing friends' wives all that cordial. That's why she only goes there for candlelight dinners in the dining room that has been fashioned around the pool. The rules prohibit swimming after six which is pleasant because who wants to see near-naked old, wrecked bodies frolicking around while dining from tables with fresh linens and bone china place settings?

Del loves his daughter because, after all, that is what parents do—they love their children. However, he does not like her very much, the woman who even as a girl refused to be called Debbie. At the time of her birth, Del said he really did not like the name *Deborah* although he did not say why. To him it sounded too stuffy. He had lived with that crap in Southampton and apparently had done exactly what he said he never would: he married a woman who was almost exactly like his mother.

Deborah has two very unstuffy daughters, Claire and Ramona. Louise has refused to put out their latest photographs, sent not by their mother who was too embarrassed to do so, but by the girls themselves, each wrapped for Christmas in sheets of newspaper— the second Christmas in which they refused to fly to be with their grandparents. Claire has high and oh-so-spiked hair in a wild array of colors. Her lips are black and condensed. Del wonders how she did that. Once they were perky little lips, almost seductive. Her face seems to have been painted some type of clown white. Ramona is like a banshee, her hair a web of knots—or so it seems. They are exactly eleven months apart, now twenty and twenty-one, living at home but not spending much time there and taking courses— or maybe not—at community colleges. Both had dropped out of high school but did manage to earn G.E.D.s thanks to money sent by their grandparents for high-paid tutors. Del suspects they sell drugs. He knows his wife discusses this topic with Deborah. But the topic has never come up between the two of them, even when Louise is on her third martini, at which point almost any subject is apt to fly out of that mouth in the middle of her skull-like face. She was a handsome woman—once. Now he avoids looking at her.

His breasts have become somewhat womanly at the same rate hers have become crinkled bags. They sleep, fortunately, in separate rooms. He cannot remember—nor does he wish to— the last time they had sex. Certainly not since they moved here.

"So, do you think he has another woman on the side?" Louise, still harping on her son-in-law, is looking annoyed and does that little thing with her free hand, a mime of sorts, suggesting she is drinking. She wants her martini. He has not sat down yet but is fussing around with the little strainer so as to catch ice cubes as he pours the martini into her glass. Louise hates that he uses so much ice. He lets ice cubes fall into his glass even though it is one designed for straight-ups.

"You think I drink too much," she often says. "That's why you put all that ice in it."

She's right, of course. But he will not acknowledge that. Will not say what he is thinking: "You're a nasty fucked up alcoholic bitch!"

He does not wish to listen to this conversation. Sometimes during cocktail hour Del plays a disc of something classical into what they both call a record player. They have not owned an actual record player in decades. However, recently Louise said she wanted to hear something more upbeat, that fugues were inappropriate for a time when people should relax. He does not have a single fugue in his collection. But he doesn't argue about music. Or much else.

"Put on Julie Andrews!" She says this after taking her mouth away from the phone and after taking a big slurp. It has been ten minutes since he poured her first drink and now she's ready for a refill.

Louise starts with sips and moves into slurps.

Del hates *The Sound of Music.* It has to be one of the most god-awful musicals ever written, one to which Louise has dragged him too many times. She mentioned that she thinks it is coming to the Adrienne Arsht Center where he detests going, what with the way people drive in Miami and the parking problems and the snobs who go to that place. He retired to get away from those types—and those types retired and, wouldn't you know it, moved to the Miami area and can't find enough places "to be seen."

None of the furniture in the house is comfortable, not even his designated chair in the room they call his office, the little ell off the kitchen. It is leather, as he wanted, but not overstuffed. She'd insisted he would grow to like the fit of the wing chair. He had not.

He has not yet started on his cocktail although he did pour a tiny bit into his water drinking goblet on the kitchen counter, something he does now if Louise isn't looking, an appetizer of sorts as he cuts up that awful soy. Recently he has left some of the crackers in their virgin state. She has said he does not give his taste buds a chance to get used to the soy cheese.

It seems now that the moment something liquid enters his mouth, Del has to use the toilet which he hopes Louise doesn't see because he sits for reasons he will not discuss with her—and he sure as hell isn't going to one of those bladder specialists that apparently she might be doing because she's brought it up. God, does she ever love medical appointments. So when he returns—not that he wants to return—to where Louise is still talking on the phone, he catches something that probably Louise hadn't intended him to hear.

"Emmanise is her name. Your father thinks she's so nice. Sure, she smiles a lot, but let me tell you this. I can't understand a damned word she says." Louise never swears, at least not until she's well into the martinis. And then she's like a pirate's parrot.

When they moved, Louise insisted that they had to have a black maid, that it was a fashionable thing to do "in the South." So they have had a series of black maids who actually are housekeepers and cooks, not one of whom has pleased Louise.

Del is the one who takes what Emmanise has prepared for their dinner—it is always on the second shelf of the refrigerator—and does whatever needs doing so that it is ready by eight. It gives him one more opportunity to be away from Louise who, of course, might be well into her fourth or even fifth martini at that point. After all, *someone needs to empty the pitcher* seems to be her motto. And once she's onto the third refill she no longer needs him to wait on her.

Emmanise is Haitian and raising four boys without any assistance from their fathers. Yes, plural. This Del knows because she's mentioned little things as she prepares the dinner. Louise has nothing to do with the kitchen, spending the late afternoon taking a shower and dressing for the cocktail hour and the candlelight dinner. On Emmanise's two days off—Sundays (she won't work on the Lord's day) and Mondays—they go out, but only to places where people "of our class," as Louise puts it, dine.

Tonight Louise is dressed casually in baggy black slacks purchased from Neiman Marcus. Louise detests that many women no longer use the term blouse. But suddenly she feels that she is wearing the wrong outfit. A large splash of martini finds its way down Louise's throat before she makes her way, both hands on the railing, pulling herself up to her dressing room where she plans to change from a white silk to a bright red silk blouse. She will wear a single strand of pearls instead of the other assorted pearl necklaces in the top drawer of her dresser. But maybe not. "You fucker!" she yells, attempting to fasten the strand.

When she had finished talking with Deborah she knew damned well Del probably heard her say, "Look, darling, don't you worry about the cost of an attorney. We will pay for that if you can get up enough courage to file for divorce."

He had, of course, heard because he was sitting on the toilet in the half bath just off the library—Del wonders sometimes if his deaf friends might, in fact, be luckier than he is with his perfect hearing—when she said it except she'd done so with a lot of slurring while at the same time Julie Andrews was climbing that goddamned-fucking mountain again.

Fortunately Louise knows absolutely nothing about their finances. He always makes sure that when it's time for her to sign her name on the income tax return that she does so just before dinner when she would have no idea what she is signing.

That drunk.

Emmanise seemed delighted when he made the offer, telling her that she would receive the same pay and have much less to do and could take off another day, if she wished.

While Louise is up there—oh, my God, the woman is screeching, apparently trying to get into Julie Andrews's range when there is still more mountains to climb!—Del has taken out the dinner and is putting it on the kitchen counter and leaving it there because during the past few days he has managed to remove all he wants from his closet and has nothing left, has done so by placing the items in a garbage bag, telling her he is taking out the garbage on his way to his club.

So he steps out of the house—he's left both of his keys to the doors on the counter next to the fillet of sole but without a note—and opens the door of his white Audi, lowers his tall, slender frame into the seat and in ten minutes, depending upon traffic, he'll be opening the door of the little two bedroom condo over in Coconut Grove where Alicia will be waiting, hopefully in the white see-through thing these women call negligées.

Alicia is exactly Deborah's age and has no interest in marriage, just a little place to nest in. They'll just see what happens.

One day at a time.

PERFORMANCE POETRY

By Alan Gardner

CINDERELLA

(The True Story)

As with every great rhyme
It starts, "Once upon a time
In a town that is far, far away,
Cinderella sought out fame.
Please remember that name.
I'll tell you what happened one day.

Cinderella lived with her kin
In the house her mother lived in.
Milking the cow gave her hands great big blisters.
Her mother was a witch;
Some say she's a bitch.
Also there are her three less-than-lovely step-sisters.

The sisters were ladies in waiting
Who couldn't wait to be dating,
But the wait was getting them nervous.
Mom, who once was a romancer,
Came up with the answer:
Send your profiles to a good dating service.

An e-mail was read
From the prince, and it said
That the royal family was giving a ball.
At his stage in life
The prince wanted a wife,
But he knew the potential pool was very small

Grizella, Pugella
And Barbella, the elder,
Made plans to spring some man-traps.
They all bought new dresses,
Fixed their faces which were messes,
And purchased support bras to get their breasts out of
their laps.

The sisters treated Cinderella badly
Though she served them all gladly.
She'd cook and she'd sew and she'd fetch.
She yearned for the day
She'd be carried away,
But she never even let out a kvetch

Cinderella's godfather was scary,
In fact a bit of a fairy.
He said he'd help her land her man.
"Your clothes are a mess,

But I will confess
I'll help you as much as I can.

"You'll need a ride that is nice.
I won't need the mice.
With mice you won't be conniving.
If you have a big veggie or fruit
I'll build you a carriage, a beaut,
And I'll even make it self-driving."

She wouldn't disparage
To ride in a horse-less carriage,
So inside a pumpkin she sits
Okay! So it's round
And has a squishy sound,
And where she sat it was all full of pits.

So the night of the ball
Cinderella had no problem at all.
She had a complete body makeover.
She took off her flop-flippers,
Changed into glass slippers,
And her scent was oil of clover.

The ball went along good.
The prince danced with every lady he could.
The ugly sisters danced as if they were crazed.
They cha-cha'd that night
With all of their might.
But the prince's eyes just seemed to be glazed.

By the time they finished the shag,
Cinderella had the prince in the bag.

He lost his heart and also his mind.
He asked her where home is.
She said, "None of his business"
It would make her harder to find.

As midnight drew neigh,
The prince wondered why
She screamed and started to run,
Not that it mattered.
Then her glass slipper shattered!
Maybe she wasn't having much fun.

The prince glued together the shards,
Sent out all his guards
To see who the glued slipper fits.
From house to house they would lurch
As they continued the search
Until they landed where Cinderella's house sits.

The guards hit every street,
Checking all feet,
Any size that might fit into the shoe.
Only heaven knows
How many tried to squeeze in their toes.
It seemed that there were quite a few.

It didn't take long
To see the shoe was glued wrong.
It would only fit a foot misshapen quite badly.
Barbella's foot slipped right in.
The guards said, "We have a win!"
And notified the prince very gladly.

Barbella was not quite right in the head,
But she gladly went to be wed.
She was a royal princess now.
Her mom was ecstatic!
Her actions erratic,
Cinderella went back to milking the cow

Well, what did you expect
When you sit back and reflect?
The old story needed a little unbending.
The fairy godfather was spurned.
Into the closet he returned.
Alas, for Cinderella there was no happy ending.

BOXES

So it won't be a mystery
I'll give you a history
Of the mother of Sona, my wife.
On the eve that she died
She wanted to confide
Her thoughts on her understanding of life.

My very first paragraph
Takes the form of a monograph
To explain the piece that I penned.
The words are quite sage
On reaching a certain age.
Her words and perceptions I'll send.

Several years ago my mother-in-law passed away. Freda was a vibrant woman who worked for years side by side with her husband, Al. After retirement they spent time together seeing the world and enjoyed visiting with relatives from the northeast.

338

Freda and Al seemed to know everyone, and everyone they met became their dear friends. When Al passed away, Freda's circle of friends narrowed a bit as. I guess it's human nature for couples to tend to socialize with other couples and widows tend to be looked upon as a "fifth wheel."

Freda suffered a massive stroke and was, to a degree, confined to a wheel chair in her home. Soon she had to have a 24/7 caregiver to share her home and to do the cooking, cleaning and shopping.

After a time she went into a nursing home. With the exception of the field trips that the home provided, she was more or less confined to her room and soon became all but bedridden.

In the year before her death, her ability to communicate diminished. In the final days she could no longer eat and her only visitors were her children.

At the time of her death, her daughter (my wife) and I philosophized as to how, as old age and infirmities overtook her, her world became smaller and smaller. During those last days her world had shrunk down to the size of a hospital bed.

I thought of this and, thus, I wrote...

Boxes

Excuse me if I ramble
And write no preamble,
But I'm old, and it's late in my life,
So let me be clear:
I felt my first box appear
When the doc cut my cord with his knife.

Even before I could talk,
I started to walk,
Exploring the vastness around me.
With every step that I took,

At new wonders I'd look
And the landscape did really astound me.

My box was my home.
Within it I'd roam,
Experiencing the wonders it had.
I could wander at will.
At each turn was a thrill.
Constraints were just Mom and Dad.

Each year I would grow
And my box too. You know
It contained a playground and my little friends.
As if obeying a rule,
My box grew into my school.
How big it would get just depends.

Then the married life
Seemed an end to all strife.
Into constraints I was no longer curled,
And perhaps with no care
I could go anywhere.
My box now contained the whole world

Then the family grew,
Created life that was new,
And with surprise I started to think:
I was quite astounded
That my box now seemed bounded
And around my family it started to shrink.

I was defined by my job
Though my friends were a mob.

Then age started thinning their ranks
With the faint sound of taps.
My box continued its collapse.
I could feel it grow close to my flanks

Now it's difficult to roam
Too far from my home,
Away from where my doctor resides.
An array of pills
To ameliorate my ills:
I can see now see how close were the sides

I write this tome
In my nursing home.
My visitors have become less and less.
In my box all that's there
Is my bed and my chair.
I feel so alone, I confess.

So now, truth be told,
I'm feeble and old.
They've sold all my assets and stocks.
My family's not here today.
They've all gone away
To pick out my very last box

THE GAME

You look back many years
And can still hear the cheers
That rang at your last football game,
And wouldn't you know
That the cross-town foe.
I won't mention that hated school's name.

At great energy cost,
We had not yet lost.
Here, in the season's final try,
We were favored by one point.
As a champion they'd anoint
And shower the team with a fame only bounded by sky.

It was personal for me,
That the scouts there would see
Me be a quarterback with a great deal of skill.
A scholarship hung in the balance.

If I could demonstrate my talents,
All of my dreams I'd fulfill.

Previous seasons wasted,
A championship not tasted,
But on the field there wasn't a soul
Who didn't think of the glory
When he one day told the story
Of raising that number one championship bowl.

I remember that night when
The lines painted white
Rampant on a field of green grass
In our uniforms we stood.
We really looked good.
The band had a special shine on their brass.

The girl who was my steady
On the sidelines was ready
To wave her pom-poms and cheer.
Tonight I'd be her hero.
Rivals would be zero.
In a few hours I could hold her so near.

The other team ran onto the field,
But our resolve would not yield
We'd send them home with their wounds licking
And deservedly so.
Our most hated foe—
Our rivals deserved a good butt-kicking.

On the field we ran,
A cheer from each fan.

It was time to start the fray.
Lights shown down from above.
I was watched by my love.
My god, how I remember that day!

Things went bad from the start.
Although we each played our part
To our goal line the other team marched,
It seemed as tough as stopping a bus.
Coach yelled at us.
He felt our spines should be more starched.

Their fans did applaud
When their team went in and scored,
And then insulted us by making a two point play.
Their plays could not be rejected,
And we were all dejected,
But no one wanted to give in that day.

But we had our pride.
At half-time we were tied;
Then we swapped the sides of the field.
It seemed in the cards.
We each made a few yards,
But it seemed that neither would yield

I'd sell my soul.
Had they not made a field goal?
And time was running out.
We trailed by three,
But visions I'd see
Of us carrying the trophy about.

As the clock ticked ahead,
I gathered my team-mates and said,
"The clock says two minutes to go!
We've no time to muddle.
When we break from this huddle,
A pass I am going to throw."

Those soaring goal-posts
I looked on as hosts,
Inviting me to come on through.
I would win the game.
I would garner the fame.
I knew that's what I would do.

I could see in my mind's eye
In the air it would fly.
It would be such a perfect spiral.
My receiver broke free.
No one near him would be.
I was sure that that pass would go viral.

I would be known
For reaching the end zone.
By all the fans I'd be adored.
I took the snap
As they started to clap,
And from my hand the ball soared.

Well, that was the plan!
I would be the man
To stand in front of all my fans' faces,
But I fell on my rear.

The ball went nowhere near.
I tripped over my own open shoe laces.

Embarrassed by my gaffe,
From the stands erupted a laugh.
The scouts folded up all their note books.
The newspapers were unkind,
Pictures of me on my behind,
And it was really much worse than it looks.

I am dumbfounded.
My life never rebounded.
My girl married a guy from the other team.
I soon had the knowledge
I'd not go to college.
Someone else was living my dream.

Now I could curse.
Everything got worse.
I became a pariah in town.
I have to dress like a slob
Because I can't get a job.
I can't get up 'cause now I'm so down.

So that is my story.
It ends not in glory.
I know now the agony of defeat.
My parents disowned me,
And no one has phoned me.
Tuna from cans is all that I eat

It's this that I learned
If fame you have yearned,

If you have a challenge and have not yet met it,
There's no reason why
You can't aim for the sky,
Or maybe you should just somehow forget it!

OLD MAN RIVER

Up the mountain clouds climb,
Though it takes so much time.
It seems no higher could they go.
And as those clouds rose,
The moisture froze,
And then it started to snow.

When the snows melt
From the mountain's hoary white pelt,
The first water begins slowly dripping,
A trickle to start.
Each drop played its part.
Its hold on the land was now slipping.

So here was the birth
So high up on earth,
The first place to see the sun in the sky.
Then as the peaks warmed,

Small creeks were formed,
And began their way to land parched and dry.

Over long days, even weeks,
Down flowed these small icy creeks,
Over slopes that are craggy and gray.
As fingers entwined,
Individual paths they initially find,
Past the spots where massive glaciers lay.

The creek's water purloined.
Now into a river they're joined.
The river is now the sum of its parts.
The destination seems blind,
Its course not yet defined.
The odyssey of its journey now starts.

Over rocks it pours.
Through ravines it roars,
Churning, eddying and spraying its foam
As it comes crashing.
The banks it is lashing
As the river begins heading home.

Toward meadows so lush,
The river's water can rush,
Past forests with trees reaching so tall
To an azure blue sky,
Puffy clouds floating by
The trees' palate of colors will arrive in the fall.

Birds on the wing
To each other they sing,

Mating calls to each other bird.
Look up to see
The flocks in the tree
In colors that are almost absurd.

The river that rushed
Is now somewhat hushed
As it begins its meandering ways,
As downhill it is flowing.
It is constantly growing,
Broadening with each passing day

Then a delta is formed
Down from where the river once stormed.
It is now a shadow of its once formidable form.
It can hear the sea calling,
Insisting there is no stalling,
Just a fraction of what once was its norm.

With its energy sapped,
Now the water just lapped
On shores that have twisted contours.
What was once mighty and swift
Now it just seems to drift,
Just tired, though the journey endures.

The water can no longer flow,
And then it surely must know
As the river turns its last bend
The destination is in sight,
And its movement is slight
As the river now comes to its end.

As it becomes part of the ocean,
There's no independent motion,
Just part of a new realm that's vast.
Its life's been fulfilled.
All motion has stilled.
Only memory of the river will last.

Think of the river as we,
Born wild and free,
Maturing into something peaceful and calm.
As we flowed through the land,
We brought new life as was planned,
Giving the earth no cause for alarm.

But just as the river with age
Reaches its terminal stage
And inexorably rounds those final last bends
No more able to roam,
We are both going home
To the place where everything ends.

ANCHORS AWRY

In the summer of '61
My college days had been done,
And the military beckoned, I fear.
I wanted to write
About a physical plight
That influenced my naval career.

Some people that knew
Said I looked good in blue.
Besides, camouflage didn't go well with my eyes.
And the Air Force wouldn't do
'Cause when they got hold of you
Then they dropped you out of the skies.

So the Navy made sense.
They had ships quite immense.
It seemed like a good place to be.
I was taken by surprise

When I learned from some guys
That those ships actually went out to sea.

"See the world," they had said,
But the thing that I dread
Was sailing the bounding main.
A fish could eat you out there.
No one seemed to care.
My protests were sounded in vain.

I went to officer's school.
I was nobody's fool.
My orders were sent out one day.
I almost died
When I saw my ship tied
To a dock in Norfolk, VA.

The ship was an old one,
And I was told one
That it had fought in the Second World War.
As the sea water lapped,
It should have been scrapped.
It couldn't have lasted much more.

Now what did they do?
They gave me a gun crew
And told me to teach them to fire.
It gave me such pride
That these men at my side
Became Uncle Sam's guns for hire.

But then came the day
When we got under way,

And the rudder was put hard alee.
It didn't take long
To find something was wrong:
This was not where I wanted to be.

Now out on the briny
With the brass gleaming shiny,
I held a death grip on that gun;
Then the deck started to roll.
My mind took its toll.
I wasn't having much fun.

My uniform was dark blue,
And my face was blue too.
I really wanted to leave.
They didn't give me a pail,
So I stood at the rail,
And into the sea I did heave.

Four years on the foam,
And I yearned for a home
On some land that never could move.
Any place but a ship,
But you can't let that slip
'Cause the navy would really disapprove.

Although there was no war,
I still gave up my gore.
I tried really to just do my part.
Though I never was shot,
My insides did rot.
I developed my own purple heart

So a landlubber I
Will be 'till I die,
My years at sea are behind me.
And now don't you know
I won't even go for a row
'Cause just a look at the sea will remind me.

So I sit here with you.
These words were all true.
I'll never skipper a tug or a carrier,
No more words to be blending
Because now I am ending
The rhyme of this ancient mariner.

REMEMBER ME

When you walk through a spot
Where there's an empty lot,
There is nothing where something used to be
Where that which was built
Now lies in the silt,
Remember me, please, remember me.

If you're feeling good
When you walk through the wood
And you pass by a fallen tree
Which was mighty and tall,
In time it will fall.
Remember me, please, remember me.

When you're alone you'd be kind
If my face comes to mind,
And a long ago memory you'd see
Perhaps at a critical stage in your life

Or carefree with no signs of strife,
Remember me, please remember me.

I always tried to be there
And show that I care.
Since the times you sat on my knee,
The good times we shared,
The poems I prepared,
Remember me, please remember me.

If you look up into the night
And one star is especially bright
And reflects off the land or the sea,
Please do not frown.
It's me looking down.
Remember me, please remember me.

In the day or the night
When I'm out of your sight,
I tried to be all I could be.
As the clock's clicking down,
Smile, don't frown.
Remember me, please, remember me,

When only my words remain,
Remember sunshine not rain.
Let your thoughts run wild and free.
If a thought you'd release,
I would truly know peace.
Remember me, please, remember me.

ABOUT THE AUTHORS

ELSA GOSS BLACK is a former journalist, a recovering attorney and the veteran of more PTA and other volunteer meetings than she cares to count. A widow for over five years, she has happily rediscovered, and greatly recommends, love the second time around. She is also a mother, stepmother, step-grandmother and step-great grandmother, all of which she is proud, although, in some cases, way too young, to be. She is beyond grateful to this OLLI group, which reintroduced her to one of the labels she has treasured most in a varied and fairly well-traveled life: writer.

THOMAS L. DAVID is a retired attorney having practiced for fifty years mostly representing small businesses. As an attorney he wrote memoranda and briefs. Venturing into memoirs has provided a long sought freedom of expression. He moved to Miami from Buffalo, N.Y to better enjoy outdoor activities, some of which are described in the memoirs within.

MAGDALENA DE GASPERI is a retired marketing director who returned to university to be able to wear Chucks and rub elbows with students several decades younger. She lives with her husband Dieter in Kronberg, Germany, and part of the time in Miami, where she grew up. Like Borges, Maggie is happiest when surrounded by books. She writes poetry, has recently started writing essays again, and is currently working on her doctoral thesis at Goethe University in Frankfurt.

JOAN FISHER is exploring life after work through writing. She uses her experiences and memories as a former student, clerk, secretary, administrator, salesperson, volunteer, realtor, educator and mother in her pieces. She is a voracious reader and a compulsive crossword puzzler who lives in Miami with her husband.

ALAN GARDNER is a retired student. He has been writing poetry since high school and has never heeded the advice to stop. He has had two books of poetry published, *Torah Lite...It Could Be Verse* and *Musings and Mirth*. His third book *Thoughts I Think I Thought* will be sent to the publisher by the end of the year. The publisher has advised him to possibly rethink his thoughts.

PAUL GUSTMAN, MD grew up in Brooklyn, New York, the best place on earth to be a kid. He retired in 2013 after practicing pulmonary medicine and critical care for thirty-eight years. He has studied writing at the Osher Lifelong Learning Institute of the University of Miami since retiring and is the author of a memoir "Life's Lessons, prn", which has had a readership of at least six, the number of his grandchildren. He also writes a blog with (hopefully) humorous observations of his life and society as a whole, available at drpaulsdiary.blogspot.com.

BEATRIZ LA ROSA was born in Cuba, emigrating to the United States as a teenager. She graduated from FIU with a B.A. degree and worked for Metropolitan Dade County for seventeen years. Her daughter Betty and two grandchildren, Sophia and Alex, reside in Jackson Hole, Wyoming. Were she to be born again, she'd be a dancer.

ELLEN LEEDS KAPLOWITZ is once again venturing forth with her writings. Ellen is currently working on a book of fiction, which she hopes to publish in the future, about a diner in New Jersey. Now retired, she taught reading and English as a Second

Language to adults for over 35 years in. Today she likes to be known as an author. She lives with her husband Zooey, their two dogs, Einstein and Soldier Boy, and Sarah, the cat. Along with her writings she also has returned to her artistic side by crafting and singing in a choir. Retirement has become very comfortable for her, and with all her endeavors she has no time for domestic things at home, which she never enjoyed to begin with. You can usually find her walking every night or texting her son Leo who currently teaches social studies in Miami.

ZOOEY KAPLOWITZ is the grandson of Yitzrak and Ruchel Kaplovich, founders and artistic directors of the Lower East Side Yiddish Midget Theater. His grandparents were the legendary great actors of the Yiddish Midget stage. Zooey entered the profession at the age of two playing the baby in *King Solomon's Decision*. Appearing in over three hundred Yiddish midget productions, Zooey earned Yiddish midget stardom playing the son in the Yiddish production of *Who's Afraid of Virginia Wolf*. He retired from the Yiddish midget theater when the casts of the plays outnumbered the people in the audience. He then moved to Miami where he taught YSOSHC, Yiddish for speakers of Spanish and Haitian Creole.

ERIC SELBY is a retired teacher of high school and college English. He enjoys having an opportunity to work with mature writers as well as interested readers at the University of Miami's Osher Lifelong Learning Institute. He lives with his husband, Stefan, in South Beach.

ISABELLE WHITFIELD spent most of her childhood absorbing the richness of small town life in Alabama's Black Belt. A graduate of Agnes Scott College, a women's liberal arts college near Atlanta, she received a B.A. degree in History and Political Science while nearly achieving a third major in fraternity parties at Georgia Tech. She was a secondary social studies teacher for many years in Miami, and is also an attorney and member of the Florida

Bar. Her varied interests include playing tennis, following college football, and embarking on travel adventures. Her southern heritage often provides inspiration for creative writing, especially memoir, a new interest which she has only recently and happily begun to pursue.

KITTY WINKLER is a blissfully retired international business executive. Having once authored articles for business publications on (ho hum) subjects like employee retention and executive development, she now feels liberated to dabble in memoir. She specializes in recalling youthful mishaps and life's embarrassing moments that none of her erstwhile business associates would believe could happen to this formerly buttoned-up corporate maven.

SHARON WYLIE is a retired teacher having taught thirty-five years in the Dade County Public School system. She spent one year in England teaching on the Fulbright exchange program. She has also been a yearbook advisor and dance instructor at times. She has taught all levels of English: high school, middle school, and college. Now in retirement she has taken up photography which is a great reason to travel the world. One year she was fortunate enough to win first prize in the *Miami Herald's* travel photography contest. She practices Iyengar yoga at the Yoga Institute of Miami. She also quilts, often making quilts for charity, with the Ocean Waves Quilt Guild. She has a son, a daughter, and five grandchildren.

Made in the USA
San Bernardino, CA
03 September 2017